# BLUE MAGIC

## The People, Power and Politics Behind the IBM Personal Computer

James Chposky
and
Ted Leonsis

Facts On File Publications
New York • Oxford

**Blue Magic: The People, Power and
Politics Behind the IBM Personal Computer**

A portion of this book's revenues, at the authors' arrangement, is being donated to the
Philip Don and Mary Ann Estridge Scholarship Fund at the University of Florida,
Gainesville, Florida.

**Library of Congress Cataloging-in-Publication Data**

Chposky, James.
    Blue magic: the people, power and politics behind the IBM personal
computer / James Chposky and Ted Leonsis.
        p. cm.
        Includes index.
        ISBN 0-8160-1391-8
        1. International Business Machines Corporation—History. 2. IBM
microcomputers—History. 3. IBM Personal Computer—History.
I. Leonsis, Ted. II. Title.
HD9696.C64I4832    1988
338.7'61004'0973—dc19                                        88-509
                                                             CIP

Text design: Jo Stein

Printed in the United States of America

10 9 8 7 6 5 4 3 2 1

With love and gratitude, this book is dedicated to our wives:

Judith Witt Chposky
and
Lynn M. Leonsis

Any sufficient developed technology
is indistinguishable from magic.

—Arthur C. Clarke

All stories, if continued far
enough, end in death, and he is no
true-story teller who would keep that from you.
—Ernest Hemingway, *Death in the Afternoon*

# Personal Dedication

My life and the lives of those on the PC team who were privileged to work with Don Estridge will be affected forever by the story of the IBM Personal Computer. It is to these people that I have dedicated my efforts on this book.

I participated in the telling of this story not for any personal gain, or to relate a one-sided version of the facts. For the truth is, during our individual and collective efforts on the PC team, we did many things right and many things wrong. But when we stumbled, we learned to pick ourselves up and try even harder the next time.

We never had to look over our shoulders to wonder if Don Estridge would be there to support us in our risks and efforts. He was there and he supported us. That was the magic in the man.

—Dan Wilkie

# CONTENTS

# Acknowledgments

We have always looked to a special few to give meaning to our common experience, to carry forth from the past something we haven't seen, could never have seen without first being shown, and having been shown could never see again without knowing, without remembering.
—From the introduction by Alex Harris to *A World Unsuspected*

BLUE MAGIC is a sincere and unbiased attempt to tell the factual story behind the development of the IBM Personal Computer.

The text is based on interviews with senior members of the original team commissioned to do something that had never been done before at IBM: within one year, to design, develop and bring to market a singularly outstanding machine that would anchor IBM in what was for the company a new niche in its industry—personal computing. These scores of hours of interviews were supplemented by other interviews with major individuals connected with or close to the microcomputer industry.

Finally, we pored through general-interest, business and computer-trade newspapers and magazines that reported on IBM's microcomputer activities during the 1980 through 1985 time frame. Dozens of anecdotes and hundreds of facts were sorted and classified. Eventually, certain pieces of verifiable evidence emerged. From this evidence, we were able to establish facts that reveal why the original IBM PC was such a remarkable achievement.

These facts, of course, are only as accurate as the recollections of those who were actually part of the team during those heady days from mid-1980 until the PC was formally introduced in August 1981. In the majority of instances, there was substantial agreement on the facts surrounding particular episodes. When conflicts arose among individual accounts of what happened, we have reported this fact.

As the evidence accumulated, we were able to draw certain conclusions that, until the publication of this book, remained as fragmented facts. The result has been what we intend to be a cohesive, sensible and simple narrative.

Throughout the book, conversations and episodes have been reconstructed according to what was often the vivid recall of those involved. The passing of time apparently did not dull their recollections of these memorable days.

*

While we choose not to present this book as "the unauthorized story behind the IBM PC," it is worth noting that IBM did not cooperate directly in the preparation of the text. The corporation refused to permit its executives to be interviewed and the only information it furnished was confined to documents that had been previously released to the concerned public. In other words, IBM neither endorsed nor authorized the publication of BLUE MAGIC.

When the text was completed, we submitted a copy to IBM for review. This copy was returned with such marginal comments as "not true" and "conjecture," but in no instance did the company offer to state its version of the points in alleged dispute.

This would have been a far different book than it is if IBM had managed to keep key members of the former PC development team on the corporate payroll. These men left the company in disillusionment because they had worked day and night and weekends to make the PC what it was and then the company attempted to fold them back into the IBM bureaucracy with only cursory recognition for what they had accomplished. So they left the company, went elsewhere, made important decisions, earned more money, and built up their estates. Now, free of the corporate procedures regarding speaking with the press, they took this opportunity to tell their inside versions of this fascinating story. The result is a book that is as true as can be possible.

As another attempt to enhance integrity, the text of this book was written on an early model of the original IBM PC.

*

Among those who left IBM and contributed significantly to the preparation of this book, we especially acknowledge Dan Wilkie, H.L. "Sparky" Sparks, Bill Sydnes, Joe Sarubbi and Jim D'Arezzo. Wilkie is named first because his contributions to this project were especially significant.

Many, many others eagerly cooperated by providing valuable insights and fresh information on the condition that they would remain anonymous. For reasons of their own, they did not wish to rile IBM.

When this project was still in its proposal stage, Reid Boates, our literary agent, convinced Ed Knappman at Facts On File that this was a book that demanded to be published. Without Reid and Ed, it is very likely there would not have been a book.

Kate Kelly, our editor at Facts On File, is a gifted professional and valued friend whose contributions to BLUE MAGIC were truly invaluable.

Among others who gave us their untiring support and steadfast encouragement during the research and writing of this book, we especially wish to acknowledge:

Linda and Hugo Ortega; Laura and Leslie Chposky; Ira Gerard, Dennis Haase, Vincent McConnell and Sally Sutton; James E. Cartwright, Ray Lee and Wanda Minton; Leah and Nicholas Braak, Margo Coleman, Charles and Leone Davis and Jane and John Regan; Donna Philo, Nora Crann, Mark Ballard for cover design, Greg Leary for cover photography, and Jordan Gold, Betty Clark and Ron Errett.

James Chposky
Ted Leonsis
New York City

# Prologue

On Friday August 2, 1985, at 5:43 PM, Eastern Daylight Savings Time (EDST), Delta Airlines Flight 191, bound from Fort Lauderdale, Florida, prepares to land and establishes contact with the Traffic Control Center at the Dallas-Fort Worth Airport.

The air traffic controller tells the pilot he has "a good area to go through."

Moments later, the pilot spots a thunderstorm cell and asks to go around it. Because the pilot had taken the plane aloft, the copilot routinely takes over the controls for landing as permission is received to fly around the gathering thunderstorm.

At 5:52, Delta 191 connects with the first of three air traffic controllers who will attempt to guide the plane into a safe landing at the airport. At this point, a recorded weather alert reports there are 10 miles of visibility, calm winds and no rain. Four minutes later, the weather report is invalidated; the control tower spots rain slightly to the north of a landing runway—but at this time of year the sudden change is not unusual in the Dallas-Fort Worth area.

At 16 seconds before 6 o'clock, an air traffic controller reports that he sees "a little bitty thunderstorm" in the path of Flight 191's designated runway. A passenger on the flight, who has been sitting in a window seat in the rear of the airplane, would later say the disturbance looked like a dust storm or heavy rain, "because it was solid black."

At four minutes after 6:00, the copilot of Flight 191 tells the pilot he sees lightning coming out of a cloud "right ahead of us." But there are still no warnings from the control tower. Earlier planes have been landing safely at the airport. So Flight 191 continues on its path.

At 6:05, the speed of the plane suddenly, inexplicably accelerates, as if it was being pushed forward by an unknown force. The airspeed races to 157 knots—then to 162 knots. Three seconds later, it is 173 knots. (It should be 150 knots.) When the plane is only 754 feet above the ground, it suddenly drops to 171 knots.

Then heavy rains buffet the plane. Now the airship is less than 700 feet above the earth and the airspeed slips to 137 knots—dangerously close to the point at which the airplane will cease to remain aloft.

The pilot loses his composure. "Push it up!" he screams. "Push it way up. Way up!" The airspeed miraculously increases. One second later, it plunges by 20 knots. The plane rolls, now out of control, and the left wing tilts 20 degrees toward the ground.

A device with a synthesized voice is automatically triggered in the cockpit. The voice sternly warns, "Pull up! Pull up! Pull up!"

The pilot shouts, "TOGA! TOGA!" (An acronym for Take Off and Go Around.) The plane is less than 200 feet off the ground. The warning device keeps repeating, "Pull up! Pull up!"

But the plane strikes the ground. It then bounces back into the sky, then bounces again to the ground. It grazes a highway and destroys an automobile. It skips along crazily, snapping off two light poles, and skims across the ground on the other side of the highway, until its left wing knocks down a huge water tank. The fuselage cartwheels into another water tank as the plane breaks in two, and its tail, set free, slides backward.

The tail of the plane sits alone, clear, safe—as flames from the ruptured fuel tanks engulf the front of Flight 191's fuselage. It is transformed into a crematorium, burning fiercely despite thousands of gallons of water soaking it from the toppled water tanks.

For a few moments all that can be heard is the crackle of the flames. Then all is quiet. Suddenly, the rains come, whipped by winds of up to 70 knots.

The few survivors—shocked, injured, traumatized—hear a metallic screech, then a creak, as the damaged tail of the divided plane settles on the soft earth.

More silence. Only the wind and the rain assure the survivors that they are still alive.

Faintly, then growing stronger, comes the whine of a solitary siren. Another siren sounds, and yet another and another.

Now the sirens surround the survivors with an earsplitting crescendo, until the air and the earth and the sky seem to shriek.

*

Near midnight on this day, 1,000 miles from the fall of Flight 191, a man sits alone, his head in his hands. He is stunned by the horror of the crash—yet still mercifully unaware of how the destruction at Dallas would change the way he would work and live for the rest of his life.

# 1     The Vixen and the Rocket

· 1 ·

A rendering of a vixen was the first image to appear on the monitor screen of an IBM Personal Computer (PC). The next image depicted a rocket ship ejecting a capsule-like projectile across the screen and beyond its borders.

The suggestive imagery was not lost on the members of IBM's Corporate Management Committee (CMC) at Armonk, New York, on a morning during the dog days of August 1980. So the committee said "Go!" when their approval was sought to permit the innovative infant to find its own crib among the company's otherwise utilitarian family tree of computing machines.

But the infant (which matured to become *l' enfant terrible* of the IBM product family) was almost involuntarily aborted only hours before its birth. Everything had worked well when this prototype personal computer was born at IBM's small-systems facility in Boca Raton, Florida. The machine was thoroughly tested and apparently perfected and ready for its debut at the corporation's world headquarters in Armonk, a hamlet in the Hudson Valley about an hour's drive from New York City. The small machine was carefully coddled—but a couple of hours before its scheduled appearance at the CMC meeting, the unit went haywire.

It may have been an instance of science imitating life, but at least some quick rewiring saved the demonstration. This done, the machine performed admirably, and the development team returned to Florida with a mandate to build it. They also returned with only initial funding and the backing to establish a development team that would lead to one of the world's most profitable industrial enterprises. The product did not even have a name, so for the time being, the embryonic machine was dubbed Acorn, under the aegis of an overall development project code-named Chess.

· 2 ·

That a corporation as straitlaced as IBM would deliver a mandate so cavalierly had a lot to do with the business climate around Armonk in those days. By mid-year 1980, the company was pulling itself together after a close brush with the federal government. The Justice Department had mounted an all-encompassing antitrust suit, accusing IBM of engaging in "monopolistic and anti-competitive practices." The suit dragged on for 13 years until the government admitted that the charges against IBM were patently "without merit."

According to *Time* magazine (July 11, 1983), Frank Cary, the company's chairman, stopped grinning long enough to say, "The suit was a tremendous cloud over the company. It couldn't help influencing us in a whole variety of ways. Ending it lifted a huge burden from management's shoulders."

The suit also caused IBM to proceed with so much caution that its share of the computer market dropped from 60 percent to 40 percent during the 1970s. As Cary explained, "This was a time of planning and consolidation."

Among the plans developed during this time was a concept the corporation calls Independent Business Units—referred to as IBUs (just as the International Business Machines Corporation is IBM). To this day, no one person at IBM takes sole credit for the phenomenon of the IBUs nor, for that matter, for the singular idea behind the development of the IBM PC. In fact, at IBM, concepts and ideas tend to evolve as a consequence of the corporation's collective reasoning process, rather than from the solitary inspirations of individual employees. At the time when the idea of IBUs was evaluated as a concept, Frank Cary was still chairman of IBM, though he confidently shared his authority with John R. Opel, who, almost a year to the day before the antitrust suit was dropped, became IBM's president and chief executive officer.

While Cary found great humor in noting that IBUs "might even teach an elephant [IBM] how to tap dance," John Opel simply said,

"You have to have people free to act, or they become dependent. They don't have to be told; they have to be allowed"—a remark taken as his way of saying that the management at IBM was, perhaps, as anachronistic as the keypunch card-tabulating machines on which the company built its reputation.

· 3 ·

John Opel spent his entire business career at IBM. He joined the company in 1949 after graduating from the University of Chicago School of Business. His first job was as a salesman in Jefferson City, Missouri, his hometown. During his first decade with the company, IBM shifted Opel around—but always upward. In 1959, the ultimate direction of his career was marked when he became administrative assistant to Thomas J. Watson, Jr., who was IBM's president and, upon his retirement, U.S. ambassador to the Soviet Union. Opel's final step up came when the board of directors approved his selection to the top spot at IBM, effective on the first day of January 1981.

Opel was philosophically and temperamentally cast in the IBM mold, yet he was not timid about using the power of his office to guide the corporate ethic into his vision of how IBM should present itself for the rest of the century. Accordingly, he set in motion a number of aggressive programs aimed at rectifying the imbalance between IBM's reputation for expertise in marketing and the general perception that the company sold reliable but technologically unimaginative products.

Even suggesting that the latter might be so invariably caused indignation at IBM. Its representatives pointed to the corporation's position as the leading computer company in nearly every one of the 130 countries where it maintained a presence. IBM even went so far as to mount a direct attack on the detractors who charged the company with being a technological laggard. The attack was based on a broad and aggressive advertising campaign calling attention to the more than 11,000 patents that the company's inventors acquired during the past quarter century. But the perception persisted that the company paid more attention to selling its products than it did to establishing itself on the technological leading edge of its industry.

Still, there was a grain of truth in such contentions. IBM would be the first to acknowledge that the foundation of its existence was based on a finely honed regard for customer relations. The company's business *was* selling its products, but its founder, Thomas J. Watson, was canny enough to realize that its relationships with its trade only began when the customer signed the dotted line.

IBM was and is totally dedicated to servicing its accounts, and has no hesitation about dispatching platoons of its people to a customer's site. Sales plus service has been IBM's equation for success and—since its founding as the Computing-Tabulating-Recording Corporation in 1914 (renamed International Business Machines Corporation 10 years later)—the company has never veered from this fundamental approach to business.

For a while, this was enough. After all, once the basic electromechanical design of a keypunch card sorting machine was established, further evolution of the process was limited to cosmetic innovations (not unlike the internal combustion engine). IBM did establish itself at one time as the global leader in typewriter sales, but even here the company scarcely improved on the technology first developed for practical application by Frederick Remington in 1868.

Its commitment to efficient marketing was not altered when the company entered the data-processing industry in 1952. Within four years, IBM had captured 85 percent of the domestic computer market—not necessarily by creating better products, but rather by doing all it could to dispel its customers' fears of computers.

Before long, the company discovered that there is a lot more involved in developing computers than in building typewriters. As the established revenue leader in its field, IBM was naturally expected to produce a steady stream of technological advances. But a well-disciplined enterprise structured with high compensation and special rewards to attract and advance high-powered sales performers had scant appeal to the technological innovators motivated by independence and professional challenge as much as by money.

In other words, a typical computer person who might otherwise balk at an IBM job would jump at the chance to join a Project Chess and develop a product like the Acorn.

· 4 ·

IBM, in its subtly secretive way, tries to conceal what it's working on until a development project produces a market-ready product. To enforce this policy, IBM (like other companies in highly innovative, high-technology industries) requires that anyone inside or outside the company privy to a project in development must sign a non-disclosure agreement. The agreement states, in effect, that the company can levy severe penalties on anyone who acknowledges IBM is working on a new concept.

So the episode of the vixen and the rocket remained tightly guarded when the PC team returned to Florida in August 1980 with their prototype. They had been commissioned to continue, which meant not only to perfect the machine but also to devise detailed marketing and distribution programs and to have the entire project completed and ready for introduction within one year.

At this particular time in mid-August 1980, Project Chess was headed by William C. Lowe, laboratory director of IBM's Entry Level Systems (ELS) Unit in Boca Raton. As manager of Project Chess (in addition to his other duties), Lowe directed a tight cadre of 13 project planning engineers. It was this group that, just a month earlier, had convened to assemble the prototype. Lowe had recruited the baker's dozen (known internally as "The Dirty Dozen") by phoning them at their homes over the July 4th holiday weekend.

Months later, Project Chess became one of seven IBUs chartered by the Corporate Management Committee under Opel's leadership. The others, which dealt with such concepts as robotics and medical systems, had their own reasons for existence.

# 2 Putting a Toe in the Water

· 1 ·

Every so often IBM introduces a product that would have been better left on the drawing board.

Such was the case with its first, fumbling attempts to produce desk-top computers, most notably, the so-called 5100 series. The company actually sold some of these small computers to customers in the late 1970s, but in most instances the purchasers, unless they had a knack for computer technology (or an infinite quotient of perseverance), were frequently frustrated by such idiosyncrasies as disk drives labeled "40" and "80" instead of "A" and "B," or even "1" and "2." And to make matters even more restrictive, only software written by IBM worked on the machines, which had a display so small that it could barely be seen. The 5100 series proved to be an embarrassment, and it was quietly withdrawn from the market.

This early failure at producing a small computer was part of a process that began at IBM in 1975, about a year after a small company in New Mexico called Micro-Instrumentation Telemetry Systems produced a $400 kit that let hobbyists put together a bare bones table-top computer called the Altair. Despite the absence of software for the machine and with minimal promotion, the company easily sold 1,500 Altair kits during the first year. Obviously, there was a need for a new kind of computer. The Tandy Corporation, owners of the Radio Shack stores, picked up on this need. In 1977, the retail chain introduced its version of a table-top computer, and this machine did so well that the Radio Shack stores couldn't keep them in stock.

Originally the machines could be used only to play games or to maintain such information as personal telephone directories and recipe logs. But Tandy, which understands what it does best, saw to it that more sophisticated programs were developed for businesspeople, such as accounts-payable and -receivable packages and programs to maintain tax records. Still, the desk-top units were generally regarded as glorified toys despite the delight they gave to the owners of small- and medium-sized businesses who could justify these little machines as legitimate tax deductions.

· 2 ·

Certainly among the celebrated stories of entrepreneurship in 20th-century America is Apple Computer and how this company grew from a $1,300 start-up operation in a garage in Los Altos, California, in 1976, to an international corporation with more than $2 billion in revenues just 10 years later. This achievement was built from a machine called the Apple II, which is given well-earned credit for starting the personal computer revolution.

In 1978, the development of an accessory called a modem (modulation-demodulation device)—pioneered by Dennis Glayes of Glayes Microcomputer Products, Inc.—allowed personal computers to use telephone lines to exchange information and to tap into mainframe computer data bases. This opened a wealth of information to pc users and helped legitimize the practicality of the machines.

Then, in the spring of 1979, a software program called VisiCalc was developed by two graduate students at the Harvard Business School. VisiCalc (visible calculator) received rapid recognition as the first practical spreadsheet for personal computers. It enabled people to sit at their desks and perform endless permutations of arithmetical possibilities. For the first time, they did not have to stand in line at a mainframe computer to access "what-if" forecasting and its applications to the variables essential to managing a business.

For example, "what if" a certain amount of products is sold in a given number of weeks? How would this affect profits? And "what if" executive perquisites were increased? How would this action influence profits, taxes and stock dividends? VisiCalc harnessed desk-top computer power to develop such answers within seconds.

For a full year, the program was marketed exclusively for the Apple II computer. That was a shrewd move on Apple's part because, in a number of instances, customers would go to a computer retail store to buy VisiCalc, and then ask for "something to run it on." The program was a deserved success, and it is often credited as the impetus behind the rise in Apple's revenues from $800,000 in 1977 to almost $48 million only two years later.

· 3 ·

As the personal computing industry grew from the Altair to Apple II and VisiCalc, IBM's Bill Lowe carefully and quietly did his homework.

Bill Lowe was neither an impatient nor impulsive man; he had spent his first 13 years with IBM as a testing engineer in Raleigh, North Carolina. At that time—the year was 1975—Lowe was named director of development and manufacturing operations for the General Systems Division in Atlanta. It took only two more years before his promotion to director of strategic development for the entire division. Then, in less than a year, Lowe became manager of IBM's Entry Level Systems (ELS) unit at Boca Raton. By the end of 1978 he was promoted yet again, this time to the post of overall laboratory director at the IBM Boca Raton, Florida site.

One of the best ways to get ahead in IBM is to achieve visibility. The idea, if one is not stationed at Armonk, is to find good reasons to visit Armonk. While there, the ambitious visitor should ingratiate himself so that the senior staff at headquarters will welcome more visits. After a while, somebody at Armonk will surely say, "Let's move him up here."

To move toward the top at IBM, one has to have contact on a daily basis with those who've already arrived. And because the truly top people at IBM are all at Armonk, it doesn't do an ambitious executive much good to eight-to-five-it at a place like Boca Raton—then spend his free time frolicking on the white sands of Florida's east coast.

In the late 1970s, Lowe spent nearly as much time at Armonk as he did at Boca Raton. Not all of this time at headquarters was spent meeting with the all-powerful IBM officers including the Corporate Management Committee (CMC). But when he did request an audience with the CMC, the members of that group were familiar enough with Lowe and his style to know that he wouldn't waste their time or energy.

Lowe's string of successes in Boca Raton earned him attention outside of IBM as well. *Business Week* (January 20, 1986) reported: "William C. Lowe is the very picture of an IBM executive: blue suit, conservative tie, square jaw and icy blue eyes. He's known as a consummate manager."

Somewhat more caustically, the *Wall Street Journal* (April 7, 1986) characterized Lowe as "an old-style IBM man," adding that "his wooden public image has prompted some critics to dub him the Gerald Ford of the industry."

What the newspaper called "wooden" is, at least to those who know Lowe well, a trait more charitably defined as "determined." And so, given his determination, "the Gerald Ford of the industry" took the responsibility to tell the Corporate Management Committee why and how IBM should hasten to join the personal computer revolution.

Lowe requested and was granted an appointment to address the CMC in the middle of July 1980. He seized the opportunity to outline the progress of personal computing, emphasizing the visibility and viability of the hot "new" industry. Then he concluded: "The only way we can get into the personal computer business is to go out and buy part of a computer company, or buy both the CPU (central processing unit) and software from people like Apple or Atari—because we can't do this within the culture of IBM."

# 3    Assaying the Golden Apple

· 1 ·

Lowe had been correct when he told the Corporate Management Committee (CMC) that a personal computer could not be built successfully within the current culture of IBM as it existed in mid-1980. He didn't, however, want to leave his analysis simply at that by telling the powers at IBM that they'd literally have to go out and buy its technological expertise just to get into the low end of the computer business.

IBM: the name synonymous with computers throughout the world. IBM: the most profitable company on earth. Now, even to suggest that IBM had to use its money instead of its people's talents to invent a workable machine—well, just who was Lowe?

But—as he hoped might happen because, like a good IBMer, he had done his homework and he knew his audience—the CMC said, in effect: "You say we can't build a little bitty toy of a computer because of our 'culture'? Then go back to Florida and forget all about this 'culture' and you can do whatever needs to be done inside or outside of this 'culture.' But come back within a month from now and tell us how it should be done."

· 2 ·

Lowe discovered that fewer than 10 percent of the 14 million small businesses in the United States were at that time using personal computers. Things were hardly much better in the big corporations, where more than half of the nation's white-collar workers were employed. Here, not even 3 percent of the employees used personal computers on a regular basis. So there was this vast number of people just sitting out

10

there waiting to be enlightened, while the principal players in personal computing—companies like Apple, Tandy, Commodore and Atari— hadn't been able to take a significant share of the market.

Apple Computer, until then the leading producer of personal computers, was especially vulnerable. Technologically, it seemed as if Apple had done everything right, at the beginning. Indeed, it was this company, more than any other, that had proved desk-top computers could have a future. But in 1980, an analysis of Apple's management, marketing, and research and development revealed that the California company had made critical mistakes that were never really rectified. In other words, Apple's market (which had hardly been tapped) was ready for a company with business knowledge like IBM.

· 3 ·

The president of Apple at that time was Steven Jobs, a cofounder of the company. When hardly past his teens, Jobs had helped his high school pal Steven Wozniak build the prototype for the first practical personal computer. Jobs, by his own admission, lacked Wozniak's technological intuitiveness. So Jobs balanced the partnership with his high enthusiasm and a gift for marketing. His was a superb type of promotion, interpreting the mood of the times to present the Apple computer as the machine that best typified the spirit of the counterculture.

Industry observers, in their confidential assessments of Apple, discerned that Jobs exhibited a sort of schizophrenia toward the conduct of his company's business. For example, Jobs espoused a personal aestheticism that mirrored the Zen Buddhism of Jerry Brown, California's often-enigmatic former governor. Jobs, who claimed to be a Republican, slept on a mat in his sparsely furnished mansion and, at one point, sought out an ashram in India.

But this was just one side of Steven Jobs; Lowe was amazed to find that the other was akin to a sort of Citizen Kane of the computer business. Jobs obviously realized that the true market for his company's machines was in businesses of all sizes. IBM, of course, was the dominant factor in this market, though it was not yet Apple's direct competitor. Meanwhile, Jobs, inspired by a remarkable prescience, was already striking away at Big Blue.

In a rambling and frequently cryptic interview with *Playboy* magazine (February 1985), he typified IBM as a company that "absolutely wants it all," then went on to say "When you're shipping 10 million computers a year, even IBM does not have enough mothers to ship one with every computer. So you've got to build motherhood into the computer." This, he mysteriously averred, is something Apple had been doing from the beginning. In the same interview, Jobs warned: "If, for some reason, we make some giant mistakes and IBM wins, my personal feeling is that we are going to enter sort of a Computer Dark Ages for about 20 years."

· 4 ·

While Lowe could not philosophically agree that his company would foment a score of dark years in the industry, he did see that the mistakes Jobs referred to had already been made.

For one, Apple had fumbled its advantage as the first company to introduce a product successfully with potentially broad uses in the thousands of businesses that did not require the raw power of a massive mainframe computer. Because Apple was for a long while the only company to "own" this market, it was uniquely positioned to achieve strong growth and high profit margins. But the company never realized its potential, and it was apparent to Lowe that a competitive machine could be introduced, offering more performance for about the same price as the Apple models.

Lowe also found another of Apple's flaws when he balanced its service and support capabilities against those of IBM. Because it entered the computer business nearly 30 years before, Big Blue always knew that higher profits on its products could be consistently achieved by selling increasingly versatile and expensive machines. To market its upscale products successfully, IBM would emphasize the benefits of its broad-based commitment to service and support, which for the most part were already in place when the company moved beyond keypunch card-processing machines.

In early 1980, for example, IBM had nearly 8,400 salespeople in the field, working out of 650 sales branch offices. Apple, at the same time, had about 100 full-time sales personnel scattered among 12 branches.

In its first attempts at the international market, Apple came up against such Japanese giants as NEC, Oki, Fujitsu, Hitachi and Sharp—all of which receive favorable competitive treatment in their homeland. In Europe, Apple tried to make a name against entrenched companies such as Olivetti, Philips, Triumph Adler and Nixdorf. But, all the while, IBM *was* the internationally recognized computer maker, principally because the marketing-oriented nature of the company meant it was a major employer and, thus, a national asset in every country where it did business. Apple, for all its ambitions, would need a decade to position itself effectively against IBM's highly visible image overseas.

Lowe soon realized that the success of IBM's projected line of personal computers would depend on their compatibility with the company's established line of medium-sized and mainframe machines. IBM was obviously in a position to make a linkup of machines a reality; Apple was not. Because IBM had extensive patent protection on its machines, Apple was restricted to operating within its smaller product universes.

· 5 ·

In 1980, nearly every personal computer on the market (and, at one time, there were nearly 200 of them) was incompatible with its competitors; that is, a software program that ran on a Commodore machine would not run on a model from Radio Shack, and vice versa. Since it was regarded as the best-engineered machine of its type at that time, the Apple II became an ad hoc standard of sorts, and it was usually selected as the machine-of-choice by independent developers of software and hardware.

This proved something—but not much. The people using small computers desperately needed a single operating standard, but despite Apple's overall leadership in the field at the time, its operating system simply could not win universal acceptance as the de facto standard for business applications. Lowe predicted that the prestige of the IBM name on a personal computer would act to force Big Blue's operating standard on the rest of the industry.

Apple chose to maintain the proprietary nature of its operating system and the machine's read-only memory (ROM). While this meant that third party software and hardware developers could make products for the Apple, they would have to be licensed by the computer manufacturer to do so. In most cases, their products, such as printers, were sold under the Apple name. It was as if companies like Goodyear and Firestone sold their tires under the names General Motors, Ford or Chrysler—and then paid a premium to the automobile manufacturers for doing so. Lowe believed there was a better alternative than the Apple approach to dealing with third-party developers and suppliers.

Originally intended for hobbyists, the Apple II used a computer chip that was practical for its target market but rather limited for the broader needs of a business. The machine's random access memory (RAM) grew in fragmented increments from 16 kilobytes up to 128 kilobytes, which was regarded as its practical limit. The machine used a cassette recorder storage system instead of disk drives. Its monitor was a 40-column television screen that had no highlighting capability and could not show more than 128 characters. Nevertheless, the machine was certainly acceptable—especially considering the quality of the competition in 1980.

But Lowe could see that Apple was having trouble winning mass business acceptance by its market. He also had pride in and respect for the way his company had proven its ability to serve American business. Still, he was convinced that IBM, as it ran its business in mid-1980, was as inept in its own way as Apple was in finding the best way to enter the emerging market for small computers.

# 4  Riding the
# Fast Track

· 1 ·

As described, the pc project would by definition have to be structured outside of the traditional organization. If it should fail—and God knows, every other attempt at IBM to build a desk-top computer had—it would be a devastating loss. Lowe weighed what the benefits of success on such a mission would mean to an eager IBMer like himself. By heading the project that brought the best of all possible pcs to market, he would at the very least enhance his reputation within the corporation.

In summing up, Lowe recommended that a task force of hand-picked engineers should be immediately assigned to build a prototype machine. Once this group was in place, the prototype could most likely be completed within a month, he said. At that time, Lowe would return to the CMC for a demonstration. In the meantime, the project would be shrouded in IBM's usual secrecy.

Lowe returned to Florida and waited. He was not anxious. His presentation had been courteously received, and he knew the CMC was still pondering his suggestion that IBM should either buy from a company that really knew how to build pcs, or bend its intractable approach to how it did business. Either way, the company needed a pc on the market to round out its product line and to fulfill Chairman Opel's pledge to have IBM make its presence known in every area of the computer industry.

Meanwhile, the CMC was giving more than usual consideration to trying once again to get the company into the desktop computer market. The force and logic of Lowe's well-researched presentation defeated the arguments of any naysayers. Lowe would have his way. The CMC would look forward to a preview of the prototype within the next few weeks.

Since in 1980 the Fourth of July fell on a Friday, Lowe put in a modified version of a full workweek. He "slept in" until 7 AM, dressed in sport clothes as a concession to the holiday spirit and went to his office.

The CMC had granted enough funding to recruit 12 engineers to build the all-important prototype pc. Every engineer on the project would have to be an expert in the development and implementation of this special technology. Each should also be a free-spirited iconoclast—the sort of responsible rebel who appreciated the benefits of being at IBM, but who is always ready for and reflexively responsive to any opportunities that challenge established order.

In short, what Bill Lowe wanted to start with was a man like Bill Sydnes.

· 2 ·

After three years in the Navy, Sydnes joined IBM in October 1965 as a test engineer. His first job at the company was to test the radio frequency assemblages used to track the Saturn satellite system. He then became involved in designing small-computer systems before his promotion to first-line engineering manager in the spring of 1972. Four years later he was promoted to assistant for technical development, and less than two years after that, to senior engineer and manager of systems design and architecture at IBM's Entry Level Systems (ELS) Unit at Boca Raton.

Along the way, he earned five formal IBM awards, including cash and plaques signed by division presidents. The awards saluted Sydnes' skills at "design excellence" and his accomplishments in "technical/ management excellence." As if it weren't enough to win those honors while ascending the corporate ladder and raising a family, Sydnes also found time to graduate from Florida Atlantic University at Boca Raton with what he remembers was a straight-A average.

Lowe had spotted Sydnes early on and correctly assessed him as a clever rebel within the system—a technical wizard whose personality and style were polar opposites to Lowe's but who, nevertheless, was a remarkable achiever, even if difficult to "tame."

Sometimes Sydnes seemed like a wild man, attacking a project with a fierce intensity, oblivious to time, eating on the run (if at all), his tie askew, his shirttail flapping. More than once, obsessed by his work, Sydnes would push himself until he couldn't go on—at which time he would collapse into sleep on top of or under his worktable. And when he awoke, he would go back to work.

And he was one smart engineer. The man seemed to do everything right, never failing to produce what was expected of him. He delivered, and he did so on time. When he was involved with the ultimately aborted 5120 computing system, Sydnes, as manager of the project, had guided the machine through conception and design and into production within only 90 days.

It was this singular accomplishment with the 5120 that so impressed Lowe. He had told the CMC that he would return in August with a working conception of what he envisioned as IBM's first successful desktop computer. So for him to say that he had the capability (without further explanation) to take this project from scratch and make a machine in record time was based on his experiences with Sydnes at Boca Raton and earlier at Atlanta.

Lowe was confident because all along he knew that he had Sydnes down in Florida—a man who worked day and night and slept under his desk and sometimes forgot to eat, but proved he could put a whole computer together in weeks—not months—and make the machine good enough to merit the IBM name. So what did it matter if the 5120 machine didn't impress its potential customers? The machine worked. It did what it was supposed to do. That's what counts in engineering. Selling the machine is somebody else's job.

So when the CMC asked in July, "How soon?" Lowe was ready. "Less than 30 days," he stated. Some members of the CMC recalled the record turnaround of the 5120 from conception to production in 90 days, but no one remembered, or even seemed to care, how that minor miracle came to pass. It was enough that Lowe knew.

· 3 ·

Bill Sydnes was on vacation in Alabama when the call came from Lowe. They had known each other since the late 1970s, when Lowe was director of strategic development at the General Systems Division (GSD) in Atlanta and Sydnes was assistant for technical development at the GSD. When Lowe went to Boca Raton as the ELS manager, he brought Sydnes with him to work on a project called the Datamaster.

The Datamaster was running almost two years behind schedule because its software development was lagging. When Roger Abernathy, the manager of the project, took a leave to attend an IBM school, the ever-adroit Sydnes, acting on his own initiative, prepared a proposal suggesting that a machine, to be called the 5120, should be spun off from the bogged-down Datamaster project. Sydnes received the go-ahead, and, when Abernathy returned from school, he was furious at what had happened in his absence.

During the holiday weekend phone conversation, Lowe told Sydnes that the pc development project would be far divorced from the daily bureaucracy at IBM. If Sydnes accepted the assignment, he, as the first member of the task force, would also be in charge of day-to-day work on the project. Of course, Lowe added, the time frame on the task was so tight that Sydnes would once again be working day and night, and the rest of his team would also be expected to do so. If the task force could put together a working machine within a month, there was every reason to believe the CMC would approve further work on the project, and Sydnes, working those weird hours, could continue to stay well away from the overbearingly conventional way of doing things at IBM.

That was the clincher. By this time, Sydnes was well schooled in and thoroughly frustrated by IBM. Still fresh in his mind was the Datamaster experience—the project so far behind schedule that it even ceased to be a joke. Sydnes had been the only person to see the way out, and he made it work. And what did he get for that? A scolding by his boss and, somewhat belatedly and certainly ironically, another of those Technical/Management Excellence Awards for "inventing" and implementing the 5120, even though no one could sell the machine.

Now here was Lowe giving Sydnes yet another opportunity to make a new machine, but with the guarantee that it could and would be done "outside the culture of IBM." With that promise of independence, the offer was too tempting for Sydnes to refuse.

Since Lowe had steered him into the opportunity with his "Bill, this is Bill calling" Fourth-of-July firecracker, Sydnes, at this point, might have assumed he would head the project all the way through, reporting only to Lowe when and if it was necessary. After all, he had known Lowe for years. They had worked together at Atlanta and had come to Boca Raton as a sort of team. This, of course, was the way it should be done, and so Sydnes said, "Count me in."

# 5 The Finest
Task Force
Ever Assembled

· 1 ·

The task force assembled soon after the long holiday weekend. Sydnes, who had cut his Alabama vacation short to join the task force, met with Lowe when he returned to Boca Raton, and they handpicked the balance of this first team. Straight away, neither man had any trouble deciding that Joe Bauman should be a member of the group.

After graduating from the University of Kansas with a degree in mechanical engineering, Bauman joined IBM at Rochester, Minnesota. He was quick to recognize that technical expertise alone would carry him just so far at IBM. So he refined his administrative skills and used them to move upward through several management positions at Rochester, Atlanta and overseas. After 18 months in Vimercate, Italy, he returned to the United States to work in engineering at Rochester. By this time, however, Bauman had savored the better life at IBM, and he deftly maneuvered to get out of Rochester. He wanted a transfer to Boca Raton, which in the late 1970s was already building its reputation as one of the more lively places to work in the corporation.

Bauman moved to Boca Raton in 1978, and worked on an earlier, failed version of the pc. Meanwhile, he received a promotion to functional manager of manufacturing. In June 1980, Bauman accepted Lowe's invitation to join the pc task force. He worked day and night to hammer out a plan for the pc's business and manufacturing strategy. Bauman's plan was so well conceived that its basic premises remained unaltered throughout the duration of the product's development.

Looking back on the formation of the task force, a cynic close to the scene later remarked, "There were really only 13 people on the project, but since it worked out as well as it did, you could go through IBM today and find 500 people who'll tell you they were members of the original task force. It all depends on who you want to believe."

· 2 ·

Task forces were not unique at IBM. One of the more successful examples of the concept sparked the development of the System 360, a well-received mainframe computer introduced in April 1964. The 360 task force set an operational standard that is still the model at IBM.

Members of the 360 task force worked closely together. They met every day. They had access to whatever information they needed. The 360 task force was permitted to sidestep the company's bureaucracy to work on solutions—rather than reports. As a result, the System 360 proved to be an eminently practical product for its time.

With this and similar experiences to guide them, the members of the pc task force settled in to develop an appealing prototype that would stimulate the interest (and, ultimately, the sensibilities) of the CMC.

The task force realized that the demonstration model that had to be rushed through production to satisfy the Corporate Management Committee (CMC)'s early July deadline would hardly be the same as the final product. Still, merely to demonstrate that they could build a desktop computer that featured amusing graphics would be insufficient to get a commitment from the corporate heavyweights on the CMC.

In the course of daily brainstorming sessions, the task force members gambled with their reputations in the corporation when they decided to propose that the new machine should have an "open architecture"; to save time, its operating system should come from a source other than IBM; its principal components should be open for competitive bids; the machine should have a 16-bit capability and—to complete the "apostasy"—the new machine should be sold through retail channels divorced from and even alien to IBM's sacrosanct sales organization.

· 3 ·

The "open architecture" concept was not only revolutionary for IBM, it was almost unheard of within the computer industry. The architecture of a computer is the machine's internal workings; that is, it is the structure of the thought processes that go into the design of a machine and how they are applied to make a computer perform its operations. Since this applied thought is often the result of highly specialized knowledge—as well as intuition, inspiration and ingenuity—its expression in a computer is what gives a particular machine its unique, intrinsic value.

The basic components of a computer—its case, chips, boards, wiring and power supply—are all pretty much the same; they represent only a fraction of the value of the machine. The true worth of a computer is directly related to the skills of its designers. A well-designed machine, backed by a reputable manufacturer, has the potential to be a profitable piece of merchandise. This is why the architecture of a computer is so valuable and why, until the pc task force thought otherwise, the architecture of computers was always protected by layers of patents. This is how Apple Computer made so much money so quickly through the late 1970s; its machines had what was then an ingeniously designed architecture, and the company put patent protection on its value.

By seeing the architecture in another light, the IBM task force was choosing a radical alternative. Their justification was that the machine could not make it to market in a tight time frame unless the hardware and software development were performed independently. The idea was to rush through the basic hardware, that is, the computer itself. When this task was completed, in about three to four months, the primary machine could be released (as is usual, on a confidential basis) to a select cadre of software developers. Then, at the same time the hardware was being fine-tuned and its cosmetics set in place, software development for the machine could start. That way, when the machine was ready, it could be introduced with practical software packages already prepared. The computer would, in effect, be a fully capable system, ready to plug-in and operate its own practical software applications.

The idea was, quite simply, a stroke of genius. To this day, no one individual on or close to the task force takes credit for the "open architecture" inspiration. It was an idea that developed out of the freewheeling, brainstorming framework of the task force. It is a classic example of what can be accomplished when people are allowed freedom of thought in an environment guided by the principle that there is no such thing as a dumb idea.

· 4 ·

Of only slightly less importance was the task force's idea to acquire the machine's operating system outside of IBM. The operating system in a computer is akin to the transmission in an automobile. Both systems give "instructions" to the machines; without these systems, the machines would sit doing nothing more than blinking or chugging.

The operating system of a computer is separate from yet essential to the hardware itself. This means the system can actually come from any competent source; though, until the task force came up with its idea, the operating systems for all IBM computers were traditionally developed within the company. That's simply the way it was always done.

The task force had correctly reasoned that by buying the machine's operating system outside the company, the pc project would be able to proceed on or even ahead of its brutal schedule. While dedication to meeting the deadline was certainly a factor behind this recommendation, the task force also weighed the questionable ability of IBM to develop efficient software on a tight schedule. Everyone in the group quickly conceded that the structured disciplines of the corporation did not tend to attract the innovative, independent thinkers that excel at systems development. In time, of course, even the software programmers at IBM would come up with some sort of a workable operating system, but in how much time?

· 5 ·

The task force's recommendation to buy the components for the pc on the "open market" was not a ploy to pull further away from the IBM supply lines. As engineers, the members of the task force had a high respect for the quality of the components developed by IBM and sold under the company's label. What they had less regard for was the company's pricing structure for such essential parts of a computer as disk drives, circuit boards and the so-called peripherals, such as printers.

IBM's refusal to rush computer components through its internal supply lines is not actually a fault. For good reasons, the company is obsessed with testing, retesting and then testing again every essential piece of hardware that goes into its machines. This is, perhaps, the principal reason why the company's products tend to have an introductory lag in the marketplace. Quite simply, by bending backward to build its machines to be both sturdy and reliable, IBM avoids future service problems.

In its brainstorming sessions, the task force reasoned that user demands on the new desk-top computer would not be as severe as those on its more conventional machines—some of which run around the clock every day of the week. When a computer operates on that tough of a schedule, its parts must be engineered for endurance and reliability.

But a desk-top machine, operated by two or three persons at most, is unlikely to be processing words and numbers 24 hours a day. Therefore, while the new pc's components would need to be reliable, they would not require the extensive fail-safe testing used for the hardware in, for instance, a complex guidance system for a space satellite. Furthermore, the parts to be used in the design had been available and applied for almost six years.

The research, development and extensive testing that goes into the perfection of a computer's components obviously influences its eventual cost. The goal of the task force was to make the pc as simple and effective as possible. The components would be basically "off-the-shelf," that is, the testing accepted as an industry standard would be adequate for what had to be accomplished. The fussing with component testing indigenous to IBM, commendable though that may be, would make it impossible to bring a price-competitive pc to market within a year.

If the CMC accepted this recommendation without qualification, it would establish a precedent, because never before in its history had IBM allowed an entire computer sold under its name to be built from parts obtained outside the company.


· 6 ·


A microprocessor is a silicon chip about the size of a small fingernail. It contains the operating instructions for a computer. By mid-year 1980, the personal computers on the market were using what is called "an 8-bit microprocessor configuration," which was an acceptable standard for hobbyists and computer tinkerers but deficient in the power and sophistication necessary to satisfy the more demanding needs of the business market.

The pc task force wanted to move up to a 16-bit architecture because it not only ran faster than the 8-bit configuration, but with 16 bits, the machine could also be more "internally comprehensive." In other words, fewer coding instructions would be needed for the machine and software development could be vastly simplified.

Until then, the conventional microprocessor chip used an 8088 configuration. Since there was a more powerful chip, known as the 8086, just coming onto the market, the task force was tempted to use this chip. But the team prudently held back. They agreed that the more powerful 8086 chip could kill the entire project at the CMC level.

As Sydnes later recalled, "The 8086 had too much horsepower. It would essentially run up the tailpipe of the products IBM already had on the marketplace, or that they were planning to introduce. So we went with the 8088, despite its constrained performance, but also because its architecture would allow us eventually to expand to the 8086 market. That turned out to be a very wise choice, because the 8088 proposal sailed right through all of the management and other political reviews within IBM."

The task force finally chose an Intel 8088 chip. This advanced chip allowed the machine's memory to expand easily up to 512 kilobytes—a level adequate to accommodate nearly every general purpose software application available for small computers in 1980. And since the 8088 chip had been on the market for some time and was widely available, it was not an enigma to the software development community, which meant that the third-party manufacturers could build their pc-oriented products quickly, easily and inexpensively.

· 7 ·

Finally, the task force boldly suggested that the new pc should be marketed through conventional retail stores. They knew the new pc had to be competitive in its market and that its relatively low price would squeeze the compensation for IBM's commission-driven sales staff. The ultimate pc could be the finest product of its type in existence, but the salespeople would still concentrate their time and efforts on moving the company's more expensive line of mainframe and midsized computers, which, as far as the sales staff was concerned, only made sense.

It made sense, too, for the task force to heed IBM's own research, which revealed that larger companies don't normally go shopping for computers in retail stores. Historically, however, that's exactly how personal computers had been sold. Retail store sales to large businesses reflected the fact that corporations sent their people into the stores to buy personal computers. They did not wait for a computer company's sales force to call. As a result of this reversal of initiative in computer marketing, large businesses were responsible for a high percentage of computer sales in retail outlets.

The task force was especially impressed by the Computerland chain of franchised retail stores. Its founder, William Millard, was a veteran of the small-computer industry who at one time had operated a company that pioneered home hobbyist computer kits. (Millard's company made the IMSAI 8080, the computer featured in the movie *War Games*.)

Obviously, Millard was a man who respected the worth of microcomputers. Meanwhile, his growing nationwide network of franchised outlets was quickly becoming dominant in small-computer retailing. The task force liked what Millard was doing with his stores, and now they wanted to give him an opportunity to help develop and sell the first personal computer with an IBM nameplate.

· 8 ·

After returning to Boca Raton, Sydnes was put in charge of the engineering group and Eggebrecht was assigned to systems engineering. Others in the original "Dirty Dozen" (as they became known) were Joe Bauman, head of manufacturing; Jerry Benedict, in charge of financial analysis; Dick Coon, director of marketing; Larry Duffy, who took over customer service responsibilities; Ed Merrill, in charge of product planning; Larry Rojas, director of business and financial planning; Jack Sam, in charge of software development; Tom Wheeler, corporate programming; Bob Wolfson, product planning; and Jan Winston, who was responsible for product planning and strategy. Bill Lowe, of course, continued as overall manager of the project.

The task force had been meeting every day for three weeks to polish its recommendations and to make enough of a machine to gain a go-ahead from the CMC. While their friends and neighbors were heading off on vacations, the pc task force routinely logged 14-hour days in the summer heat of coastal Florida.

Why? Although some members would cry "enough!" when the pc prototype was completed in early August, others couldn't wait to carry on with the project.

# 6 Essential Approvals

## · 1 ·

Outwardly confident, although understandably apprehensive, Lowe completed plans to return to Armonk in early August. He was accompanied by Bill Sydnes, who in turn brought along Lewis Eggebrecht, an engineer who had worked side by side with Sydnes on building the prototype. Sharing the passenger cabin with the trio on the flight from Florida was the precious prototype of the still-to-be-named desk-top computer.

Despite the machine's malfunction shortly before its demonstration to the Corporate Management Committee (CMC), the demonstration with the vixen and the rocket proceeded as planned.

Sydnes and Eggebrecht were then asked to wait outside the boardroom while Lowe alone presented the task force's recommendations on how to get IBM quickly and effectively into the bottom tier of the computer market.

On the other side of the closed doors, the two engineers waited with mounting impatience. While their purpose in being at Armonk was to shepherd the machine through the first part of the presentation and to give Lowe moral support, Sydnes and Eggebrecht had not intended to stake their careers in the company on the whim of the CMC.

They knew that the corporation, with its seemingly inexhaustible resources, had a habit of marshaling men and money to explore the feasibility of product introductions. Such work would be assigned to an ad hoc task force that might or might not continue to have life, depending on the decision of the CMC. These projects were often abandoned at some point in their life spans, for any number of reasons.

· 2 ·

If the CMC kills a project, the basic proposal behind the project could be recast in a fresh form and win approval. "No," with its implications of finality, is hardly ever heard at a CMC conclave.

Somewhat indirectly, the genesis of the pc project originated with the CMC and, in particular, at the behest of Chairman John Opel, who would not concede defeat despite prior failures to bring a successful desk-top machine to market. Firm believer that Opel was, his instincts told him that somewhere, somehow, someone within IBM had the capability to lead the way in filling the embarrassing gap that existed at the low end of the product line.

Succinctly: There was to be an IBM desk-top computer. It had to be developed within the corporation and it must, in every way, merit the IBM nameplate. This was not just a wish. It was a direct command.

The situation created an obvious advantage and source of consolation for the members of the pc task force, since the decision that their work would be scuttled was not likely. There was, for instance, the time element, and here the pressure was clearly on the CMC not to be finicky about such usual concerns as who would produce the parts for the machine, where the operating system would come from, if the machine's architecture would be open or closed and even how the pc would eventually be marketed.

Sydnes and Eggebrecht were still riding the high they got during the meeting when the CMC as much as admitted that the prototype had great potential. Of course, the sticky business of getting approval for the project to continue was something else; that end of it was for Lowe alone to handle: Lowe, with his inimitable polish and keen regard for the sensibilities of the CMC.

· 3 ·

Finally Lowe emerged from his stand-up session before the CMC. Sydnes and Eggebrecht leaped to their feet. Teasingly solemn at first, then breaking into a reassuring grin, Lowe told his two anxious associates that the CMC had agreed to the proposal as presented and had given its imprimatur to upgrade the task force to a full-scale Product Development Group.

This meant the pc project and its product-under-development would have their own code names and special funding to bring the group into operation. For the next 60 days, the IBU task force could attend to staff recruitment, continue its work on a fully functional prototype pc and, in its spare time, work out the details of manufacturing and marketing the machine.

In early October, the development project would reach a "checkpoint." At this critical juncture, additional work on the project would be held up pending approval by the CMC of the Independent Business Unit (IBU)'s progress report and its proposal for further activity.

In the meantime, it was full speed ahead. Much work would be involved, and the rewards might be unparalleled glory and gratification within the corporation and throughout the computer industry.

Lowe, Sydnes and Eggebrecht were ecstatic as they boarded the plane for the return flight to Florida. For the engineers, this was the first time in their careers that they'd entered the privileged fast track at the usually staid and stodgy IBM—and it was all being done with the full approval and eager encouragement of top management.

For Lowe, this day marked yet another victory with the CMC. He would have his own way of getting along and getting ahead in IBM.

·  4  ·

In keeping with corporate policy, no formal announcement was made of the project's formation. Within the company, though, word spread rapidly that a new unit was in place down in Boca Raton, operating under a series of liberal mandates without precedent in the company's history.

The news and details of the project sparked strong reactions within IBM. Some IBMers felt the CMC had lost its wits in a desperate, last-ditch effort to close a gap in its product line that many believed was better left unfilled rather than resort to daring departures from the IBM way.

Others looked on the project as another career dead end, seeing it as nothing more than a recast of an inevitably doomed effort to develop a machine that the typical engineer and salesperson at IBM were fundamentally inept at designing and marketing.

Still, many at IBM were attracted to the new project. They saw it for what it was—an opportunity to build a brand-new computer in a

Silicon Valley environment, but with a unique plus: The machine would be backed by the personnel and financial resources of the most powerful industrial entity on earth, and the final product would carry the corporation's nameplate, which, by itself, would all but guarantee the machine's ultimate acceptance in the marketplace.

Later, the most adventurous of these positivists set about finding a way to transfer to Boca Raton.

### · 5 ·

Lowe, perhaps more than anyone else, was responsible for the fact of the new group—now known as "Project Chess," developing a product called the "Acorn."

Lowe had shown that he could recognize a reasonable idea, burnish it, develop it, present it brilliantly and win acceptance for it.

His strategy was to continue as a sort of godfather for Project Chess, while the day-to-day management of the effort—which by now was essentially a crash project—would be turned over to a reliable senior program manager.

This person would have to be technically competent and have an excellent reputation for managing and motivating the type of disparate rat-pack mavericks that were drawn to Project Chess.

Because of the project's excruciatingly tight timetable, Lowe was not in a position to experiment with managers. He had to be right the first time. Typical of Lowe, he knew all along whom he wanted to succeed him on Project Chess. He wanted Don Estridge.

# 7    Just Call Me "Don"

· 1 ·

Philip D. Estridge was known as "Don" since his high school days in Jacksonville, Florida. He had a natural affinity for the sciences and was skilled at working with his hands, which led him to his first job as an apprentice electrician while he was still in high school. Later, while still a high school student, he worked for a civil engineer.

In 1955, he enrolled at the University of Florida in Gainesville. During his sophomore year, he confirmed his decision to become an engineer and, this same year, he met a coed named Mary Ann Hellier from Jensen Beach, Florida.

In June 1958, Estridge married Mary Ann Hellier, graduated with a bachelor of science degree in electrical engineering and, at his father's earnest urging, he joined IBM. For the rest of his life, he never seriously considered working for another company.

His new employer started Estridge at its Federal Systems Unit at Kingston, New York. He spent four years at Kingston working on a contract IBM had with the air force to develop an early warning radar system known as SAGE, an acronym for Semi-Automatic Ground Environment.

In his fifth year with the company, Estridge became a systems programmer for IBM and started work on the Apollo moon missions. "There was nothing like watching Borman come from behind the far side of the moon for the first time," Estridge would recall. "We knew to the tenth of a second when he would appear and that if it didn't happen, then he'd never come out. And there he was."

In 1969, giving credence to the tongue-in-cheek joke at IBM that the company's initials really mean "I've Been Moved," Estridge returned to

Florida, where the company had opened a new plant built the year before at Boca Raton.

For the first time, the Estridges were able to hang their pictures and begin to build their lives around their daughters in their home state.

· 2 ·

IBM built its plant at Boca Raton to experiment with what the company calls "Entry Level Systems." This is a euphemism for small, low-cost computers—a product area in which the company was, at that time, woefully unsophisticated.

Even then, more than a full decade before the pc project had life, the company sensed that something might be stirring in the segment often scorned as "the low end of the business." IBM did not attain its global dominance by staying in one segment of its industry, no matter how profitable the big mainframes might be. The company had already achieved a certain degree of success through its General Systems Division at Atlanta, which had moved significantly into the midsized computer market against such formidable adversaries as Wang Laboratories, Digital Equipment Corporation and Data General Corporation.

When the Boca Raton plant opened its doors, Steven Jobs was still in junior high school and an apple was something to be polished for the teacher. Personal computer technology, as such, was essentially undreamed of at the time—though there were indications that products like separate terminals might be used to access data from mainframe computers in a process that would come to be called "networking."

But for the time being, what was later to become the Entry Level Systems facility at Boca Raton was content to live with its reputation as an outpost of experimentation isolated from the corporate mainstream: a shirtsleeves operation in a comfortable climate.

· 3 ·

His being six-feet four inches tall didn't hurt, though it was Estridge's style and attitude that made him outstanding. He had that ineffable quality press agents call "charisma." His associates remember Estridge as "charming," "likeable" and "a regular sort of guy."

As one of his admirers recalled, "You always knew when Don was in the room. There was a magnetism about him. He attracted people and he could bring out their best when he wanted to."

He had a loose, lanky gait; he used his hands and arms when he talked; his mannerisms were totally unaffected. A trade-journal columnist called Estridge "the Cary Grant of microcomputers"—a well-intentioned appellation that occasioned no small amount of teasing in the corridors at Boca Raton.

Unquestionably, he was a leader. Such leadership is not necessarily rare at IBM, where it is identified, encouraged and nurtured as an ideal by-product of the corporation's competitive culture.

Had Estridge been stationed elsewhere within the company, such as at Armonk, he would probably have been just one achiever among many. He might have distinguished himself there, but it is more likely that the corporate restraints on individualism that are strongest near the center of power at IBM might have stifled him.

But, at a place like Boca Raton where nearly unbridled initiative is encouraged, someone like Estridge, almost by his presence alone, would naturally gravitate to the top.

He shined as a programmer—one of those who starts with a blank screen on a computer terminal and then proceeds, in a totally logical and orderly manner, to compose a plan that quickly taps technology to solve any series of problems.

One of the first problems Estridge was assigned to was the accursed Series 1 project. The machine was essentially ready, but it lacked functional software. Estridge was put in charge of an operational group whose assignment was to complete a segment of software for the machine.

Every day, the project fell further behind schedule. Estridge would alternately threaten and cajole his group. He would take the reins and then relax his grip. Eventually, 18 months behind schedule, the Series 1 operational software was completed. Estridge then formed another team to handle the successful development of an IBM Series 1 computer for the State Farm Insurance Company.

When the CMC gave its approval for the formation of the pc project, Estridge let it be known that he wanted to join the development team. He had been fascinated for some time by personal computer technology. He had an Apple II at home, and to relax after a day at the plant working with computers, he would tinker with his Apple. The problem was that Estridge, who by now was an established group leader at the company, could not be slotted essentially downward on an equal operational level with engineers on the pc team who generally lacked his administrative experience.

If Lowe's personal vision for the future held, Estridge could be advantageously moved in to head the project. That meant no "stranger" from outside the Boca Raton outpost would be transferred to the assignment and it also meant that Lowe, by handpicking his successor, would be able to maintain an intimacy with the project that he'd shepherded to this point.

Meanwhile, Estridge was building a reputation as a creative marketer somewhat beyond the corporate norm. His loyalty to the company for the past 10 years was beyond debate; he was held in high regard by both his superiors and peers; he did not grumble and chafe when the company's way of doing things conflicted with what he may have perceived as a better way.

All in all, Estridge was safe. He could be trusted. He was a candidate for promotion.

# 8  Tasks at Hand

Now it was mid-August 1980, and the engineers were intent on putting together a fully functional prototype of the Acorn. This would be the machine that would lock in the basic technology. Duplicates of the machine with details of its layout, components and architecture would then be made available to the carefully chosen outside companies responsible for developing the operating system, software and printers.

Pressed by the one-year market-ready deadline, the engineering staff was quickly doubled to 26, even though by IBM standards this was still a small staff to tackle the building of a new computer.

At this point, a final name for the machine was the furthest thing from the engineers' minds, and although they weren't even sure how much space on a desk-top the machine would require, they did know that it wouldn't forge any technological breakthroughs.

In fact, all the components of the new computer had to have been already proven in the market, so all the principal components would be drawn from technology that was already four or five years old. The parts would, of course, be laid out in an original manner, but even these specifications would not have any leading edges in such key areas as logic or high-memory density. Rather, everything specified was to be state-of-the-art and have high reliability. The point was to minimize risk taking, and to avoid getting caught up in IBM's extensive testing procedures. The result, ideally, would be a machine that people would take a look at and say, "Hey! Technologically this computer is really nothing."

Joe Bauman, who was in charge of the machine's manufacture, recalled:

Our strategy was to simplify everything, devise a sound plan and not deviate from it. Since we didn't have time to develop and test all of our own components, we shopped for completely functioning and pre-tested subassemblies and put them together. That cut development and test time. But we assembled and tested the final product ourselves.

The pc planners on Project Chess were intrigued by the idea of IBM being in what amounted to a special position to develop standards for the microcomputer industry. For the time being—but only for the time being—consideration of setting an industry standard was officially postponed while the staff concentrated on grasping the existing infrastructure of the personal computer industry as it related to marketing, distribution techniques, pricing, customer alternatives, software suppliers, hardware add-on suppliers and manufacturers of peripheral devices.

· 2 ·

As their knowledge of the field increased, the staff decided it would be best for IBM simply to fit in as a new player in the game. To attempt to be different, they reasoned, would be too much of a risk. This reasoning was based on their assessment of an industry that gave every indication of being poised for a dramatic breakthrough in customer acceptance during the 1980s. Despite the staff's reverence for the marketing power of Big Blue, they could not accept the proposition that any single supplier of hardware, software or peripherals could provide the final answer to an emerging market's demands.

While there was agreement among the staff not to take the machine to the outer limits of microcomputer technology as it existed in 1980, they did push cautiously past certain standards.

For example, they opted for using a 16-bit input/output channel, though 8-bit I/O channels were the standard. The staff deduced that the 8-bit channel would limit the performance of the new machine's main processor because twice as many bits would have to be moved to execute any given operation, and so a 16-bit channel was chosen to give the machine an edge in speed against what was then available.

The first version of the Acorn would have up to "only" 64 kilobytes of main memory on the machine's motherboard, which was still 25 percent more Ks for a user to play with than the 48K standard at the time. (By 1987, 640K had become an accepted minimum for main memory.)

During one of its early brainstorming sessions, the staff concluded that the available applications software fell far below its potential because it was limited to somewhat less than 48K in order to function on then-existing desk-top computers. Each increase in main memory (typically made in multiples of 8K) would permit that much more versatility in the software.

In one of its more brilliant moves, the staff decided to build the Acorn with expansion slots that would permit insertion of accessory boards containing additional memory. When taken to its limit with expansion technology, the new machine could even then accommodate up to 640K of main memory.

The machine's floppy disk drives could handle only 160K of storage. There was a suspicion that people would wonder why there was more memory than disk capacity, which would prevent the transfer of data memory to a disk.

The staff saw this, however, as a theoretical problem. They reasoned that users of the machine would be content with saving only the data they were concerned about. In other words, the additional memory would not only permit the development of more versatile software, but it would also allow the user to have a vast scratch pad to augment customized applications of the technology.

Its designers wanted the machine to be able to work in a wide range of environments, regardless of heat, temperature, humidity and electrical interference. Given these considerations, it became apparent that the machine could not, in reality, be as small as it might have because of its electrical needs.

So the staff decided to create something more than a "marvel of microtechnology" by making the machine large enough so that its commonly available parts would not be all that close together. This would make it easier to attach otherwise hard-to-manage mechanical assemblies and result in a machine generally easier to understand and work with for both its users and the dealers who would have to provide warranty service.

But all of the design problems were not solved quite this easily. Bill Sydnes recalled:

"There were enormous differences of opinion about what the machine should look like. The IBM industrial design community went crazy when we elected to use sheet metal for the box because they felt metal wasn't dependable. We had some major confrontations with them over this till we got to the point where we told them if they didn't approve our specifications for the box, we'd escalate the matter all the way to the CMC.

"We had to be bull-headed because we knew we couldn't do tooled plastic covers for a whole machine considering the deadline we were working against. We got our way and that was a major victory for the engineering organization when the industrial design community was overruled.

"In retrospect," Sydnes said, "the sheet metal was a magnificent selection because, without it, we would never have passed the FCC (Federal Communications Commission) Class B requirements within the time frames we were talking about."

· 3 ·

Nothing could bring the Project Chess team together faster than a perceived threat from the outside, which in this case also included "outsiders" from within the IBM organization. But between themselves, the team tiffed constantly.

Out of this debate came, as a team member described, "maybe 300 changes in that product in the first year." Even so, the men on the project had their own ground rules, one of which was that any change must be functionally compatible with a prior change. For instance, if a card was designed to interface with the motherboard, any change in a component on the card could not change the output into the motherboard or affect its ability to function. There could be a circuit design change on the interface card, but the interface would have to remain constant. The idea was to make the changes functionally compatible both upward and downward so that if a new board or a new card came along maybe years later,  either would still work in the original system. That requirement put a significant criterion on the entire process by breaking the design into interface blocks. This way, if changes were made in some segments of the interface, they wouldn't have an adverse impact on the system's entire architecture.

Meanwhile, the project team was continually tempted to develop its own line of add-ons for the new machine. Apparently, the so-called joy stick attachment primarily used to play games on a computer was an example of a rejected add-on. Falling into this same category of provocative-but-unprofitable products were memory expansion cards and a host of other accessories that failed to support customary gross profit margins greater than 55 percent to justify the time, attention and management focus that would have to be directed their way and away from the central task of Project Chess, which was—most certainly—to get that Acorn machine to market within a year.

· **4** ·

Senior IBMers at Boca Raton maintain two wardrobes. One is lightweight and casual; the other, heavier and more formal—the latter especially for trips to Armonk.

By now, it was fall, and Lowe packed a suitcase from his Armonk wardrobe. Word had reached him through the company grapevine that the major IBM facility at Rochester, Minnesota, would soon be looking for a new general manager.

# 9  Microsoft Meets IBM

· 1 ·

The scenario underlying IBM's selection of an operating system and programming language for the Acorn dramatically reveals the powerful impact this giant corporation can have on the fortunes of an outside supplier.

The supplier, in this case, was the Microsoft Corporation, which by 1980 had gained recognition as the leader in the development of the standardized software that enables computers to be accessible and useful. The company was formed in 1975 by William H. Gates III and Paul Allen, former classmates at Lakeside High, a private school in Seattle, Washington.

Gates had been experimenting with computers since the seventh grade, when the school's Mothers' Club set up a fund to enable the students to rent processing time on large mainframe computers. Instantly fascinated by computer technology, Gates used the mainframes to reconstruct class schedules for the school.

Bill Gates was never a poor kid from the other side of the tracks. His father is a leading attorney in Seattle, and the family is socially prominent in the Pacific Northwest. Among their acquaintances in 1980 was John Opel, IBM's chairman, who served on the board of directors of the United Way with Bill Gates's mother.

In the eighth grade, Gates joined with high school sophomore Paul Allen in devising ways to enter and manipulate the data in giant time-sharing computer systems maintained by Digital Equipment Corporation (DEC) and Control Data Corporation (CDC).

· 2 ·

Gates's precocity eventually landed him in trouble. He entered the DEC systems and discovered flaws in the machines' programming. Gates (at this time, about 14 years old) took it upon himself to clean up the programs to make them run more efficiently.

Next, his mischievousness and his technological talent led him to invade computer security systems. While "normal" kids his age were hanging out at drugstores and school dances, Bill Gates was isolated at his computer terminal, challenging the CDC's Cybernet computer network, which was reputed to have 100 percent reliability and impenetrability.

Gates learned that the CDC computer at the University of Washington was tied into Cybernet. So, young Gates got his hands on everything he could that had to do with CDC hardware and software and the Cybernet network. He discovered that he could invade the system by seizing control of one of its peripheral processors. In doing so, he circumvented the machine's human operators, who were, of course, quite unaware that an outsider was fooling around inside their system.

But Gates went too far. Instead of continuing to tinker with the programming to improve it, he started planting unique programs in separate components of the computerized network. With the touch of a few keys, Gates was able to destroy all of the programs at once.

But he became careless, and CDC computer security officers traced the source of the "invasions" straight to the deft fingers of William H. Gates III. The unraveling of his scheme and the consequent embarrassment caused Gates to reassess the conventional pleasures of growing up as a teenager in a comfortable suburb of Seattle.

Later, according to Paul Freiberger and Michael Swaine, authors of *Fire in the Valley* (Berkeley, California: Osborne/McGraw-Hill, 1984), Gates recalled, "I swore off computers for about a year and a half—the end of the ninth grade and all of the tenth. I tried to be normal, the best I could."

· 3 ·

In this regard, normalcy was not Gates's strong suit, and when his friend and confederate Paul Allen became aware of a new and vastly more powerful microprocessor known as the Intel 8008, he enticed Gates back to the machine. (The 8008 was the first microprocessor to make 8-bit technology practical. It was the precursor of the Intel 8088, which became the heart of the Acorn computer.)

But the device itself would be of little practical use without what is called an interpreter—a translating device that takes the instructions to the computer, entered in the BASIC language, and converts them into command sequences that can be "understood" by the 8088 microprocessor.

Gates was skeptical of the 8088's abilities beyond its possible applications in hand-held calculators. But he was lured again by microcomputer technology. He came up with $360 for the microprocessor, and then Gates and Allen enlisted Paul Gilbert (another friend who was captivated by the technology) to help them build their own microcomputer. By now, Gates was 16 years old.

With an operating machine in hand, the teenage entrepreneurs wrote a software program to analyze traffic patterns. They formed a company called Traf-O-Data, which at best had only limited success, due at least in some part to the fact that its executive officers were gangly, tousle-haired teenagers with squeaky voices.

· 4 ·

Gates today will be quick to say that adversity can spawn success. Shortly after Traf-O-Data collapsed, the software products division of TRW Corporation, alerted to the expertise of these teenagers in the still somewhat foreign technology of microcomputers, made contact and offered Gates and Allen $30,000-a-year jobs as software developers. Allen, who by now was in college, found this irresistible. So did Gates, and he took what amounted to a leave of absence from high school to join Allen at TRW.

They put in almost two years there, and Gates used some of his money to buy a speedboat. But more important than the money for them was the chance to work in what was essentially a hacker's heaven. By the time Gates returned to high school and Allen headed off to a job at Honeywell, the pair had begun to build national reputations as masters of microcomputer technology. In time, word of who they were and what they could do would reach IBM.

· 5 ·

In mid-July 1980, the desk-top computer task force at IBM's Boca Raton facility took its first tenuous moves to interview outside suppliers of a BASIC programming language and an operating system for their new machine.

The best-known and most highly regarded operating system at the time was called CP/M—Control Program/Microprocessor. It was the product of a company called Digital Research, based in Monterey, California.

The founder and president of Digital Research, Gary Kildall, like Gates, was born and raised in the Seattle area. During his high school days Kildall invented a security alarm for autos and a Morse Code simulator. Not until he was a junior at the University of Washington did he "discover" computers, and they quickly became his obsession.

After college, he joined the navy and picked up a master's degree in computer science. He was then assigned as a teacher at the navy's postgraduate school in Monterey, California, where he completed studies for his doctorate in compiler code optimization for computers.

In 1972, when he was 30 years old, some mathematics formulas Gary Kildall had written captured the interest of the Intel Corporation, a pioneer maker of computer chips. The company retained Kildall as a consultant to develop a programming language for the new 8008 chip (the same microprocessor-on-a-chip that lured Bill Gates back to microcomputing).

Kildall had no trouble writing the microcomputer programs, but the only machines available at the time were equipped with awkward storage units that depended on a punched-paper process.

Developing storage devices for microcomputers was not his forte, but Kildall did some research on his own and found that a Silicon Valley company called Shugart & Associates was completing development of a disk drive data-storage device especially for microcomputers.

Although the device was not ready for the market, Kildall correctly believed that disk drives were the only sensible way that microcomputer data would eventually be stored for retrieval. So he began to work on an operating system that would be ready to coordinate the work of the microprocessor and the disk drives. Within two months, the operating system was finished. Kildall called it CP/M. He showed it to Intel, and they told him he could try to sell it on his own.

But what was written in two months would take another two years to find its niche. This came when the first primitive personal computers were introduced in the mid-1970s. The CP/M was originally sold by mail order and it quickly became the de facto operating system for the first practical generation of desk-top computing machines. In 1976, Kildall and his wife, Dorothy McEwen, formed a company to sell the system; the company came to be called Digital Research.

The following year, IMSAI, one of the first serious manufacturers of microcomputers, chose CP/M as its standard operating system. Digital Research became an overnight success as a full-time prospering business headed by Gary Kildall and his wife.


· 6 ·


In late July of 1980, the task force (yet to be named "Project Chess") made its key decision to buy the operating system for the new machine from a source other than IBM. To gather research, the task force assigned Bill Sydnes, Lew Eggebrecht, Larry Rojas and Dave Stuerwald to investigate the implications of this decision. According to Sydnes, the ad hoc team made an appointment to visit Digital Research.

When the team reached California, they told Digital Research that they were interested in its operating system, but that certain changes would have to be made in CP/M to conform with the 16-bit operating standard IBM wanted to introduce. (At the time, CP/M was not structured to take advantage of the more powerful 16-bit technology.)

The IBM people also presented a copy of the company's standard nondisclosure agreement which, they said, must be signed before they could even begin to talk business.

Signature to the agreement, which is mandatory for any outside suppliers who want to do business with IBM, essentially protects IBM from lawsuits and stipulates that the outsider will not tell IBM or its representatives anything that is confidential. If something confidential is subsequently revealed to IBM, IBM cannot be sued if it acts on the information. On the other hand, the agreement insists that IBM has the right to sue the outside supplier if the supplier reveals any information that IBM considers to be confidential.

Kildall is a free-spirited sort who has his own airplane, boat, sports cars, motorcycle and jet skis. Bearded, iconoclastic and fiercely in-dependent, he is the antithesis of The Corporation Man. Recurrent reports persist that Kildall, an avid amateur pilot, had argued with his wife shortly before IBM's scheduled visit and, to "cool off," he went to a nearby airport and took a solo spin in a private plane. He was allegedly aloft when the IBM team arrived and, without the president of Digital Research on hand, his wife and the company's attorney refused to sign the standard non-disclosure agreement.

What is clear, however, is that someone at Digital Research told IBM what it could do with its one-sided nondisclosure agreement. He also added that CP/M would not be changed to suit IBM's 16-bit technology, even if IBM changed the provisions of its contract with Digital Research—something which, of course, Big Blue was not about to do. So that was that.

The company's attitude baffled the task force team. When IBMers approach a potential subcontractor, they are not accustomed to rejection.

Stunned but not discouraged, the task force team had another call to make while they were still on the West Coast.

· 7 ·

After graduating from high school, Bill Gates entered the pre-law program at Harvard University in 1973. Here, according to the *Wall Street Journal* (August 27, 1986), "he spent his time playing poker, fiddling with electronics and, in his words, 'sitting in my room being a philosophical depressed guy, trying to figure out what I was doing with my life.'"

His high school pal, Paul Allen, was by now working at a Honeywell facility not far from Gates. When the pair would get together in early 1975, they would work on a BASIC programming language for microcomputers using the more advanced Intel 8088 chip.

The program was an outstanding success, causing Gates to leave Harvard and Allen to quit Honeywell so the pair could form Microsoft to market their product.

The first headquarters for the new company was at Albuquerque, New Mexico, the home of MITS, a corporation founded to make and market the first generation of microcomputers. (In 1979, MITS, after changing hands two years earlier, went out of business altogether).

Since there was no more reason to remain in New Mexico after MITS was sold in 1977, the 21-year-old Gates decided with Allen to move Microsoft to Bellevue, Washington, not far from Seattle, where they had spent their boyhoods.

Unquestionably due to the brilliance and total dedication of its founders, Microsoft prospered as a company known for making some of the most reliable operating systems on the market for microcomputers such as the Apple II, the Altair and the Commodore PET. Microsoft was, of course, in direct competition with Gary Kildall's Digital Research and its prime product, the CP/M.

· 8 ·

The Acorn task force team was favorably impressed by the good reviews for Microsoft's BASIC language. Pressed for time and uneasy while away from their teammates in Boca Raton, they had phoned Gates in July 1980 to set up an appointment to visit Microsoft. According to various published accounts this was the key meeting that would lead to making Bill Gates a billionaire by age 31. But at this time, when Microsoft had only 32 employees, Bill Gates was 25 years old, though he looked like he was, at the most, barely old enough to vote. Yet here was a young man wise well beyond his years—a genius at programming and a born master of his business, gifted with remarkable instincts when it came to controling what would be his company's extremely profitable relationship with IBM.

Gates, surprised though he was, was perceptive enough to take the call from IBM personally. Gates wanted to see them the following week. The IBM man said, "Can you make it tomorrow?" Gates checked his calendar. He had an appointment the next day with Ray Kassar, the chairman of Atari. In order to accommodate IBM, he cancelled the meeting with Kassar, for whom he was developing a version of his BASIC language, the language that formed the bread-and-butter of Microsoft's product line.

· 9 ·

When the IBM task force team arrived at Microsoft the following day, they were greeted by Gates, Paul Allen and Steve Ballmer. Gates had met Ballmer at Harvard in 1974, and the two had quickly struck up a close friendship, though Ballmer—who was sales oriented—never approached Gates's acumen at the art of microcomputer programming. After Harvard, Ballmer entered the MBA program at Stanford University, dropped out, took a marketing position at Procter & Gamble, then joined his friend and confidant, Bill Gates, at Microsoft in 1979.

Before the meeting began, the IBM people introduced their in-famous nondisclosure agreement. Gates, Ballmer and Allen read the agreement and, without the benefit of legal counsel, they shrugged and signed. To Gates, the whole matter of the agreement was a pointless formality. He wanted to get down to business. He wanted to know what IBM wanted from tiny Microsoft.

At that time (still a month before Project Chess received final approval and its code name) IBM was being coy and altogether vague. Still, Gates did not have to use much of his genius to deduce that IBM had not abandoned the idea of a desk-top computer, and that his com-pany, Microsoft, might have an opportunity to provide the BASIC programming language for whatever kind of a machine IBM had in mind.

But nothing of the sort was discussed at this meeting. Instead, the IBM people asked what Gates later recalled as "a lot of crazy questions." To the Microsoft people, this seemed like a social gathering of "good old boys." Everyone smiled a lot and the IBM guys were astonishingly laid back. The Microsoft people just sat there, smiled back, and waited for the shoe to drop. Well, it never did—not this time anyway.

Finally, because they couldn't think of anything else to talk about (and they didn't want to make any of those "nondisclosable" revelations), Gates and his pals took the IBM team on a little tour (it couldn't have been much else) of the Microsoft facility.

The hosts never really knew at the time if the IBM guys were just being polite, or if they really did want to see a few people in cubicles squinting at computer screens. Then everybody went back to Gates's office, smiled at each other some more, and the IBM team said they'd better start back to Boca Raton.

· 10 ·

Gates and his associates went back inside the office. They sat there and grumbled and wondered what that had been all about. Then all three—Gates, Allen and Ballmer—started talking at once. The consensus was that IBM wanted to buy Microsoft's BASIC language and that the men from Big Blue came up to Bellevue on the banks of Lake Washington across the way from Seattle to see if this company was being run out of a garage or a basement in somebody's house.

Microsoft, however, was a full-fledged business with a lobby, work space for its employees and real offices for its executives. Of course, this was the first day since the company was founded that all of its executives came to work in suits and ties—but that was only because IBM was coming to call and, after all, IBM is IBM.

Ballmer, the most street smart about such things, returned to his office and put together a letter for Gates's signature. The letter thanked IBM for taking the time and trouble to visit and assured their recent visitors that Microsoft continued to be eager to resume the conversations that started in mid-July.

After this, Gates yanked off his tie and began to prepare for his rescheduled meeting with Atari's Ray Kassar.

# 10 Choosing the Operating System

· 1 ·

On the flight back from Seattle to Boca Raton, the task force team completed their report to Bill Lowe. They would tell him that Microsoft, while not a dominant factor in the overall computer industry, was obviously superior in the area of its chosen specialty: reliable, easy-to-use software that enables people to write operating programs for their microcomputers.

The company's BASIC programming language for the Intel 8088 chip was regarded as a classic of its kind, an opinion that was substantiated by the growing acceptance of this language as the standard for many of the major desk-top computers now being produced.

The IBM team that had visited Microsoft was typically astonished by the unprepossessing demeanor of the company's boyish and brilliant chief executive. They were well aware of how rude and arrogant members of the hacker's generation could be. "Temperamental, spoiled brats," they called them over the lunch tables at Boca Raton.

Hackers often resented IBM because of its ethic and its strategy of noninvolvement until a market was established by the smaller and generally entrepreneurially driven companies in the industry—at which time IBM bullied its way in and, on the strength of its reputation for excellence and its superior manpower and resources, proceeded to dominate the market at the expense of the bit players who were often there at the beginning.

IBM knows that it is more effective for the corporation to ignore these detractors than to make peace with them. In this regard, Big Blue stands firm in its time-honored belief that no one person or outside institution is indispensable to the corporation's success.

Although hindsight might tend to indicate otherwise, IBM would never concede that Microsoft's products were essential to the acceptance of Project Chess. No matter how outstanding Microsoft's reputation was, IBM was not about to make a deal with people who would not show the proper respect, enthusiasm and gratitude for the privilege of acting as a supplier to Big Blue.

Bill Gates, Paul Allen, Steve Ballmer and their associates at Microsoft qualified admirably in these matters of utmost importance to IBM. When the task force team checked in with Lowe, what they essentially said was:

> Bill Gates may look like a kid, but he doesn't act like one. He is, without a doubt, brilliant at developing software and programming languages. He's smart and he knows it—but he is not a smart aleck. We like him. We can work with him. And his other executives are also okay.
>
> They're not running their company out of a garage or a basement. They are serious businessmen and they gave us the impression that they would fall all over themselves to get a chance to work with us.
>
> We say, "Let's go with Microsoft for the BASIC."

Lowe concurred with the team's recommendations, so at least this much was settled.

Microsoft could not be informed of the decision because Lowe still had to get approval for the project at his presentation to the Corporate Management Committee (CMC) in early August.

Time was running out. Here it was, going into late summer 1980, and still no one knew who would supply the vital operating system for the desk-top machine intended to justify IBM's belated entry into the market for microcomputers.

· 2 ·

By mid-August, the CMC had approved the project and designated it for code names. IBM contacted Gates again. They wanted to return to Microsoft with more people, five in all, including a corporate attorney.

When the date for the second meeting with IBM was confirmed, Gates and Ballmer decided to match the IBM contingent man for man, one of whom would be a Seattle lawyer familiar with Microsoft.

Before the meeting could convene, the Microsoft people were asked to sign another of those nondisclosure agreements IBM is so fond of. IBM's corporate attorney examined the documents carefully, making sure that each Microsoft signature was exactly where it should be.

After this formality, somebody in a blue suit reportedly remarked that the mission to Microsoft had a lot to do with "the most unusual thing the IBM corporation has ever done."

Gates and his people hung on every word. This, they sensed, was not just another casual gathering of the good old boys. These were heavy hitters from IBM: impeccable, articulate types; the sort of persons central casting would send in response to, "Get me somebody who looks and acts like they've been at IBM since the day they were born."

No one was smiling when the senior IBM executive took in a breath and confided that the company was engaged in a crash project to build a personal computer under its own name. Microsoft was being invited to supply the BASIC programming language for the machine. Perhaps tens of thousands of the new machines might be sold in its first year, which meant that Microsoft would have to make a major, immediate commitment of resources to win the contract and supply IBM's demand.

Then they showed the Microsoft people the proposed design for the new machine. Gates was enthusiastic. He knew that a 16-bit technology would enable Microsoft to write extraordinarily powerful software for the machine. Gates became animated; the IBM people were impressed.

The meeting ended with Gates agreeing to write a detailed proposal on how Microsoft, as an outside consultant, could supply the programming language for the Acorn.

Then, almost as an aside, the IBM people added that they also needed an operating system for the machine. Gates jumped. He said it was a topic he'd like to talk about further with IBM. Then the meeting adjourned.

Gates and his associates, recognizing an opportunity, stayed late at the office to consider making a bid to design the operating system a key part of the proposal to IBM.

The IBM bid, however technically challenging and potentially profitable, could hurt Microsoft. For example, Microsoft had struggled just to keep up with the demand for its programming languages. Writing a BASIC language for the new IBM machine on a backbreaking timetable could tie up the company's resources. Then there was the nature of Project Chess itself. The IBM people had made it abundantly clear that the project was embryonic and that it might be shut down at anytime. In other words, IBM guaranteed nothing.

· 3 ·

Along with Gates and Allen at the after-hours meeting was Kazuhiko Nishi, a Japanese national who was Microsoft's Far East agent. Nishi, who is known as Kay, is the same age as Gates.

According to the *Wall Street Journal* (August 27, 1986) Nishi has an "impudent style. His ability to captivate executives two and three times his age was matched only by his ability to appall them by being extravagantly rude."

The *Journal* said Nishi would give formal presentations at business meetings "and then rise from his chair, stretch out on the floor and fall immediately asleep. Other times he dozed off in his seat or stared off into space breathing noisily.

"'I am famous for random activities,' admits Mr. Nishi. He speaks in animated, cheerful bursts, pausing frequently to run his fingers through his shaggy hair, and rub his eyes with fatigue. 'I have many moods,' he says, 'high and low, and the difference is very big.'"

Gates found Nishi fascinating, and the two would chat for hours, fantasizing about a time when millions of microcomputers would be as common as typewriters and television sets in offices and homes around the world. Within three years, however, they would vow to never again to speak to one another. Nishi would call Gates a liar and Gates would counter by saying, "The guy's life is a mess."

But back in the waning days of summer 1980, it was Nishi, probably more than anyone else, who convinced Gates that Microsoft should make a serious bid to supply the Acorn's operating system.

Sources close to those at the late-night meeting said Gates, Nishi and Allen disagreed until Nishi suddenly leaped to his feet, danced around the room waving his hands in the air and exclaimed, "Gotta do it! We gotta do it!"

Gates and Allen found Nishi's enthusiasm contagious. As Gates would tell the *Wall Street Journal*, "Kay's kind of a flamboyant guy and when he believes in something, he believes in it very strongly. He stood up, made his case, and we just said, 'Yeah!'"

In a way, Nishi's outburst was anticlimactic. All along, Gates had an ace up his sleeve.

· 4 ·

True to the terms of the IBM agreement, Gates nondisclosed his knowledge of a small software house across the lake called Seattle Computer Products. The head of the company was Rod Brock, a local computer buff. Brock, like Gates, was a whiz at programming but, unlike Gates, Brock had never propelled his company to national attention within the industry.

Phillipe Kahn, president of Borland International, a software development firm on the West Coast, characterizes Bill Gates as "the best businessman and salesman in the microcomputer industry. His image as a nerd and visionary hacker is baloney—Gates is one helluva sharp businessman and a top-notch negotiator. Just look at how he worked out a deal that had Microsoft working with IBM to develop an operating system that Microsoft then turned around and sold to IBM's competitors. I can't believe it. Gates is a phenomenon!"

Bill Gates has always been a likeable, unassuming person who sometimes seems a bit embarrassed by his success. Before that success he was—as he is now—the type who makes friends easily. So he called his friend Rod Brock who, he knew, had been working on an operating system for microcomputers that was designed to exploit the power and potential in 16-bit technology. The system was called the SCP-DOS (Seattle Computer Products Disk Operating System).

Brock had been working on the project for some time, and Gates guessed that the system was probably close to completion. Now that the heavy work was nearly finished, the final debugging and fine-tuning of the SCP-DOS could likely be handled by anyone competent in advanced programming; anyone, that is, but, in particular, someone like Bill Gates.

So he contacted Brock, they struck a deal, and Microsoft became the new owner of an operating system for microcomputers originally designed to be sold by Seattle Computer Products. Because Gates considered himself still to be bound by his signature to IBM's nondisclosure agreement, he did not tell Brock why Microsoft wanted the operating system. (Half a dozen years later, his reticence at the time of the deal with Brock would return to haunt Gates.)

On Tuesday morning after the 1980 Labor Day weekend, Gates and his colleagues would have to begin work on the "consulting" report for IBM: the document that must convince IBM to buy the programming language and operating system for its new microcomputer from Microsoft. There would be no second tries at this, no opportunities to "go back and run it through again."

· 5 ·

All through September, the Microsoft management team fussed over the report. Kay Nishi stayed on in Seattle to make his contributions in what was known as "Nishi English," a convoluted syntax that Steve Ballmer once called, "copy that always needs editing."

The document finally was ready for submission, and this time, the Microsoft people went to Boca Raton. It was the last week of September.

On the 3,300-mile overnight flight from Seattle to Miami, Gates, Ballmer and Allen finished revising, proofreading, paginating and binding the report that specified how Microsoft could supply the BASIC language for the new machine and also convert SPC-DOS to act as the machine's operating system.

Eventually they agreed that the report was complete. No more changes. This was *it*.

# 11 Tying Loose Ends

For a while, it looked as if Project Chess was going to be handled at an IBM site much closer to Microsoft's far western headquarters.

To increase the size of the staff working on the project, the Entry Level Systems (ELS) facility at Boca Raton wanted to recruit hardware and software engineers and manufacturing specialists throughout the corporation.

This was in fall 1980, when the IBM facility at Boulder, Colorado, was in a relative hiatus. It manufactured large disk drive components and photocopying machines, and at the time both product lines were not succeeding in their markets.

The Boulder site's state-of-the-art, high-volume production facilities were almost idle. Even worse, backing up this on-line capability was a concentration of some of IBM's foremost engineers and manufacturing specialists whose skills were atrophying because of the downturn in the market for their products.

Lowe found this situation and the accelerated timetable for the Acorn's introduction to be a timely and intriguing concatenation of circumstances. He summoned Bill Sydnes, the chief engineer on Project Chess, and Joe Bauman, the project's director of manufacturing; and sent them to Boulder with instructions to recruit competent staff people for the Acorn and assess the facility as a manufacturing site for the new desk-top machine.

As Sydnes later recalled:

> The top-level approval for the project and the tight timetable for delivery obviously meant that a fair amount of staffing had to be done and it had to be done quickly.
>
> When we went to Boulder, we expected to interview maybe 30 or, at the most, 40 people. As it turned out, almost 400 people at Boulder

showed strong interest in what we were doing. We had to take over the cafeteria to conduct the interviews and even then the two of us we were so swamped that we had to bring in more people from Boca Raton to help out.

Back at Boca Raton, Lowe was pleasantly astonished. With a strong response from the staff at Boulder, coupled with the manufacturing facilities already in place there, he proposed that the headquarters for Project Chess be moved from Florida to Colorado.

But the senior management at Boulder was not happy with this suggestion. Quite simply, they did not want to get involved. They assessed the project and agreed among themselves that the timetable for Chess was absurd—meaning that the pc would never be ready for its scheduled introduction which was, by then, less than a year away, and the people at Boulder were well aware of the false starts and failures that had seemed to typify IBM's plans to introduce a practical desk-top machine.

This was not a rash conclusion, given their collective years of experience with the traditional IBM way. Of course, the senior men at Boulder reasoned, the project was quite alive at the moment, but when it began to slip behind schedule it would be a candidate for cancellation.

And that cancellation would probably not be subject to further consideration by the corporation. The Boulder executives were also well aware of the unspoken tendency within IBM to blame failed projects on their staffs. "Guilt by association" was a sure way to be labeled as a loser. At IBM the assumption is that losers are finished; there are no second chances; winning all the time is everything and the system is tuned in such a way that the sorting out of the winners from the also-rans is a continual and merciless process.

So they said no. The powers at Boulder did not want Project Chess to be laid in their laps—no way! But they would not stand in the way of staffers who recklessly defied the wisdom of years to associate with what could only be an ill-fated adventure that would turn their careers into dust.

"We got some excellent people out of Boulder," Sydnes recalls.

·  2  ·

The overnight flight from Seattle touched down on a runway at the Miami International Airport, and minutes later, Bill Gates, Steve

Ballmer and Paul Allen were driving a rented car on the Florida turnpike, bound for Boca Raton.

They had not had a restful night. By now, they were taking advantage of the resilience of youth and a rush of adrenaline.

At the Entry Level Systems facility, they were ushered into a small conference room, where the IBM people focused on Gates. They wanted to know what he could do, when he could do it and exactly what he could produce.

The questions fired at Gates were polite and precise but pointed. The IBM people had done their homework; nearly every question was read from the yellow, legal-sized notepads favored by the task force team.

No one really wanted to destroy Gates as a supplier, nor, for that matter, did they fluster him. While his hosts were, of course, interested in his answers, they were just as concerned with how Gates and his associates appeared and how they handled themselves. After all, this meeting was intended to be the beginning of a uniquely symbiotic relationship between IBM and Microsoft.

It was one thing (as IBM had often done in the past) to forge an alliance based on the ability of an outside supplier to furnish machine screws and monitor screens. But this was a relationship IBM had never had before. If the task force were satisfied with Microsoft (pretty much on the basis of this one meeting), then the two companies would become almost like family. It would essentially be a quasipartnership, with each company dependent on the other for the accomplishment of a single goal.

When the meeting broke for lunch, Gates, confident and self-possessed, took Ballmer and Allen aside and told them his impression that the deal with IBM was all but in the bag. By then it was, but before Microsoft could actually begin work on the project there were the matters of secrecy and security so important to respect at IBM.

· 3 ·

At Boca Raton, the IBM people told Gates and his associates that Microsoft's ability to produce the operating system and BASIC programming language for the Acorn was not in question. But, they continued, before contracts could be signed, IBM would have to be comfortable with security precautions at Microsoft. Gates squirmed in his chair at this one, because, until then, Microsoft had no so-called security precautions, a situation that would have to change immediately if Microsoft intended to get the contract. Aside from IBM's concern about security procedures, the meeting ended on a high note, and the men from Microsoft caught the next plane back to Seattle.

· 4 ·

While IBM was checking on security at Microsoft, the Corporate Management Committee called for a checkpoint on Project Chess. This came in mid-October 1980, after the highly detailed plans to bring the Acorn to market within a year had been developed into final form. The checkpoint was to update the senior executives on the progress of the project and it was one of the few traditional IBM procedures the task force was expected to honor.

Joseph Sarubbi, who would become a key man early in the program, explained the significance of the checkpoint.

> This is where determinations are made of the tasks that can be accomplished. It's like a feasibility study: What are the objectives? What is the status of the operational hardware? What are the specifications and specific functions for the machine? And this is only the beginning of the questions that have to be answered.

Sarubbi compared the process to the construction of a house from scratch. Using this analogy, the checkpoint in October can be compared to the submission of a first architectural rendering. When the outline of the Acorn was settled on, following critiques from the CMC, the task force was able to proceed with details such as the delicate matter of obtaining parts for the machine and the software to operate it from within or outside of IBM.

At the mid-October session in Armonk, the CMC approved additional millions of dollars in funding for Project Chess. Among other things, this money was used to add 100 more people to manufacturing.

Before the October checkpoint, everything to do with the project was handled according to IBM's standard corporate procedures. After the session, an unprecedented amount of freedom was given to the Independent Business Unit working under Entry Level Small Systems at Boca Raton.

In other words, the power was passed. The corporation and its rules and regulations, checks and balances, procedures and protocols, standards and traditions—and all that has to do with its bureaucracy—well, perhaps almost all, was tossed out.

What remained were the reporting procedures. While the project was to enjoy a remarkably free rein, headquarters at Armonk was not about to let go of its long leash.

· 5 ·

John Opel had laid his personal blessing on this most-favored of all projects. He was the person people had to answer to directly when they tried to screw with the IBU. And they had better be able to make their point well, because Opel, on whose desk the buck finally stopped, stood firm as an oak when the Acorn was threatened.

Until now, Opel's term as chairman was characterized more by caretaking than groundbreaking. Somewhat diffident, his Teutonic rectitude was no match for the Gallic charm of his predecessor, Frank Cary, who is credited with a famous remark about the IBUs being an attempt "to teach an elephant how to tap dance."

Now Cary was gone and Opel was in charge. And there was still time before he, too, stepped aside—time to make his mark at IBM, time to prove that it was under his regime that the corporation brought a low-end, desk-top computer to market. It could be the fulfillment of a career's ambition.

· 6 ·

Meanwhile, back at Boca Raton, Bill Lowe was on the brink of fulfilling his ambition to become a vice president of the corporation. By now, it was the middle of fall, and Lowe's network of contacts at Armonk believed that he was in line for promotion to vice president of the Information Systems Division (ISD). The announcement would be made after the first of the year, and it would likely mean a transfer to a position of greater responsibility for the company's operations.

Lowe could trust his sources. So now it was time to pull away from the fledgling Project Chess in order to concentrate on more lofty matters. Besides, even with Opel protecting the project's independence, there could be no guarantee that it would not be stopped at any time. In early November 1980, the project appeared to be an unacceptably risky venture for someone with more traditional notions of how to get ahead at IBM. No matter what its future, Project Acorn had already succeeded for Lowe.

An apocryphal anecdote says that the Vatican moves with less caution to canonize a saint than IBM does to name a vice president. Although that may be a less-than-reverent stretch of the truth, the fact is that Big Blue will probably not promote a person unless someone nearly as equally qualified is ready to assume his prior position.

This unwritten policy makes a lot of sense. For example, it all but avoids the creation of empires-within-the-empire. Ideally, no one at IBM is ever personally indispensable because, across the corridor or down the hall, their successor is being groomed. If an executive is so unsure of himself that he does not share responsibility, this fact is made known through the grapevine, and the person finds his responsibility systematically eroded and his career at a halt.

Not so for Lowe. His chosen successor was right down the hall.

· 7 ·

If Don Estridge wanted the job, it was his; this matter had already been cleared through the CMC. Should he accept, the transfer of day-to-day responsibility would begin immediately. Estridge had just completed a tedious programming project for an insurance company. He was, as they say, "between projects," but never, as he later confided, did he foresee going on to a project like this one. He was well known as an IBMer who worked with hardware and software all day, and then went home at night to play around with his own little Apple II microcomputer. He couldn't get enough of computers. He was fascinated, hooked, addicted, and dedicated. He would sit at a keyboard and become one with the machine. Estridge was like a kid at Christmas when he got his hands on new software. The line was indistinct between his work and his second love, the computer. His first love was his family.

# 12  A
# "True Blue"
# Family

Don and Mary Ann Estridge were each other's best friend. Together, they played tennis, enjoyed classical music and raised three daughters. When the parents of one of their daughters' best friends were killed in an auto accident, Don and Mary Ann took the orphaned girl into their home, which gave them four young girls to raise.

Bringing up the kids while her husband worked for a company whose initials to many meant "I've Been Moved" was not an easy task for Mary Ann. But Don was a better-than-average breadwinner. He caught on fast and, as it is said, "the man did not have a lazy bone in his body." Mary Ann didn't have to work to help pay the bills, so she chose to devote her life to her husband and children. They'd already planned for the time when the two of them would be alone together.

When IBM transferred Don back to the only state he really loved, the Estridges bought a serviceable home in Boca Raton in a shiningly clean, middle-class neighborhood. Later, as Don's salary and bonuses pushed his income toward the six-figure level, the Estridges decided to buy a tonier home in a fine, old-line area of Boca Raton.

The Estridges loved the outdoor life almost as much as they loved their children and one another. Don even fancied himself something of a tenderfoot cowboy. He bought a pair of expensive leather cowboy boots and kept them in better condition than his everyday business shoes. The cowboy fantasy inspired him to suggest to Mary Ann that a dude ranch would be ideal for their next vacation.

· 2 ·

Lowe had given thoughtful consideration to his choice of the best person to assume leadership of Project Chess. Even so, when he gave the job to Estridge, he could not have fully known what a wise choice this would turn out to be.

There were, of course, others on or near the project who were more technically qualified than Estridge. Many in the IBM organization with records of remarkable accomplishment could come in, take over, and get the job done by following traditional company techniques. The problem was that those who were technically qualified lacked the leadership skills Lowe saw in Estridge, and no IBM bureaucrat stood a chance of getting the Acorn to market on time.

Estridge, in his unstudied way, had a remarkable gift for playing the maverick without ever appearing disillusioned with or disloyal to the corporation and its heritage. He was, as they say, "IBM all the way."

Certainly not in 1980, but not so long afterward, Estridge would become one of the most famous personalities in American business. Job offers would come to him from across the nation and around the world; the salaries would always be in excess—often very well in excess—of what he was earning at IBM. During the peak of his appeal, Estridge and a fellow IBMer sat together on a long flight when Estridge confided that he was being flooded with offers to leave IBM. The other IBMer asked Estridge what he was going to do, and Estridge, adding that he was most certainly flattered by the offers, said, "I guess I'll never leave IBM. I can't describe what a kick it is when someone asks me who I work for and I tell them, 'IBM' and they are always impressed. Gee, that really means a lot to me—it's something money can't buy."

· 3 ·

This attitude of Estridge's—his way of getting his way without creating enemies—likely had its roots in his Catholic school upbringing. The nuns would tell him that the only thing we really know about the character of Jesus is that he was meek and humble of heart.

And so, recalling these times, Brendan "Mac" McLoughlin, a sales manager who reported to Estridge said, "Humility was his best characteristic. Some people can be arrogant and pompous and still be successful. Don was the exact opposite. He was humble. He taught me that we can't allow ourselves to be cocky. We have to remember to be willing to beg for business. There was a magic in Don's saying that we should remember to be humble."

· 4 ·

Listen to any one of IBM's legions of detractors and they will say that humility has never been Big Blue's style. Yet, instead of sitting around congratulating themselves for getting jobs with IBM, the Project Chess members began to act as if their destinies as mortals depended on getting the Acorn finished and out to market on time. To this day, no one connected with the project has anything but fond memories of those halcyon times.

Dan Wilkie, who became a senior decision maker on how to build up the pc business, was a close friend of Estridge. Wilkie recalls:

"Don would give us an assignment, or our assignments would require us to take some action and so we would just go and do it. We didn't have to wade through the layers of the corporation's bureaucracy. We knew what counted and we could see the results. It was like the brass ring. You could see it, it was right there and you could touch it and you could quickly reach out and get feedback on it.

"For example, during my first 14 years with IBM, I don't think my neighbors once asked what I was doing. Then word about the pc gets out and people are calling me up to talk about it, neighbors are stopping me on the sidewalk, everybody could relate to it. It was great. After all that time, I finally knew that what I was doing mattered because I could identify with the machine and so could other people—even people outside of IBM. I mean, it was just phenomenal.

"Before I went to work on the team, I helped develop a printer at IBM. That printer was in development for seven years! I kept telling myself, 'It's coming . . . it's coming.' But the printer was hopelessly mired in design changes and bureaucracy. After a while, those layers and layers at IBM really get to you. This happens, I guess, because every job at IBM is so vertical, so specialized. No individual, or any group, has a clear, visible identity—not even an opportunity to see what I call 'the whole pie' of a product, including the research and development, the marketing expenses, the direct costs, everything—the whole pie.

"But with the pc project, I saw the whole pie for the first time. We saw the costs, we solved the problems ourselves, we lived with the good and the bad. It's no exaggeration to say that I made more decisions in my first 30 days with that group than I made during my first 14 years with IBM. I mean, these were real decisions! And with the Acorn, we were going from start to finish in a year—in only 12 months it would be there. It would be real," Wilkie said.

So there was Estridge in King Arthur's spot at the round table, surrounded by his *parfait* knights. It was like no other time in IBM legends. According to Wilkie, "It was just like Camelot."

# 13    The Pace
# Quickens

· 1 ·

By fall 1980, word about Boca Raton had spread throughout the corporation and soon Don Estridge's desk was piled high with the resumés of engineers and technicians eager to sign up with the PC IBU. The problem was that nearly everybody wanted to help build the machine, but no one wanted to take charge of selling it.

But then Estridge remembered another IBMer, H. L. Sparks, who lived down the block from the Estridge home in Boca Raton. "Sparky," as he was known since boyhood, lived up to his nickname; he was a vibrant ex-Texan who was a "born salesman" with strong feelings about how marketing accomplishments should be achieved. And he was loyal.

Every now and then, Estridge or Sparky would need a ride home from the office, so, on those days, they would check in with one another. At the office, Estridge, working on Project Chess, had only occasional call to work closely with Sparks, who was managing a marketing group supporting the sales of medium-sized computers to the financial industry.

So, only days after his talk with Lowe, Estridge phoned Sparky's office. Rather than leave a call-me-back message, as he usually did, Estridge told Sparky's secretary that he would return the call. Later, when Sparks received the message that Estridge had called, he told his secretary, "When Don calls back, tell him I'm going out of town and I can't give him a ride home."

A few minutes later, Estridge called again and insisted on speaking to Sparks. "Hey Sparky, I don't want a ride home. I want to offer you a job." "A job doing what?" Sparks asked, and Estridge answered, "Don't ask. It's really a great deal. Trust me and just say 'yes.'"

Sparks, who by then had been with IBM for going on 18 years, did not hesitate to give Estridge the reply he wanted. Sparks liked Estridge. He knew him as a straight shooter—an honest, solid sort of guy, a man who could be trusted. And so Sparks, without doubt or misgivings, laid his career on the line with Estridge.

The mystery of what he'd be doing was solved a few days later when he returned to Boca Raton. Estridge wanted Sparks to head up the sales and marketing for Acorn. He would have an essentially free hand and report directly to Estridge.

Years later, looking back to that time, Sparks recalled, "Our biggest problem and the greatest point of contention within the organization was how to gain the acceptance and the needed approvals to take a product with the IBM name and get it away from the company's sales staff and into the hands of outside dealers."

Ever a man of his word, Estridge gave Sparks full rein to do whatever he considered necessary to sell the Acorn. Sparks reasoned that the nature of the product demanded a marketing scheme and servicing plan quite unlike anything else that had been done in the past at IBM.

Sparks knew this: The proposed price for the Acorn meant that it wouldn't be enthusiastically received by the quota-conscious, bonus-driven IBM sales force. "And so," he said, "we started thinking about ways to get into mass merchandising—an area where IBM had no experience whatsoever."

·  2  ·

At that time, late fall of 1980, Jack Rogers, a senior group executive at IBM, held a seat on the board of directors of Sears, Roebuck and Company. According to Sparks, Rogers "made some suggestions" to the Sears board which, as it turned out, were well received since, by the most happy of coincidences, the giant retailer was investigating a broader base of business opportunities.

Sparks was invited to meet with the Sears Corporate Planning Group to discuss the possibility of selling through its outlets what was then known only as an "IBM home computer." More meetings were held, and these sessions formed the genesis of the Sears Business Centers, which would be among the privileged few retail dealers to join in the introduction of IBM's secret new product.

Sears was never led to believe that they would handle the new product introduction on an exclusive basis, but, since this was IBM, the retailing organization quietly settled for half a loaf.

· 3 ·

Most of the rest of the loaf went to the Computerland stores, which were now beginning to thrive under the direction of William Millard, the marketing genius behind the early IMSAI computer kits. Millard was chairman of the Computerland organization, but the bulk of the business' day-to-day operations were in the hands of Ed Faber, the president.

As Faber recalls, IBM expected Computerland to do more than simply clear its shelves for the new desk-top machine. "We started working with IBM at least 10 months before the machine was announced," he said. "I headed up a group composed of a couple of our headquarters officers and a half dozen of our franchise holders. We acted as consultants to IBM on how to get into the retail business since they knew absolutely zilch about what to do. But of course, before we could do anything for them, we had to know what we were talking about, so out came the confidential, non-disclosure agreements from IBM."

With this vital formality out of the way, Faber and his people were cautiously introduced to Project Chess. Here was the trade-off: Every Computerland store would become a charter dealer for the new machine. In return for this privilege, Faber and his staff would use the benefit of their experience to help IBM design and market the Acorn. It was an uncharacteristic relationship for Big Blue and testimony to how Estridge learned that humility can be a concept with more than religious value.

Faber can still recount details of the brainstorming sessions with Estridge and his team. "They asked us everything including our ideas on what to name the product, to what it should look like and what its relative position should be in the market. The IBM people were less concerned with pricing than with the values dealers and customers wanted. The idea was to place a properly competitive retail price on these values within the framework of a good markup for the dealers.

"They wanted to know all about displays, promotion, advertising and all that it takes to make a product move in the stores. They readily admitted that they had no experience and no background to speak of in selling directly to the consumer. The IBM people did have some preconceived notions, which were fairly accurate; this showed that they'd been doing their homework. But many of the important things we talked about were matters that IBM hadn't even considered."

This process had ironic overtones for Ed Faber. He had first learned about the computer industry sitting at the knee of IBM. He spent 12 years as a sales rep for the corporation before heading off on his own. This experience, he would recall, gave him a special familiarity with an unwavering respect for the company and its business ethics. Unlike other third parties who found themselves cautious about "getting too involved" with IBM, Faber, who was only returning to a previous wavelength, dove right in and, as he said, "We quickly worked out a mutually supportive relationship and held regular meetings at our facilities on the West Coast and at the IBM operation in Boca Raton. In time, we developed some really good relationships with the IBM guys and I had a very warm, personal relationship with Don Estridge who, as far as I'm concerned, is the real father of the IBM PC. Period.

"Don Estridge had something that is quite rare," Faber said. "He was exceptionally bright when it came to technical competence and he matched this with very strong capabilities in organization and management. This combination isn't found that often. And the man was the kind of person you absolutely knew was telling the truth—even if IBM's confidentiality policies prohibited him from telling all of the truth. When we got into one of these tricky areas, he would clearly state that this was something he couldn't discuss. His level of believability was at the very top."

The two of them would get together and talk about any number of things, such as the ever-present possibility that Project Chess could be cancelled. Estridge did admit that the information from Computerland was "really invaluable. Very important to us. We really need you guys."

What he couldn't confide was the identity of the other principal charter dealer, which turned out to be the Sears Business Centers. (Naturally, the product-starved IBM Product Centers would also sell the machine, but that was no surprise to anyone.)

Throughout the late fall of 1980, Faber could only guess at whom else was working with IBM on the project. Like most, this is an industry that thrives on gossip, and the easily affable and instantly likeable Faber is well known and broadly connected. But, despite Computerland's intimate involvement with the Acorn, he still didn't know for sure that Sears was involved, that outside software developers were busy writing programs to coincide with the machine's introduction and that Microsoft was already working day and night to develop its operating system.

In the past, Computerland had cooperated on an informal basis with other computer manufacturers, such as Apple. This time it was different. "That's because there is simply no way to compare the size, the scope and the resources of IBM with any other company in the field," Faber sai     "1, e meetings would center on some specific aspect of the machine     BM had a specialist and a code name for every-thing."

Eventually    'I  itside participants in Project Chess were called together to fe     ad hoc advisory committee. According to Faber,

> Each of t'    ipants was communicated with individually; no one
> was awar      o else was being invited to join the committee. The
> airplane  ei  rrived a day before the scheduled departure and it was
> only the      e committee members knew they were going to Florida.
> Some (      ple didn't even know IBM had a facility at Boca Raton.
> When  y g  everybody there, IBM put them all up at the same hotel. It
> was oi      hat we knew who else was involved. I'd come into the hotel
> lobb\     somebody I knew and we'd laugh and we'd both say,
> "Wh  Yc  too?"

· 4 ·

Meanwhile, senior members of the initial IBM task force like Bill Sydnes and Joe Bauman were lining up outside companies to supply key components for the Acorn. Eventually, they signed agreements with Intel Corporation to make the 8088 microprocessor chips. The disk drives were made by the Tandon Corporation, the power supply came from the Zenith Corporation, SCI Systems made the circuit boards and the first printers were manufactured by the Japan-based Epson Corporation. Piece by piece, the machine was coming together.

· 5 ·

It's not that things were exactly coming apart at Microsoft's headquarters in early November 1980, but Bill Gates recalled that, from the time his company signed its agreement with IBM, "We were basically three months behind schedule."

IBM wanted the operating system to be finished by March 1981 and, to establish this point, they inundated Microsoft with interminable timetables and schedules.

The operating system was the key piece of software for the Acorn. Until it was completed, the applications programs for the machine could not be written. If the schedule for delivery of the operating system was not met, Acorn could not be delivered on time—which meant within a year of the project's inception, just as Bill Lowe had promised to the IBM Corporate Management Committee.

Although no one from Boca Raton came right out and said so, unmistakable hints of all sorts of dire consequences were given to Microsoft. The principal message was not lost: Without a workable disk operating system and a bug-free BASIC programming language, the project would miss its deadline and probably be scuttled. The pressure was on.

To improve the efficiency of communications between the two companies, IBM and Microsoft established an electronic mail system. This, in turn, was supplemented by Bill Gates and his staff shuttling back and forth between Seattle and Boca Raton. If anything, everybody was certainly earning his salary.

Gates assumed personal responsibility for converting Microsoft BASIC so it could run on the Acorn. He, in turn, put Paul Allen to work on the disk code while other programmers tussled with details of converting the language as it was originally written for the now-ancient Altair computer.

· 6 ·

By late November 1980, IBM shipped the first "bare board" prototypes of the Acorn to Microsoft and the other third party suppliers. Another 15 units to be used for internal testing and quality assurance were close to completion.

Sparky Sparks had his marketing plans in order—but then Sparky always had everything in sight in order. When guaranteed anonymity, one of his associates at the time recalled:

> Sparky was really great at getting the marketing pulled together and the dealer organizations in place. But beyond that, well . . . Sparky could be in a presentation session and he'd be more worried about where the staples were in the documents than in what the documents had to say. He was, to say the least, very finicky. For instance, his office and conference area had to be spotless—I mean absolutely spotless—and people couldn't put down coffee cups or leave finger marks on things. And God help you if you spilled anything!

Don Estridge was also sharpening his style. Project Chess was turning out to be the most challenging assignment he had ever undertaken at the company where he had spent more than half his life.

He was under heavy pressure by this time. His family life, which meant so much to him, was sacrificed to workweeks that often took up 60 to 70 hours. His days began with scheduled meetings at 8 AM, and the meetings would run back to back and the meeting rooms would be packed wall to wall and if he ate at all, he did so on the run as he juggled everything from sales to planning to manufacturing to software programming to status reports like, "Is Microsoft staying on schedule?" and "What time does my plane leave tomorrow?" and "Tell my wife I'll have to call her back." A short day would end before 8 PM.

· 7 ·

As Christmas 1980 approached, Don did what he could to get home in time for dinner with his family. Around the table, the Estridges made plans for their traditional Christmas Eve coming together of close friends and relatives. Over the years, Mary Ann had achieved an enviable reputation as a hostess.

In 1980, Christmas Day fell on a Thursday and many businesses across the country—including IBM—remained officially closed on the following day.

As a concession to the long weekend and the spirit of the holiday, Don Estridge did not convene his first meeting at the office on the day after Christmas until 9 AM.

· 8 ·

As the New Year began—the year when the wraps had to be lifted off the Acorn on schedule—advertising and promotion plans for the machine moved to center stage.

Specialists in these areas had to be recruited, so the General Business Group, headquartered at White Plains, New York, was asked to supply communications support for the project.

Sparky Sparks tapped Jim D'Arezzo, a communications specialist with experience in promoting low-end machines, such as typewriters and copiers. D'Arezzo had also been responsible for introducing the IBM Displaywriter in June 1980. The Displaywriter, a dedicated word processing machine, used a 16-bit technology and was, at the time, probably the closest machine in the IBM product line to the Acorn.

When D'Arezzo got his opportunity to join Project Chess he was an advertising program administrator for IBM's Office Products Division

(OPD), at Franklin Lakes, N.J. As D'Arezzo recalled, "The management at OPD told me this could be the chance of a lifetime, or it could be a total bust. That happened to be my career they were talking about here, so I looked for some guarantees that there would be something I could come back to if the project at Boca Raton folded. They told me they'd do everything they could to help me if the project didn't pan out. Now this was all within the communications fraternity at IBM, which is a fairly small group within the company. By that, I mean we had, at the time, about 600 people around the world responsible for all the communications activities pertaining to IBM products. This included advertising, sales promotion, public relations, promotional literature and related activities."

D'Arezzo didn't want to make any commitments until he visited the Boca Raton facility and met with Estridge. This was arranged and, when they got together, "I went into his office and sat down with Don Estridge," D'Arezzo remembers. "He had an Apple II on his desk. He was grinning and showing me what the machine could do with some of the applications software he had on hand. Then he said the problem with the Apple was that it couldn't be expanded with extra boards and drives. He dug into a pile of papers on his desk and came up with some charts and he said, 'This is what we've got as a product.' I saw right away that this thing was fantastic and I knew that it was going to be a barn burner as one of the biggest items of all time in the IBM low-end product category.

"When I returned north," D'Arezzo continued, "I went to management and said, 'This is something we must have. We've got to get this product.' By that I meant we should be promoting and selling it through the Office Products Division."

The decision makers at OPD did not share D'Arezzo's enthusiasm. They didn't want to get involved with the Acorn, supposedly because they had no experience in selling directly to consumers. The IBM Product Centers were under the OPD umbrella and so, according to D'Arezzo, "They said they might want to think about maybe selling a few of the new machines through the Product Centers and that was the extent of it. But the important thing is that here we had a terrific opportunity for any number of divisions within IBM to take on this machine and, in every case, the opportunity was passed by.

"Meanwhile," he added, "down in Boca Raton this small group was saying, 'Look, we don't need those guys. What we want to do is go out in an entirely new direction for IBM. We'll be responsible for selling the machines ourselves.' And that's where Sparky Sparks came in. He was the one who decided the group should sell the product itself. So he worked with some outside consultants and retailers to develop an entirely new distribution strategy that had never before been used at IBM."

It is now understood that this distribution revolution begun by Sparks did not please some very influential groups at the International Business Machines Corporation.

# 14   The Peddler
# Is a Tramp

## · 1 ·

In early 1981, Richard Young was president of IBM's Office Products Division (OPD), and, according to Jim D'Arezzo, Young looked at the Acorn and said he had no intention of "pushing it off" on his sales force.

"Dick, we need this product," D'Arezzo insisted.

"No we don't," Young countered.

Then, in what could be interpreted as a concession, Young did allow that the Acorn might have a place in the IBM Product Centers as a sort of marketing experiment.

*But that was it.* He told Sparky Sparks that he didn't want the new desk-top computer to be sold through a network of outside authorized dealers because, in effect, this would make the dealers competitive with the IBM Product Centers. Furthermore, he declared, if the dealers were permitted to sell the Acorns, absolutely dire consequences could result. What the hell—let outsiders sell one machine, and the next thing they'll want to do is retail IBM typewriters, the unit sales of which, in 1980, came close to the one million mark and accounted for multimillions of dollars in profits for the corporation. At that time, IBM practically owned the market for office typewriters.

There is a principle of conduct that states: Avoid beginnings. Dick Young was its apostle.

## · 2 ·

Sparky, of course, saw things in a different light. Young's attitude infuriated him. Sparky went to Estridge with his Dick Young problem and Estridge told him, "Do what you have to do."

73

To Sparky this meant he had to do battle. "The best defense is a good offense" was the principle he would use in his affairs with Young. And so the pair often had run-ins. Young could not bring himself to trust this new cadre of dealers; these Computerlands and Sears Business Centers and God knows who else would be selling the Acorn and encroaching on what he called, "My Product Centers." When he put forth this argument, Sparky blew up. When the smoke finally cleared, Sparky had won.

Someone close to this argument reported, "Young stood his ground for a long time, but, at the end, he just kind of rolled over and said he disagreed with the decision to let this bunch of crazies in Boca Raton step in and take an unprecedented mandate at IBM."

The decision Young disagreed with had come down from the equivalent of Mount Olympus at IBM; that is, it came from John Opel himself, the man who started his New Year by becoming the corporation's chief executive officer. Of course, the Opel directive had been instigated by Don Estridge, who was well regarded at Armonk as just one helluva guy—a true-blue mover, shaker and doer who only had to get his way in order to fulfill the promise to get the Acorn to market in a year.

· 3 ·

Jim D'Arezzo had faced south when he toasted the New Year of 1981. A few days later, he was on his way to Florida and his new assignment as manager of communications for Project Chess.

The assignment did not include a honeymoon. During the first hour of his first day on Project Chess, he sat down with Don Estridge. To this day, that experience is still vivid to D'Arezzo:

"There's Estridge and he's not smiling as much as he did when I came down there a few weeks ago to look things over and go through the interviewing process. This time, he leans forward at his desk and tells me this product, the Acorn, has to be announced in six months and I have to get all the communications plans together before then and that, till then, nothing—absolutely nothing at all—had been done about a communications plan for the project.

"I was sitting there taking notes and so I asked him what the product was going to be called when it was introduced. He said he didn't know.

"I asked how the product was going to be packaged and he said, 'Packaged? We don't even know what its size will be!'

"About this time, I started to get a bit apprehensive and I wondered if I should go home and pack my bags and head back north.

"So," D'Arezzo said, "I asked Don what the machine's capabilities were going to be and what specific markets we were going after. He looked kind of blank and said that's something we still have to figure out.

"What that all meant was here was this super-crash project half the company seemed to oppose and the other half didn't think would amount to a hill of beans and here was this guy in charge of the project who didn't know what the product would look like, what it would really be good for—or who would even buy it—and he's telling me to get together a full-scale communications plan for the product and to have the plan ready to go in a few weeks.

"I'm sitting there trying to keep my mouth from dropping open and, all of a sudden, I start to get a headache—and I never get headaches. Then, before I can say anything, Don tells me he's busy and I have to go and he points me down the hall and tells me to get started on the communications plan. I started wondering how many days I could get in on the beach before this whole thing fell apart and I had to go back north to the snow and ice."

Snow and ice would have likely been the least problems for D'Arezzo if Project Chess had collapsed. Speculating on the possibility of something that never happened, D'Arezzo said, "If this had turned into a fiasco, I probably would have been transferred back to the New York area. From there, the company would put me in a job as an 'administrator' buried in some division. I'd forever be known as one of those reckless guys—and there are a lot of them around the country—who had been associated with aborted projects.

"Needless to say, that would not have been a good thing. It would not have helped my career at all and, up to the point where I went to Boca Raton, my career at IBM was in very good shape.

"Sure, I was taking a gamble going from being an administrator—which is not a very big role—to the manager of communications on a new project which, if it worked out, would mean I'd have a sizeable staff reporting to me and there would be a lot of significant responsibility."

What D'Arezzo was doing, of course, was stepping outside of the traditional career path as it was defined at IBM in the early 1980s. As he explained some years later:

"At that time, there were only two places in the country—or maybe even in the world—where things were happening at IBM. One was at or near the New York headquarters; the other place was Atlanta where the

General Systems Division is located. No major activity was going on anywhere else. Sure, there were plant sites sprinkled around where somebody like myself could go and do things like put together the plant newsletter and organize the annual picnic and softball game—which, to me, would be like going to Siberia. So then comes this new, hot site at Boca Raton where the grapevine says all sorts of exciting and revolutionary things are happening. And I had a chance to be there and have unheard of authority to do whatever I had to do to make things work. I was a young guy at the time, I wasn't even 30 years old—how could I not agree to go?"

· 4 ·

D'Arezzo put the communications plan together in record time, outlining what Project Chess needed in the way of advertising, sales promotion, public relations, packaging, design and product literature. The plan's total cost came to more than 20 percent of the first year's expected sales revenues from the Acorn. D'Arezzo knew he'd never get that much money and, as it turned out, he had to fight to end up with nearly half of his original budget projections.

Advertising was the big item in the budget. Apple Computer had been promoting its line with a series of carefully crafted print ads that effectively conveyed their products' technical advantages and the array of applications programs—such as the popular VisiCalc—that could be run on an Apple machine. The company's radio and television ads featured the erudite and urbane Dick Cavett. The perception of the company and its products as warm and friendly was conceived by Apple's president, Steve Jobs. The campaign was executed by Chiat, Day under the supervision of Jay Chiat, president of the Los Angeles-based advertising agency.

IBM loves research, and won't make a move without exploring and weighing every facet of potential consequences. This respect for research is shared by the advertising industry so, when it was time to set an ad campaign for the Acorn, research meant everything. Research revealed, for example, that there was a definite market for in-home computers, but that there was a fear of these quick-witted machines among consumers. One source, a professor of behavioral psychology at the University of Michigan, opined that people who are afraid of computers are the same people who have a dread of being caught making mistakes. As a rule, neophytes will blunder about for a while until they get the hang of the technology; in the process, they will inevitably make mistakes. If these mistakes are an embarrassment, and if they fear such embarrassment, then they will be cautious about exposing their ineptitude with computers—or so this theory asserts which, if it is true, indicates that Apple and its ad agency were on target with their user-friendly computer campaign.

Somehow, IBM had to create an image for the Acorn that was even more "friendly" than Apple. Add to this the problem of overcoming what D'Arezzo described as "the almost universal perception among consumers that IBM was as cold and heartless and methodical as its famous line of mainframe computers.

"Since there was so little time to develop a campaign and because of the tight security on the project," said D'Arezzo, "we decided to go with one of the ad agencies IBM was currently using. This was the suggestion of my senior managers in New York and they didn't have to twist my arm because it meant we wouldn't have to take valuable time to educate a new ad agency on IBM, explain the corporate culture, go through the whole thing with security and only then get down to talking about the product. By doing this, we automatically narrowed the field to four agencies. I talked to all of them and we finally settled on Lord, Geller, Federico, Einstein, a New York-based agency that we felt could do a real class job."

The agency's assignment, in so many words, was to find a way to sell the new desk-top machine while, at the same time, dispel fear of computers in general and a certain revulsion toward IBM in particular.

· 5 ·

Dozens of campaign themes were painstakingly prepared and summarily rejected. Somebody suggested, "Let's put white coats on all of the guys that developed the machine and pose them in front of the lab at Boca Raton and have the headline say that all of IBM's expertise in computers went into this little product." There would be a battalion of so-called scientists standing around this little box and looking into the camera. "Oh boy, talk about dry!" D'Arezzo said.

Then someone else chimed in, "Have a picture of the computer and above that a headline saying, 'Pick this up at an authorized IBM dealer, take it home and plug it in and start being a computer user.'" This idea was taken up at first, but then dropped, and, once again, D'Arezzo's head started to ache.

When all else fails, Madison Avenue turns to celebrities as salespersons. In this instance, Lord, Geller was no exception. They put together storyboards for a TV commercial that moved the camera through a stage setting, while an unidentified voice talked about how the new IBM machine helped them do this or that. At the end of the commercial, a door would open and there would be someone (or something) like Kermit the Frog, Beverly Sills, or Tommy Lasorda. In D'Arezzo's judgment, this campaign bore more than a passing resemblance to the American Express Company's world-renowned "Do you know me?" commercials. Furthermore, it lacked essential credibility because it did nothing to polish the patina of IBM as a company. So D'Arezzo sent the agency back to their drawing boards while he reached for an aspirin bottle.

About this time, as reported by *Time* magazine (July 11, 1983), "The agency was talking about using the Muppets or Marcel Marceau, the mime, when, according to [the agency's] Creative Director Thomas Mabley, the idea for the [Charley Chaplin] Tramp 'sort of walked in and sat down.'"

Now, finally, D'Arezzo was intrigued. "I took it from there," he recalled, "and sold it throughout the company. It was not an easy sell, by any means. After all, here we had an internationally known American corporation that prides itself on its presentations, its people and their selling skills and we were going to use a tramp that doesn't talk. And the tramp is identified with Charley Chaplin, who some people thought was a communist, so he left the United States and never returned. To make matters even worse, in *Modern Times*, one of Chaplin's most famous movies, his tramp gets tangled up in the giant gears of a machine, which, to some people, represents the trouble with technology. But I really loved the concept and when I got together with the agency to show the idea to Estridge, he asked, 'Now how are you guys going to sell that?' And we showed him exactly how we were going to do it."

· 6 ·

The way they did it was by introducing the tramp character almost as an afterthought. As part of this strategy, the agency prepared a series of three initial print ads—none of which had anything to do with the tramp.

By this time, the Acorn had evolved to become the IBM Personal

Computer—though no one really expected the name to stick—but it was useful nevertheless for the introductory series of ads pegged on the theme: "The IBM Personal Computer and Me."

The first ad showed a businessman sitting relaxed, with his tie unloosened and his feet up on the desk—which was another "first" for IBM. He was contentedly pecking away at a keyboard on his lap, while the headline announced: "Introducing the IBM of Personal Computers." Another ad in this miniseries was in a cartoon format with the headline: "Dad, Can I Borrow the IBM PC?"

Before the campaign could be started, it had to be presented to the Corporate Management Committee (CMC). D'Arezzo was in charge of the presentation, and he planned his strategy carefully. Looking back to that all-important meeting, he recalls:

"There I was, fresh from Boca Raton, standing in front of some of the legendary figures at IBM. First, I showed the ads with the relaxed businessman and the kid asking to borrow the PC. I explained where the ads would appear and discussed some general concepts of how we'd promote the machine. Then, toward the very end of the presentation, I pulled out a picture of the tramp and said, 'We're looking at this for television. We'll produce a commercial and see how this works.' Then I let it drop. I did not say that we were going to build the whole campaign around the tramp. To get the campaign going, we used a traditional approach and from there we gradually added the tramp."

Since the CMC made no connection between the taciturn tramp, communist leanings and an antitechnology bias, D'Arezzo told the agency to start the campaign.

· 7 ·

Permission to use the tramp image had to be obtained from Bubbles, the company owned by the Chaplin family, to license use of the actor's name and characters.

The next step was to cast the role of the tramp for these modern times. "It took us months to cast for that character," D'Arezzo said. According to *Time* (July 11, 1983), "the agency interviewed some 40 candidates in New York City and 20 on the West Coast." The winner was 5-foot 6-inch Billy Scudder, who'd been doing tramp impersonations at Knott's Berry Farm in California since 1971.

"I still remember hour after hour of looking at tapes of those people who would come and do the tramp," D'Arezzo recalls. "And Billy

Scudder stood out—I mean, he just popped out! There was absolutely no question that he was the guy. It was Scudder from day one."

With the licenses obtained and Scudder cast as the tramp, the vital presentation of the first IBM PC began to evolve. As far as D'Arezzo was concerned, the character of the tramp was the key to the image of the PC.

"This was all based on the Chaplin movie, *Modern Times*," D'Arezzo said. "The initial tag line for the tramp in the campaign was, 'The IBM Personal Computer—a Tool for Modern Times.' We were always careful to say, 'This is not Charley Chaplin. This is the tramp, a character made famous by Charley Chaplin many years ago.'

"The *Modern Times* film became a catalyst to show that here was a guy caught up in the modern world and that he represented a clever person, the one who, at the end, always did things by the book and always seemed to get himself out of incredible scrapes. And because of his wits and his capabilities, he was able to be successful.

"So here he was representing a true tool for modern times—a tool that was friendly, supposedly easy to use and that didn't cost too much. This character embodied that complicated concept for us. The tramp did a beautiful job of communicating the impression we wanted of an effective, low-end product. The idea worked perfectly."

*Time* (July 11, 1983) lent prestige to the campaign by stating, "The Tramp campaign has been so successful that it has created a new image for IBM. The firm has always been seen as efficient and reliable, but it has also been regarded as somewhat cold and aloof. The Tramp, with his ever-present red rose, has given IBM a human face."

# 15    Choosing the Mail Carrier

· 1 ·

Dan Wilkie has a way of getting ahead in the world without the benefits of an old-boy network, impressive academic credentials, an aristocratic family, a socially advantageous marriage or a flamboyant personality.

Wilkie's winning formula is the essence of simplicity: "I am a mail carrier," he says. This means the man gets the job done no matter the obstacles in his way: not rain, not sleet, not dark of night—not even corporate bureaucracy. It also means he delivers on time with no regard for his personal feelings, comfort or convenience. Wilkie makes the Protestant work ethic look like a code for dilettantes. Of course, they loved him at IBM.

Wilkie wanted in the worse way to be a member of the Project Chess team. He had the advantage of being stationed at Boca Raton as a functional manager of engineering and materials, where he developed friendships with Estridge, Bauman, Lowe, Sydnes and other members of the PC task force.

He was fascinated by the freedom they enjoyed from the conventional corporate constraints. Since he was not a man blinded by envy and jealousy, he saw that Project Chess was not a ballet of futility, nor were the guys on the project the "pack of crazies" they were becoming known as among the battalions of resolute IBMers. But more than any other single aspect of the project, there was the leadership of Don Estridge, and this, matched by the personality and demeanor of the man himself, completely captured the heart and mind of Dan Wilkie.

He dreamed of joining the Estridge team. But then, in the fall of 1980, and through the early days of 1981, there was no place on the project for someone with Wilkie's particular talents and skills—capabilities that were being adequately furnished by Joe Bauman.

81

He was a man not unaccustomed to being passed by during the first round of personnel selections. And so, once again, he was disturbed by the nagging notion that an exciting project at IBM was getting past him.

· 2 ·

Such notions meant nothing to Bill Lowe. He was on target and on schedule, and this was proven when, in March 1981, he was named a vice president of the Information Systems Division and general manager of the IBM plant at Rochester, Minnesota.

At his going-away party in Boca Raton, no one thought it unusual that Lowe spent so much time in private conversation with Joe Bauman, the director of manufacturing for Project Chess. After all, they had known one another for years, and Bauman had even followed Lowe from Atlanta. They were probably rehashing old times.

· 3 ·

Steadily and inexorably all of the scattered pieces of the project were coming together. Tucked away on the shores of a lake near the far corner of the continent, Microsoft was on schedule with its development of the operating system and programming language. The first 15 production units of the machine were in the hands of trusted software developers. Final contracts were being signed with outside suppliers of components for the PC. The IBM plant at Greencastle, Indiana, was tooling up to handle spare parts for the machine. At Boca Raton, test runs of the manufacturing pilot line were underway. Estridge constantly shuttled between Boca Raton and New York, furnishing status reports to senior management, and he always seemed to return with more money for the project. Meanwhile, Wall Street and the business press were having limited success following up rumors that something big was happening at the IBM plant in Boca Raton, which was the first news for many of them that the corporation even had a facility there.

And Dan Wilkie continued to "carry his mail" and keep his hopes high and do his best to bide his time.

· 4 ·

More than a few of IBM's principal areas of business were not having the best of times in 1981. Many companies were holding back on mainframe computer purchases to see if IBM's new models would make the current technology obsolete. Meanwhile, upstart innovators such as Wang Laboratories and Digital Equipment Corporation were making steady advances into the market for mid-sized computers—always at the expense of IBM, which never achieved the dominance in this segment of the industry that it had in mainframes. Although Big Blue was hardly in danger of folding, as a corporation it was not performing up to its standards.

This circumstance caused down-the-line cutbacks throughout almost every area of the company. The belt-tightening stressed freezes on hiring, reductions in capital spending, and restrictions on travel and entertainment. The exception was the Entry Level Systems Unit in Boca Raton, where the only variable that exceeded the budget for Project Chess was the adrenaline level of the staff. Estridge could switch roles fast and wear any number of hats. Depending on the circumstances, he was a father figure, knowledgeable mentor, big brother, patient listener, gentle coaxer, stern disciplinarian, loyal friend, kindly teacher and a coach based on such role models as Knute Rockne, Vince Lombardi and Bobby Knight.

He also knew how to get what he wanted, and in early June of 1981 Don Estridge wanted somebody to carry the mail.

· 5 ·

Dan Wilkie had just been promoted from a functional manager of production control to materials manager at the center of operations at Boca Raton when Don Estridge came into his office, unannounced, and sat down. Wilkie thought he was going to offer congratulations on a recent promotion. Instead, Estridge said, "I want to talk to you about running my manufacturing operations for the PC group."

"Estridge took me by complete surprise," Wilkie said. "I just sat there for a moment, then I asked, 'Well, what happened to Joe?,' because I knew Joe Bauman very well and he hadn't said anything to me about leaving as director of manufacturing for the group.

"Don said that Joe had an opportunity to go somewhere else and everyone agreed that it would be in his best interests to leave. It was only later that I found out about Joe Bauman. Guess what? He was leaving Boca Raton to be Bill Lowe's new plant manager at Rochester.

"Before he approached me, Don had talked about this matter with Howie Davidson, who was the general manager of the Boca Raton site, and Howie—who was kind of a mentor to me—recommended that I should get the job. So with that, Don sat there and looked at me like he expected me to say 'Yes' in about half a millisecond.

"The thing was that this came so out of the blue that I had to let it sink in. So I said, 'Well, I don't know if I really want to do that, because I just received a nice promotion and, besides, how can you be making a change like this when you're only a few weeks away from announcing the product?'

"Don didn't hesitate a bit. He came right out and said, 'I believe that when any of our people gets an opportunity for something better, I shouldn't hold them back, regardless of the program.
shouldn't hold them back, regardless of the program.'

"That really impressed me," Wilkie said. "So I told him I would consider his offer and he got a funny look on his face like he was thinking, 'My God! This guy is going to turn me down.'

"So he got up and headed for the door and I asked, 'Does Howie Davidson [the general manager at Boca Raton] know you're talking to me about this?' And Don says, 'Why yes, of course he knows.' Then he looks back at me and I get up from my desk and I say, 'In that case, I don't need to think about this anymore. I'll come to work for you.' And Don acts like this tremendous weight just came off his shoulders and we shake hands and he is grinning from ear-to-ear and so was I. And that started it for me. It was a decision that I have never, never regretted," Wilkie recalled.

· 6 ·

This decision was not necessarily another step along a destined path of glory for Dan Wilkie.

He was the first member of his family to join IBM. His father had done production work for Lever Brothers in Whiting, Indiana, where his son was born in 1943. Eleven years later, his parents separated and young Dan was raised by his mother, who worked in a succession of waitress jobs.

After graduating from high school in Indiana, Dan Wilkie entered the Chicago Technical College. Looking back to those days, he recalls, "The college was tucked away in an old office building in the middle of Chicago's loop. The left campus was a flowerpot on one side of the front door and the rest of the campus consisted of the flowerpot on the other side of the door.

"It was one of those places where you went to school from seven in the morning till noon, or from noon till five in the afternoon. This is because the students had jobs the rest of the time; when you weren't working or sitting in class was when you studied. It was an all-male school and there was no social life to speak of—there wasn't time for any. I just went to school, studied, and worked at two or three jobs I held during my time in college, which were four of the toughest years of my life. Graduation was nothing special. I took my degree, walked out the door for the last time and said, 'Well, that's that.'"

But at least he had a degree and, armed with that credential, Wilkie applied for a job with IBM. "I not only got a rejection," he recalls, "but I also got a letter back from some guy at IBM that implied why was I even writing to him in the first place. 'So who needs you, you jerk?,' is what I thought. Initially, I got a real sour taste for IBM, so I ended up going into the steel industry, then I got a job in aerospace engineering at Pratt-Whitney."

Wilkie is a large-boned, hefty man with a thick handshake and a cautious manner developed, perhaps, from dealing with more than the usual share of disappointments. But there is nothing about him that indicates he is weak, timid or a quitter. He may call himself "a mail carrier," but he is really the tortoise, as in Aesop's fable of the tortoise and the hare. The confidence he radiates is grounded in the sure knowledge that he will prevail because he will persevere. So, though his feelings were hurt by his initially abrupt treatment from IBM, he was not about to wallow in self-pity for the rest of his life. The only problem he had with IBM (and he always recognized this) was that his timing was wrong the first time around.

And so, some years later, when Wilkie, an avid angler, was reading the fishing column in a Florida newspaper, his attention wandered to an employment ad. It was an ad by IBM, and they were looking for a mechanical engineer. Wilkie took the bait and he landed the job. Some years later, he would recall, "This taught me that life was all timing. It's not who you know, as a lot of people think it is, though that can certainly help. But the whole thing is being in the right place at the right time and by always applying two secret little four letter words called 'work hard.'"

# 16    Bidding for
#        Bucks

· 1 ·

The team was solidly in place. Every key spot was filled. No further
turnover was anticipated. Along the way, however, Estridge would spot
a problem with a staff member, do what he could to redirect his efforts
and kindle his enthusiasm, but if he still did not respond to project
standards, Estridge would turn away and say, "He hasn't got what it
takes. He can't keep up with the pace. He has to go." And then the
laggard would be gone, no matter who he knew or how well he was
liked. Always ticking away were the clock, the calendar, the timetable,
the deadlines, the fate of the project. The members of the PC team
would holler and scream and curse but they *worked*. "We were a strange
bunch," Wilkie mused, "but we were strange in a way that worked for
the success of the project. What we had was quite a combination of
factors. And how! I could shut my eyes and think that I was almost
anywhere else but at IBM.

· 2 ·

It had been IBM's custom to build its computing machines with parts
made by divisions within IBM. Until the advent of Project Chess, this
practice was all but sacrosanct—the sole exception being the acquisi-
tion of the highly sophisticated silicon chips known as microprocessors.
Here, IBM lacked the expertise of such specialized corporations as
Intel, National Semiconductor and Texas Instruments.

As Joe Sarubbi, who was handling the technical procurement and component qualifications for the project, said, "We purchased components from third parties and then took their designs and the data sheets from companies like Intel, National Semiconductor and Texas Instruments and we'd use our own data sheets to lay out logical designs to see if they worked. Then we could proceed to get the necessary certifications for these off-the-shelf components from independent testing labs and from our own engineers at Boca.

"In the past," Sarubbi said, "most of the semiconductor activities would be handled by the IBM Component Division, or by the General Technology Division, then portions of the development would be handled by outside labs. This would cover only 10 or 20 percent of a system—not 100 percent as it did in our case."

If Project Chess had been forced to follow conventional IBM procedures, Sarubbi estimated that it would have taken up to another two years to complete the PC project. "We would have had to start from scratch to deal with so many different areas within the company. Coordinating something like that in the timetable required would have been an unmanageable task."

· 3 ·

Initially, the administrators of corporate procurement at IBM seemed not to care. According to Dan Wilkie, their attitude at the time was, "Those guys at Boca aren't going to buy any technically sophisticated stuff. They're looking for state-of-the-art stuff, crumbs lying around on the floor, so let them have the freedom to get it wherever they want to. What's the loss? Big deal!"

That's what they thought back then, eons ago in late 1980 and early 1981. Now it was the fall of the following year, and the excitement simmering at Boca Raton began to scorch the corporate buyers up north.

Joe Sarubbi, who knew his way around the corporation, worked with Estridge to keep the corporation out of their way, but no amount of effort could keep them from trying to get a piece of Project Chess. This was a typical phone call to Wilkie:

"Hey, Dan, we want to come down to Boca and take some worries off your shoulders. You guys have been doing a great job, but now that you're getting big, we want your business, so we're coming down. Okay, Dan?"

Wilkie refused to play the genial boniface, though these callers must have expected as much. He would listen politely, then say, "Well, thanks, but no thanks. But I'll tell you what—you can bid on the job."

Then the caller, who never was treated like this before within the closed fraternity of Big Blue, would sputter and snap, "What in the hell do you mean, you'll let me bid?"

Not everyone went away mad. Some guy would gulp and add, "Uh, okay. What do I have to do to make a bid?" That's when the fun would begin.

"I'll send you a quote package like I sent to all the other suppliers bidding on this job," Wilkie would say. "So you can give me a bid and put in your fixed-cost guarantee, then, if your cost overruns, that's your problem. I'll treat you like all the other vendors, which means you have to submit a sealed bid." Then the guy on the other end would sputter.

Later, Wilkie recalled, "Oh, did that cause turmoil in the company! In fact, we probably gave the company more strength by going through this process than by anything else we did. By this, I mean, when I look back 10 or 20 years from now, I'll know I had something to do with making IBM finally become competitive with itself and more aware of outside pricing."

But at the time, the corporation—at least those facets of it that tried to "do business" with Project Chess—attempted with all of their collective might to resist change as the only constant. Wilkie said, "I recall one high corporate official joking with me that making IBMers wait in the lobby really made them angry. I wasn't doing this on purpose, of course. Their problem came from being treated like true vendors instead of privileged suppliers on an 'inside track.' That hit them like true culture shock."

In the good old days, the facility at Endicott, New York, always made the raw cards for all IBM products. Memory chips came from the Burlington plant, and the operation at Kingston, New York, built power supplies. It's not that it *had* to be this way—it's just the way it was. Until Project Chess came into existence and started messing with the system, no one ever had conceived that things could be otherwise.

But Wilkie couldn't be concerned about whose feelings he hurt, because competitive pressures demanded lower costs. "I'd tell the other divisions at IBM that, if they wanted our business, they'd have to supply fixed prices on a volume matrix basis, which means if our volume goes up, then we pay a lower price, and vice versa. Then, when I told them we wanted to work with a fixed-cost concept, they'd cry, 'We can't do that. The financial measurement system doesn't allow it.' In other words, what they were saying was, 'We'll sell you this part for $50, but if we can't make a profit, then we'll throw in all our extra costs. If it turns out to be $55, then that's the price you'll have to pay.'"

Wilkie didn't buy this line at all. "Nope," he'd say, "if you bid $50, then that's it. In fact, I'll be back for even lower costs in line with industry prices over time." Then, unabashed, the in-house vendor would reply, "Okay, if we say it's $50, then it's $50, but on December 31, we'll reset our books as a one-time ledger adjustment and if there are overrun costs, then you have to make up the difference."

To this ploy, Wilkie would say, "No, no, no. If you say $50, then it's $50—no ifs, ands, or buts."

## · 4 ·

The IBM plant at Charlotte, North Carolina, was the first in-house vendor to sign a contract with the group at Boca Raton. The Charlotte plant would provide the central processing unit card assembly, but not before Wilkie took bids from four other vendors outside the corporation.

Initially, the Charlotte facility came in more than 20 percent high on its quote. But in an effort at least to *try* to keep some of the business inside the corporation, Wilkie went through 14 reviews of the bid with representatives of the facility and finally with Frank Metz, who, at the time, was the group executive for finance. Along the way, tempers flared and, at one point, an executive from Charlotte snapped at Wilkie, "Look, we're not some little outside vendor you can play around with. We are inside. Our badges say 'IBM.' What the hell does *your* damn badge say?"

By now Wilkie knew he was on to something so hot he sensed he could get his fingers burned and his future jettisoned. Obviously, the word had moved throughout the corporation that Project Chess was something special. The fact that Estridge had a direct line to the top of the corporation caused a lot of clean-clipped heads to turn. Then, every time Estridge walked out of the corporate offices, he would come away with more money and that was certainly reason for pause, because the rest of the corporation was being forced to cut costs. The final slap was that the rebels at Boca Raton were actually getting respect for their revolutionary in-house competitive bidding process. Project Chess was riding unbelievably high, which, in a corporation like IBM, meant that it was becoming a target for those less favored. Wilkie opted to not back down, because Charlotte was just the first of many locations that would be coming after pc business with the full force of their division and group staffs.

· 5 ·

Wilkie told the Charlotte people that they could have a piece of the project's business if they would beat by 15 percent the lowest bid from any source. (Experience had shown that final prices were about 12 to 18 percent beneath the initial bids.) He thought this would placate some sensibilities, but, instead, this is what he heard:

"Okay, we'll match their bid, but we don't know how those other guys can do it for that price. They're going to lose money, because here's their buildable materials cost, and here's their reasonable profit, and they will lose money, they'll go bankrupt, that's for sure, but we'll match their bid price anyway, because—well, it's the right thing for us to do to make this machine you're building as much of an IBM product as possible."

Wilkie winced whenever he would hear this. So once he shot back with, "Now wait a minute, we're getting closer but let's negotiate some more." That did it. The in-house people saw to it that Wilkie was summoned to group headquarters at White Plains.

Wilkie went, and he explained how he was operating. At this point, the Charlotte facility hadn't contracted with Boca Raton to do card assemblies and testing, so Frank Metz, who was acting as arbitrator for this disagreement, turned to the Charlotte people and said, "Well, do you want his business, or don't you want it? What we have here is a $6 million order. If you don't take it, I'll let Wilkie do what he wants." Then the general manager of the Charlotte plant said right away, "I'll take it. We want the business." And that, complete with detailed terms and conditions for cancellations, became the first fixed contract signed between Project Chess and an IBM in-house vendor.

Months later, Wilkie was sent to do business with Pat Toole, general manager of the IBM plant at Endicott, New York, which was responsible for the procurement and manufacturing of printed circuit boards for all IBM computers. After several sessions, Toole had given

Wilkie what seemed to be a reasonable price, but then word leaked back to Wilkie that an executive at corporate headquarters had, in effect, confided to Toole, "You don't have to worry about keeping under a vendor price with Wilkie. Just give him your price and he has to take it whether he likes it or not."

Right away, Wilkie saw that his strategy of conciliation was being exploited by people within his own company.

So Wilkie picked up his phone and dialed the Endicott plant and got Toole on the line and said, "Pat, I need a better price and with it I'll have more volume business for you. He got it. Just like that. It was good business for the pc group and good for Endicott as well."

A while later, the corporate execs tried to get into the act, but, by then, Wilkie and Toole had signed their contract. "It was a win for both of us," Wilkie said. "It was my decision to buy from within the company and Endicott gave us a superior product at a very competitive price. Neither of us needed any 'help' from the corporation to work out an agreement."

In another instance, the IBM plant at Boulder, Colorado, failed to match the standards for the PC's floppy disk drives. According to Wilkie, "Their cost points were wrong and when they got a subassembly from an outside supplier and tried to put it together themselves, the result was a terrible flop." In time, the problem with the drives would likely have been rectified, but Project Chess couldn't wait. The contract to supply floppy disk drives for the IBM PC was originally signed with the Tandon Corporation of Chatsworth, California, and other outside suppliers though, significantly, the IBM operation at Boulder was not among the chosen.

· 6 ·

Project Chess did reach agreement with the IBM facility at Lexington, Kentucky, to furnish the keyboard for the new PC. In a move that would be widely criticized, the left-hand shift key and the return key were intentionally located to be noncompatible with the universally accepted IBM Selectric keyboard standard.

In an interview with *Byte* magazine (November 1983), Estridge later admitted, "I wasn't thrilled with the placement of those keys, but every place you pick to put them is not a good place for somebody. The left-hand shift key is where it is because we wanted to have the character-typing keys inside the control keys. The arrangement with the one extra key, instead of being the shift key with the character on the outside, is just the reverse. It's not much of a problem in the long run," Estridge suggested. "Fortunately, people adjust."

Estridge could be adroit when confronted. As the *Byte* editors pressed the keyboard question, Estridge countered that the company's experience with building millions of typewriters actually helped in the design of the PC. For example, the keyboard was built to tilt at an angle, or it could be laid flat. "We don't know why people feel comfortable with one of those two positions," he told *Byte*, "but we've learned from building typewriters that these are the two popular angles for wrists."

He said studies of the human eye also influenced the final design of the PC when it was shown that there is a direct relationship between pupil dilation and fatigue. That is, the more a computer operator's pupils expand, the more tired he will become. Estridge explained that the key to fatigue reduction is to cut down on contrast changes on the face of the equipment. As he told *Byte* in this interview:

"Imagine that the center of the machine is a high-contrast area and the outside of the machine—the background—is a low-contrast area. The machine has grades of contrast as you move from the screen outward. Its highest contrast is on the display tube. Immediately around the tube is a lower-contrast border and then the cabinet curls round to form an even lower-contrast frame.

"The eye then progresses from seeing dark gray to light gray to medium white. . . . As the eye moves across those boundaries, it doesn't experience much contrast change and the viewer doesn't get tired."

· 7 ·

Those who knew him well say the *Byte* interview was a typical example of Estridge's expertise at handling the media. What he essentially did was sidestep negative comments on the controversial decision not to adhere to the Selectric standard, then he seized on IBM's experience in typewriters as a positive factor in the PC's design. Apparently, the *Byte* editors were either befuddled or mollified, since they moved from talk about the keyboard to a less sensitive line of questioning.

A few years later, Dan Wilkie recalled, "Unlike most engineers and technical types, Don had a masterful command of verbal skills. He didn't clam up when reporters came around and he didn't get tongue-tied when he had to make presentations to senior management."

The consensus of those who knew him best is that Estridge never did trust himself to be a good bull-thrower. He was good on his feet because he was compulsive about details and preparation.

Wilkie explained, "Don would make a pitch to management with maybe a dozen flip-charts, but he would have 70 more charts as back-ups. He used the back-ups more for his own preparation than as part of his final presentation. He supplemented this through a succession of reviews with his various staff people where all sorts of minor issues were approached and sorted out. With all these details and analyses in his head he was thoroughly prepared for any specific presentation."

# 17    The
# Inner Circle

· 1 ·

Saturday mornings in the summer of 1981 at Boca Raton: the streets were quiet, a few lawn sprinklers twirled, a kid here or there on a bike. The pace was so slow. It was the weekend, and a time for rest, or play, or puttering about the house. Even IBMers slept in, then moved leisurely, lazily, through the hazy morning. It was that kind of a day in that sort of a place.

But Wilkie was already late, and it was only a few minutes past 8:30. When he pulled his car into the parking lot at Project Chess headquarters, there, side-by-side, were the autos driven by Don Estridge, Bill Sydnes, and Joe Sarubbi. Wilkie yanked the car into the parking space and hurried through the door, into the building, down a corridor and on to the conference room where the others were just getting settled.

After all, it was the weekend, and a time to relax, so here was the unofficial inner circle of Project Chess eagerly engaged in their favorite form of relaxation: Talking about the project and the people and the PC in an easygoing way without phones to answer, problems to resolve, and neckties to wear.

At these gatherings (they weren't really "meetings" or "conferences" in the IBM sense of those terms) Estridge would democratically take care to sit anywhere but at the head of the table. Nobody really "ran" the meetings or called the sessions to order.

While things would get underway at the office around 8:30 on those Saturday mornings, there was no set time limit; if someone had to leave, they simply did. Around noon or one o'clock, the others would begin to call it a day and rather grumpily head back home to tend to the lawn, go to the hardware store or make the weekly trip to the supermarket.

94

(Years later, Joe Sarubbi said, "We didn't spend a lot of time at home in those days. Our wives knew we were working on a very exciting and important project and they gave us all the support we needed. Actually, the people on the project didn't see one another socially that much because we spent so much time together otherwise. When I wasn't working, I'd put in time on the beach. That was my social life—I'm a beach bum. One time I asked Estridge to give me an umbrella and a telephone, and I'd work from the beach. Needless to say, he didn't think that was such a good idea.")

·  2  ·

The Saturday gatherings proved to be invaluable to the success of the project. During the Monday to Friday workweek, there were just too many interruptions and niggling details that demanded immediate attention. As a result, there was never any time to say, "Stop! Let's take a look at where we are, where we've been and where we're going—especially, where we're going and why."

The weekdays were hectic, so the real critiques and progress reports were held on the weekends.

By mid-summer of 1981, the PC group was going at a fever pitch with scores of critical issues to be resolved daily. When a glitch did develop, this inner circle would quickly gather, sometimes without waiting for all areas of responsibility to get involved. Decisions were made quickly; there was no time for second-guessing. Wrong decisions were re-decided. Indecision was never tolerated.

They were, in effect, a tactical unit within the task force. This meant they were also firemen ready to move quickly and focus on a quick solution to a problem. (Reverting to gridiron parlance, Estridge called this team-within-the-team his "downfield blockers.") They were always on duty—Don and Dan and Bill and Joe—and, when trouble arose, Estridge and Wilkie and Sydnes and Sarubbi were the ones the others confidently turned to, especially when confidence in the fate of the project would occasionally waver.

·  3  ·

At Microsoft headquarters, confidence was king. Never did Bill Gates doubt his ability and that of his crackerjack programmers to produce a state-of-the-art operating system and BASIC language that would set a standard for the entire personal computing industry.

Privately, though, Gates would concede that his confidence in IBM was less than he wished it would be. Quite frankly, he was always afraid that Big Blue would and could at any time simply cancel Project Chess, pay its bills for work accomplished and head away toward other ventures.

It was common knowledge in the industry that only a fraction of IBM's research projects were ever carried through to product introductions. So Gates, high-strung and nervous by nature, would fret over the worst possible scenario. What other projects were running in tandem with the development of a desk-top computer? Were those guys at Boca Raton running around with some half-baked belief that they could keep on managing their own show while they were still on IBM's payroll? What about those persistent rumors that IBM was back to holding secret conversations with Gary Kildall at Digital Research? And then there was the almost-daily speculation in the press about what IBM was up to at Boca Raton. Some of the stories proved to be remarkably accurate, which further upset Gates and caused him to fear that IBM would accuse Microsoft of violating its airtight confidentiality agreement.

· 4 ·

Throughout the end of June 1981, the Project Chess team put on their ties and jackets and played host to at least 40 of IBM's top officers, all quite curious to see the midget marvel of a computer which, by now, had seized the imagination of the corporation.

"These reviews by top management were necessary before the machine could be introduced to the public," Joe Sarubbi explained. "We tried to get as many people here at once as we could so we wouldn't have to keep repeating the same information."

Essentially, Estridge and his staff were telling IBM's big brass that they should coordinate their schedules and make an effort to come all at once because there wasn't any time for repetitious private presentations.

Amazingly, management acquiesced. Where, in the past, there would be separate reviews for management at the local, divisional, group and corporate levels, in this case, just one review would have to do. Besides, it gave some of the company's top people their first chance to size up one another face to face without contention.

Contention, often accompanied by confrontation, has been a way of life at IBM since the days of Thomas J. Watson, Sr. For example, a group at one location might be assigned to develop a particular machine, while another group at another site would be working on a somewhat similar project. The choice of which machine gets to market often has very much to do with how persuasive—that is, how "successfully contentious"—one group is at getting its way over the other. This system, obviously, does not always produce the best product, but, at the level of personalities, it most certainly separates the winners from the also-rans within the company.

Like everyone else at IBM, the PC development group was nurtured on the system of contention and confrontation. But there were some subtle differences at Boca Raton. According to Joe Sarubbi:

"There was always the contention of going through corporate procedures, but we were able to re-write most of those rules. When it came to contention within the group, I could hang in with the best of them. But Donnie [Estridge] was uncomfortable with the process, so he would stop everyone and say, 'Wait a minute. What is it we have to do? What do we have to provide?' Then he'd make us stick to the point until we agreed on what we had to do and when we had to do it. The result was that nobody's ego became bigger than the goal of the group, which was, of course, to get that machine out of the shop on time."

· 5 ·

By mid-July 1981, the maiden version of the IBM PC was nearly ready for market. All that remained were the myriad final details before the finished product was ready to be unveiled before the Corporate Management Committee (CMC).

During the regular Saturday morning conclave of the inner circle, Estridge took Wilkie aside for a private chat. Wilkie learned that the PC group felt that the nitpickers and detail-compulsives in the systems assurance group had come up with a list of 122 so-called work items that absolutely had to be addressed and corrected before any version of the PC could leave Boca Raton for any purpose whatsoever.

At IBM, the systems assurance people are somewhat akin to in-house censors at a television network. Systems assurance says, "You can't do this" and "You have to do that." They lay down their edicts, then wait for the inevitable onset of contention and confrontation. When the smoke clears, neither systems assurance nor the product designers get everything they want, though each side will always get some concessions. Major points where no compromise is possible are adjudicated before the CMC, which, in such instances, acts as the court of last resort. Although the CMC's decisions are final and binding, conventional wisdom at the company insists that it is never a good idea to get the CMC unnecessarily involved in contentions better confronted and compromised at staff levels.

By now, the PC group and everyone at Boca Raton who had anything to do with the new machine were on a seven-day work schedule. This meant that the systems assurance people were standing by on Saturday when Estridge told Wilkie to solve the list of nits and details.

Looking back to that time, Wilkie said, "We spent about four hours that morning going over every item. When we were done, there was enough paper lying around to cover the walls and floor. Each work item by itself seemed to be a small detail, but when they were considered together . . . well, I agreed with the systems assurance position of nonsupport on releasing the machine for market.

"In one case, there was a problem with the operating manual; another problem had to do with customer service procedures. There were also details we had to clear up with diagnostics, quality checks, and this, that and the other thing."

The biggest problem of all concerned how to work out these items and still keep the PC's introduction on schedule. Here, again, is where the PC group's carte blanche to circumvent corporate protocols and its structured disciplines with demands for checkpoints, reviews and approvals in writing across the chains of command functioned for the common good. Wilkie brought the concerned parties together in small, flexible groups. Specific problems were addressed, trade-offs negotiated and decisions made on the spot. As a result, at least 110 of the 122 work items were fixed within less than a week. The balance were polished off a few days later.

· 6 ·

It was almost the end of July 1981 when Microsoft delivered the final version of its disk operating system and BASIC programming language for the PC.

The remaining work items were cleared, the last bolts were tightened on the machine and an IBM logotype was glued to the face of the PC's central processing unit.

The machine was now ready for its preview before the Corporate Management Committee. This was the end of the line; if the CMC was impressed, the wraps would quickly come off the IBM PC, and it could be introduced to the world.

Shuttling from Boca Raton to Armonk was now a routine for Estridge. He'd grab an early flight, land in New York, rent a car, drive to headquarters, tend to business and return to Florida—all in a single day. He would do this at least once and often two and sometimes three times a week. He was not the sort to lay his briefcase on his lap and catch up on work while the plane was airborne. Instead, this was a time to relax, to read a paperback page-turner, or to collect his thoughts out of reach and out of mind from the supercharged atmosphere at Boca Raton.

This time, of course, it was different. Accompanied by Wilkie and other members of the group, Estridge was heading north for the most crucial meeting to date with the CMC. Estridge saw to it that he was well briefed for this meeting. The contents of his flip-charts were committed to memory. In a mock dry run of the session, the PC staff peppered him with what they thought was every conceivable question that could be asked by the members of the CMC.

Estridge would have no more than 45 minutes to explain why the PC was made, what it could do, the markets it would serve and the role it would have in the corporate product mix. He would do this alone, while Wilkie and the others who had come along to lend moral support were told to wait in a room on another floor at corporate headquarters.

As it turned out, Don Estridge tapped his ineffable ability to concoct just the right mixture of charm, tact and sincerity to win the day with the CMC. When his three-quarters of an hour were up, Estridge emerged from the conference room and immediately sought out the PC team. They took one look at that grin and they knew. They knew.

Later, Estridge told them that the toughest question he had to answer was, "Why should IBM risk its name and reputation for customer satisfaction and service by selling this product through non-IBM sales channels?" They also wanted to know how the PC team would assure that customer needs were going to be properly addressed. The queries, pointed as they were, came near the end of Estridge's presentation. He was taken by surprise because, in all of the prior reviews, these matters never appeared as issues with the CMC. As Wilkie recalled, "Don said the questions were worded in such a way that he felt, 'My God, they are changing their minds!' But Estridge's quick thinking held and he carried the day. So, okay, he had won the battle, but this episode left him clearly aware that the performance of non-IBM delivery channels was an important matter to the CMC. They were satisfied with his answers and so, from that moment, the IBM PC was officially launched."

# 18   The Emergency Brigade

· 1 ·

Initial shipments of the new PC were made to Computerland outlets and Sears Business Centers less than a week before the machine was scheduled to be unveiled in New York City on Wednesday, August 12, 1981. The shipments were delayed till the last possible minute to avoid leaks to the press. Preferably, the packing boxes with the PCs inside would not even be opened until the afternoon on the day of the official announcement. Then, on August 10, a potentially devastating discovery threatened to cancel the scheduled introduction that so many people had worked so hard and so long to maintain.

At about 2:30 in the afternoon, Joe Sarubbi and his staff were running final potentiometer tests to determine if there were any high-voltage leakage on some of the new PCs. Time and again, two of the machines tested positive, which meant that there was a possible dangerous voltage leak.

The engineers quickly found that the 65-volt power supplies on the two machines had too close a tolerance between an electrical raw circuit board and the frame of the power supply. This in turn caused too close a spacing that could possibly lead to a short-circuit between the electrical current and the metal frame. The problem was brought to Wilkie's immediate attention. Then a quick call went out to convene the inner circle, along with Howie Davidson, the site general manager at Boca Raton.

Sarubbi explained that the power supplies shipped to date had been tested and were shown to be safe. But the fan in the power supply could accumulate enough dust to create a 'bridge' to the metal edge of the machine and cause a short-circuit. In addition, a look at worst-case tolerances between the printed circuit card and the frame revealed a tolerance that was unacceptably close, and a relay out of the circuit board had to be added to achieve a permanent fix for the problem. There was only a random chance that this could happen again, but that was still more of a chance than Wilkie and Sarubbi wanted to take. One power supply failure was one failure too many. Meanwhile, more than 1,700 machines—all with short-circuit potentials—were sitting innocently in storage at Computerlands and Sears Business Centers around the country.

The IBM PC was intended to be *the* product to put the Sears Business Centers on the map. Accordingly, IBM had made elaborate arrangements for a full-scale demonstration of the machine to the retailer's senior management committee at the Sears Tower in Chicago on the morning of Tuesday, August 11. Now, here in Boca Raton, less than 18 hours before the big demonstration was set to begin 1,500 miles away, there was concern that the machines at Sears Tower would not only amaze, but could quite actually shock anyone who so much as laid a finger on their casings.

Four pairs of eyes turned on Sarubbi. Estridge was the first to speak. "Okay, Joe, what do we do?" Sarubbi said, "We'll have to put a piece of insulation in every machine between the printed circuit board and the power supply cover. Fish paper, which is a non-conductive cardboard bridge, should be sufficient, but this is something we really have to do ourselves."

Dan Wilkie suggested the formation of a quick task force. "We can call them 'The Power Supply Brigade,' and fly them out to Sears in Chicago and elsewhere to put in the insulation. But we have to do it now—today. Commercial flights won't get us there in time. We'll have to charter a private jet. When they're finished at Sears, they can go back to the Chicago airport and fly on to the next destination. Frankly, I don't see any other goddam way we can get this done if we still plan to show the machine to Sears tomorrow."

Estridge winced. He turned back to Sarubbi and said, "Joe, the decision to go or not to go is yours." What Estridge really meant was, Should we stop the announcement or send out the Brigade?

Sarubbi reasoned that not to send the Brigade would mean the PC announcement might be delayed for at least another 30 days. "That would put egg on our face in the industry and throughout the company," he later recalled. "But there was also no way that we could overlook the safety of the unit."

Never before in his 30-odd years with the company had Joe Sarubbi been so overwhelmingly grateful that he worked for IBM with its vast resources and capital. He looked back at the frantic, frustrating and yet thoroughly exhilarating year gone by and remembered all the times he gazed across the ocean and said to himself, "Why in the hell did I ever get into this?" Then he pictured the other people on the project and concluded, "They're just like me. We're all of a kind. We're wild ducks within IBM and we're doing what wild ducks do and that's why I have to stay."

Then his thoughts returned to the present. "Uh, Joe," Estridge said. And Sarubbi instinctively knew what a wild duck would do at a time like this, and so he said, "Send the Brigade. And keep the introduction just as it is."

"Well, son-of-a-bitch! All right, let's go!" Wilkie shouted as he turned with a big grin and smacked his right fist into his ample left palm. Estridge had to shut his eyes for a moment to pretend he hadn't heard Wilkie, then came the famous grin. Sydnes and Davidson were also smiling, and for that moment, Joe Sarubbi, the old pro, the veteran IBMer, the self-professed beach bum—he was the king of the hill, at the top of the heap.

· 2 ·

It so happened that Wilkie had a cadre of some 30 devoted admirers on his manufacturing staff. They were a gung-ho crowd who liked to hang around with Dan because he had a tough side with a tender edge and he was eminently fair. And they were loyal to Wilkie, because most of them had never worked for anyone else anywhere else at IBM. Infants all, they thought life at IBM was just like Project Chess, which, of course, made this a very good company to work for. As Wilkie would later reflect, "The team's strength lay in the fact that most of them had never really worked under the strictures of conventional IBM standards."

Wilkie walked out of the meeting and gathered his staffers. Eagerly, expectantly, they circled around their leader as he explained what had happened and what had to be done. He said, "I want you guys to go home and get your toothbrushes and a change of clothes and then come right back here and standby to leave for Chicago tonight. You'll be going by private jet out of Boca Raton airport at midnight. We don't know how long you'll be gone, so be packed for at least three days."

They all but tore the doors off to get home, grab their gear and get back to the office to be among the first in line to stand by for that emergency flight to Chicago.

As soon as the last car squealed out of the IBM parking lot, Sarubbi's office became a war room. From this jerry-built command post, the senior staff on the PC group arranged for a private jet to be ready to leave at midnight for Chicago.

The plane landed at 3:00 AM on Tuesday in Chicago. Black limousines were already waiting to whisk the Brigade through the dark streets and to the main entrance of the world's tallest building.

Earlier, back at the war room, Sparky Sparks completed special arrangements to admit the Brigade to the Sears Tower at that late hour. The Brigade deployed to the demonstration room like commandos. Within three hours, their assignment was finished; the fish paper was secured in each PC and the machines were tested again for high-voltage leaks. The demonstration for the Sears management could go on as planned and no one had to know what happened in the Sears Tower the night before.

Back at Boca Raton a phone call came at about 7:00 AM from somewhere in Chicago: "Mission accomplished!" the Brigade leader said.

Sarubbi gave Wilkie the thumbs-up sign. Wilkie went back to his own office and took his spare shaving kit out of a desk drawer. Still not fully awake, he stumbled into the men's room and tried to remember the last time he'd had breakfast at home, followed by an uneventful working day.

· 3 ·

During the next day and a half, the Power Supply Brigade, with ample supplies of fish paper, flew to Computerland stores in Texas and California. Once again, their missions were accomplished before the debut of the PC.

But the power supply episode was still causing upset at Boca Raton. Wilkie recalled, "We were really paranoid about what happened. We said, 'My God, what if the world finds out that we had this quality problem?'

"In time, the world did find out, but the reaction was the exact opposite of what we thought it would be. People everywhere were saying, 'What a class act this company has.' Sears and Computerland told us, 'Now we know the kind of treatment we can demand from all the other companies we do business with.' And so," Wilkie said, "instead of this having a negative impact, it became a real plus for the project and an unforgettable experience for those men who flew around the country and worked around the clock to guarantee that the introduction of the PC would stay on schedule."

· 4 ·

The IBM PC introduced in New York that week had one disk drive, 16 kilobytes of random access memory (RAM) and a $1,595 price tag. (Within four years, other manufacturers would have a "clone" of the basic PC with two disk drives, 256 kilobytes of RAM and it would be available for about $1,000.)

By now, despite the company's security precautions and its refusal to give any details of the "new product introduction," enough information had leaked out of IBM to make the purpose of the August 12 announcement well known throughout the industry and on Wall Street. These reports were especially significant to Martin A. Alpert in Cleveland, Ohio. Alpert, a doctor and engineer, was president of a small company called Tecmar, a sort of anagram for "Marty's technology."

Tecmar got its start with a computer-based machine used to diagnose lung problems. But the company had the technology in place to build add-on products for the basic IBM PC. Predicting that there would be an enormous market for such add-ons, Alpert put his staff to work designing products for a machine they had never seen. Then he made careful plans to buy an IBM PC when it became available. As it turned out, Tecmar bought the first IBM PC to be sold anywhere.

# 19    The Shroud
of Secrecy

· 1 ·

Since IBM makes machines, a reasonable assumption is that an invitation to an IBM announcement has something to do with news about a machine. Invariably, IBM will officially deny this, stating only for the record that the corporation is making an announcement. Period.

This is a canny strategy, because it does not undercut the market for any of its already-existing systems by revealing before the date of the official announcement that a new system may significantly supersede its predecessor. It avoids, for instance, the debacle caused by the Osborne Computer Corporation's ill-considered announcement. In April 1981, Osborne introduced a novel portable computer, complete with all the software most users would ever need. The machine used the CP/M operating system, and it sold for under $1,800. Called the Osborne 1, the computer had top sales of 10,000 units a month, and the company's revenues grew from 0 to $100 million in less than two years. But in early 1983, Adam Osborne, the company's flamboyant president, formally announced that the company would introduce a significantly improved machine within a few months. Immediately, sales of the Osborne 1 dried up. Cash flow slowed to a trickle, the company was forced to cancel a public offering and soon thereafter the company went out of business.

Since IBM prudently keeps its product development secret, there is a constant demand for inside information. This demand is generally served by an elite corps of professional "IBM-watchers," which consists primarily of consulting firms that are typically staffed from the top down with ex-IBMers. Corporations pay these people thousands of dollars a day for their counsel on the possible impact of IBM's developmental activities on the future of a client's investment in data-processing (DP) equipment. Obviously, such inside knowledge (assuming it is correct) can influence how large sums of money are spent by DP-dependent enterprises.

The value of an IBM-watcher is directly related to the reliability of the consultant's contacts within IBM. Because the whirl of activity at Boca Raton was such a controversial topic throughout the corporation, the watchers had no trouble at all uncovering the nature of Project Chess. But since the machine had not yet been officially announced, most of the consultants fell far short in their estimates of the machine's potential.

Assured of his anonymity, one consultant recalled, "Nobody in a position of importance at IBM thought the PC would ever amount to anything. It was just a matter of some innovative people getting together to build an interesting product. Remember, IBM is a company that's controlled by its National Accounts Division—the people that handle the big national and international customers. The people who rise to the very top at IBM come out of this division and it is totally oriented toward big mainframes and large corporate accounts. Back in the early '80s, the National Accounts people uniformly looked at personal computers as toys. They'd see what was going on in Florida and say, 'Well, someday we might throw some of those PC machines against the wall and see if they stick. Maybe some of those things will sell.' The applications for microprocessor-based systems just weren't that obvious in those days. Sure, there were some advocates and enthusiasts for PCs at IBM, even then. But this is a big company with thousands of employees where you can always find advocates and enthusiasts for almost anything."

Another IBM-watching consultant, also requesting anonymity, recalled hearing about the PC before its introduction. Seeking specifics, the consultant called a source at IBM.

According to the consultant's reconstruction of the conversation, the IBM insider said, "Why on earth would you care about the personal computer? It has nothing at all to do with office automation. It isn't a product for big companies that use 'real' computers. Besides, nothing much may come of this and all it can do is cause embarrassment to IBM, because, in my opinion, we don't belong in the personal computer business to begin with."

This, of course, was a source from the mainframe end of the business, so the consultant persisted and was eventually referred to a source at Boca Raton. "Under the circumstances, I don't want to identify the guy," the IBM-watcher said, "but he was so elated to find someone really interested in the PC that he stayed on the long-distance wire for four hours. I can remember it growing dark outside and the street lights coming on, but he kept right on talking. As a result, I think I must have been the first person in the country not directly connected with the project to know what it was all about. One thing I did know: that guy in mainframes was way off the mark. It was obvious that the so-called 'wild ducks' down in Florida were on to something that could change the entire course of the industry, if only IBM handled this one right, which, to me, meant that Armonk had to keep the PC project protected from the doomsayers in the National Accounts Division."

· 2 ·

At least some of the more perceptive mainframe advocates correctly assessed the microprocessor-based PC as a very real threat to the core of IBM's business. Over drinks or on the golf course and always well beyond earshot of IBM loyalists, many of the more astute mainframe marketers cursed Opel for bringing the PC into IBM. Outside of the company, in the hands of such innovators as Apple and the chain store retailers at Radio Shack, the desk-top computer was not a menace—it was, at best, a toy for tinkerers and nerds. But now, backed by IBM, the PC was actually *inside.* It was like a Trojan horse within the Big Blue walls. Some of the mainframe guys were scared and, as it developed, their fears were confirmed.

An ex-IBMer who was not involved with Project Chess explained the basis for these anxieties. "Even before the PC was introduced, a lot of the mainframe people at IBM were very well aware that microprocessor-based systems—of which PCs are the most conspicuous example—could completely destroy the structure of the computer industry during the next decade. They can destroy it because the price-performance of microprocessor systems is so much better than mainframes that a user would have to be totally retarded not to take advantage of this where he can. And the number of areas where this advantage can be taken is sufficiently numerous to guarantee that mainframe growth will never again be what it was in the past. So there's the personal computer decreasing demand for big systems while IBM's profitability continues to be infinitely linked to its dominance of the mainframe environment.

Personal computers are inherently inimical to that dominance. The mainframe people saw the PC as IBM's worst enemy—bar none."

· 3 ·

These fears were laid on Opel's desk by men whose opinions he respected, but the chairman did not waver. He was well aware that, without his corporation's blessing, the concept of practical personal computing could wallow in the shallows and never pose—at least during his term as head of the corporation—a threat of any consequence to the mainstream of IBM's revenues.

Yet he was also aware that the microprocessor was at the leading edge of technological advancement in his industry. Someday, some company, somewhere, would inevitably focus vast resources on the low-cost production of this technology and then it, and not IBM, would pose the true threat, a threat beyond the control of IBM. Logically, it would seem that this threat would come from Japan. According to *Time* magazine (July 11, 1983), "Many outsiders believe that IBM is more concerned about the Japanese than it professes." In the meantime, aside from Apple and Radio Shack, no other factors worthy of serious regard in the United States were working aggressively with microprocessor systems.

So Opel chose to keep the Trojan horse within his own walls, which meant the short-sighted in his company had to be prevented from harming the PC. To do this, he placed an unprecedented umbrella over the entire project.

Recalling this time, Jim D'Arezzo said, "Within the company, it was us trying to get our job done without getting tangled up in the rest of the bureaucracy. That was not an easy thing to do. John Opel made sure we retained our autonomy and he kept the business with us in Boca Raton, rather than our being swallowed up by the Data Processing or General Business Divisions."

Dan Wilkie, who, in his pre-PC days, had spent some time at headquarters on the corporate manufacturing staff, recalled, "The general mentality said we had to keep an eye on the outlying divisions to prevent them from screwing things up. It was like at headquarters, we always knew what was best. But with Project Chess, the headquarters guys gave us their blessings and an almost unlimited charter to move ahead. If we needed help, that's what they gave us. As far as we were concerned, this was very uncharacteristic for the corporate-level staffs to be our cheerleaders and chief supporters. But we didn't kid ourselves. We knew the support was coming right from the top to grease the skids so we could get our job done in less than a year."

· 4 ·

That job was done well enough to permit the IBM Personal Computer to be introduced at New York City on Wednesday, August 12, 1981. The announcement came on schedule, and almost a year to the day from the time Bill Lowe promised to deliver IBM's very first personal computer. Estridge was in charge of the ceremony and, in keeping with corporate procedures, only designated IBMers were allowed to speak to the press.

Since hardware is all but useless without software, IBM also introduced eight applications programs written especially for its new Personal Computer. These included the venerable VisiCalc; a set of business programs from Peachtree Software; Microsoft's BASIC programming language; a game called "Adventure" (that enticed its fans with explorations of "a fantasy world of caves and treasures") and a utilitarian word-processing program called Easy Writer.

Edward M. Esber, who at the time directed sales and marketing for VisiCorp, the supplier of VisiCalc, recalled, "IBM, which was accustomed to a much slower-moving environment, obviously wasn't up to speed in personal computing—an industry that was changing dramatically every six months. The company needed strategic software positions in such applications as spreadsheets, word processing and accounting. By sewing up some of the best minds in the applications software industry, they assured the initial success of the pc. It was a brilliant stroke."

According to Steven Levy in his book *Hackers* (New York: Doubleday & Company, 1984), the word-processing program was written by a convict "during his stint in prison for using the Apple phone interface as a blue box." This was preceded by the convict's discovery "that when one blew the whistle that came in 'Capt'n Crunch' breakfast cereal the result would be the precise 2,600-cycle tone that the phone company used to shuttle long-distance traffic over the phone lines." There is no evidence to this day to prove that IBM was aware of the origin of its first "authorized" word processing program for the PC.

The press tries hard to be blasé at media events. The trade-press reporters like to do a "blue suit count" at IBM affairs, while the daily-press business reporters will rush in, ask their questions and leave immediately. Another product, another story.

This time was different. Although IBM had nothing to say before the ceremony, everyone knew that the PC was going to be introduced. Estridge talked for a while about what the machine was designed to do and the market it was aimed for, but, beyond this, the presentation and demonstration were rather sedate. Yet there was definite enthusiasm in the air. Everyone present sensed that history was, indeed, being made.

The press, often given to sarcastic remarks where IBM is concerned, was remarkably constrained and concerned. Only the reporters who really had to go to meet deadlines did so and then, only reluctantly. The machines performed flawlessly, and they were strangely attractive. Everyone wanted to play with the keyboard, work a routine, print out results.

The excitement level was so high that the atmosphere itself seemed to crackle and sizzle. Something was afoot, all right. It was magic from Big Blue.

This was Blue Magic.

· 5 ·

After the official announcement, someone showed Wilkie a full-page ad in that day's *Wall Street Journal*. The ad was sponsored by Apple Computers, and it saluted IBM by stating: "Welcome IBM. Welcome to the most exciting and important marketplace since the computer revolution began 35 years ago. We look forward to responsible competition in the massive effort to distribute this American technology to the world."

Wilkie couldn't wait to pass the newspaper around. It caused a lot of chuckles among the PC team because, as Wilkie later explained:

"There seemed to be a suspicion in the business that IBM was paranoid about Apple. Actually, we didn't think about them too much at all. We did think it was pretty funny when we heard that all their marketing meetings dwelled on IBM-this and anti-IBM-that. As far as we were concerned, Apple was just another competitor, a price point in the market we were going after. They already owned a large share of the market and, to be honest, the absolutely worst thing that IBM would ever want would be for Apple to crumble. If that happened, everybody would say IBM was responsible and we'd look like the bad guys."

But in at least one other opinion bearing on the IBM versus Apple matter, Warren Winger, chairman of a chain of computer retail outlets in Texas and Illinois, told the *New York Times* that IBM's strategy for its PC was obviously geared to exploit the business and scientific markets that had inexplicably not been tapped by Apple. "It appears that IBM has a better understanding of why the Apple II was successful than had Apple," Winger said.

In its news columns on the day following the announcement, the *Wall Street Journal* reported, "IBM has made its bold entry into the personal computer market. The computer giant could capture the lead in the youthful industry within two years." Later, the newspaper declared, "Now that IBM has jumped in, nobody expects the personal computer industry to stay the same."

# 20    Riding the Crest

· 1 ·

Don Estridge and his PC teammates were riding an emotional crest when they returned to Boca Raton, following the triumphant introduction at New York. The media, the dealers, the industry itself—all were under the spell of Blue Magic. The almost-immediate demand for the IBM Personal Computer was so enthusiastic that its developers were caught flat footed when it came to promising deliveries.

Officially, the machine was supposed to be available for shipment in October. But orders far exceeded the ability to deliver. In the *Byte* magazine interview, Estridge bemoaned, "It's not that you can't predict what will happen in those areas that you understand. The problem lies in the very thing that makes this product popular—its application to completely unknown uses. That's exciting, but it's also the very thing that makes the business totally unpredictable."

Still, all the PC marketers could do was fall back on the corporation's standard sales forecasting procedures. Every three months after the product was introduced, IBM would ask its authorized sales outlets for a projection of the number of PCs needed for the next fiscal quarter. The company also asked for shipment projections for the rest of the year. What the company wanted, of course, was a quasi commitment from its outlets, though no contractual penalty was attached for either the dealer or IBM.

The PC took off so fast that these projections were understated by as much as 800 percent in nearly every case. As Estridge admitted to *Byte*, "We can only handle so many factors of two." He said that the production rate was quickly tripled (it was eventually quadrupled) and added, "We're extremely pleased that we can build a quality product at that rate, but it's not enough. The demand is increasing at a very fast rate and we're doing everything we can to stay with that demand.

"If the demand keeps on going at these rates, at some point there won't be any more parts. We're not there yet, but we can see where it is from here."

Meanwhile, the builders of add-on accessories for the new machine were tooled up and waiting, pacing, impatient to get their hands on an IBM PC—even just one PC!

Recalling his eagerness, Dr. Martin Alpert at Tecmar said, "In this market, especially in those years, there were absolutely no rules. Nobody understood the market or what was happening. All we knew was that people wanted a standard. They didn't know what to buy until they heard about the IBM PC and then they figured they couldn't go wrong because it was IBM.

"As soon as we saw the machine, we believed in it and we bet the future of our company on it. We intentionally put ourselves in that situation. If the IBM PC won big, then we'd win big. If the win was a small one, well, we could at least recoup our costs. Of course, if IBM didn't ship anything, then we'd lose big, but we figured we were well protected because of IBM's reputation. After all, we were only a small company at the time and we had no delusions of grandeur. We were definitely on IBM's coattails and I'll be the first one to admit it."


·  2  ·


On Saturday, August 15, the inner circle sat down at headquarters in Boca Raton for their weekly conclave. By now, they had come down from the high of the announcement and, if anything, their mood was morose. It was time to get back to work. Estridge, appearing tired and strained, asked for his teammates' attention, and then he essentially said:

"We just went through a tough period to get our product out as quickly as we could. If we can deliver, it's a winner. But now the product is out and it's apparently going to be a success in the marketplace and we're obviously going to have much more to do and we'll have to do it at an even faster pace."

Wilkie, Sparks, Sarubbi and Sydnes didn't stir as Estridge continued. "Now our ability to negotiate and get along with the other players in this business is going to be very important. During the past year, schedules to get the job done were a definite motivation to us. We're all going to have to deal with a lot more people in all sorts of situations—both inside and outside the company. And, of course, we must still always remember to stay humble."

The four others looked at each other and said in unrehearsed unison, "Us 'humble' . . . no problem." Then an uncomfortable silence fell over the room. Finally, Wilkie got up and said he had to go to the men's room. When he returned, Estridge was heading out the door, and all he had to say was, "It's been a long week, but the real fun is just beginning."

"Well, yes, it is," Wilkie said to the closing door.

· 3 ·

Sparky Sparks and Joe Sarubbi went home soon after Estridge left. Wilkie and Sydnes lingered in the conference room. They talked about how the introduction went and laughed over what they referred to between themselves as "The Epson Episode."

It seems that the Epson Corporation had been contracted to produce a dot matrix printer for the PC on an original equipment manufacturer (OEM) basis for IBM to sell under its own name. One of IBM's standard safety check-points is printer and typewriter ribbon parts. In this instance, the tests revealed an unspecified irritant in the ink used on the printer ribbon—the testing laboratories could not tell if the substance was carcinogenic. The uncertain test results came back only a week before the printer was to be introduced.

Estridge told Wilkie and Sydnes to find a way to break down the components of the formula on the ribbon. Wilkie, in turn, went to the domestic company that distributed Epson printers where he found out that the formula is proprietary, hence secret. "I'm not giving this formula to you, I'm not giving this formula to anybody," a high-level executive in the company snapped at Wilkie.

Wilkie went back to his boss, but Estridge insisted that Wilkie and Sydnes had to solve the problem. Wilkie recalled, "Sydnes and I may have had a lot of influence on the PC team, but outside the company we were only a couple of grunts. We thought the best way to get to Epson was by going through the head of the technical staff at IBM.

"So we went back to Estridge and told him—because the head of the technical staff was an officer of IBM—that he, Estridge, as head man on the PC project, would have to call the guy. Estridge got mad and said, 'Look, I don't have time for this. You guys have got to solve the problem. Do what you must do to remove the nonconcurrence and put together a work plan that says we can demonstrate the ink is okay." Then Estridge turned and walked out the door.

So Wilkie and Sydnes tracked down the head of IBM's technical staff at Armonk. "The guy was in an all-day meeting," Wilkie said, "and he told his staff he was not to be disturbed. We knew he wouldn't come out to see us because me and Sydnes were grunts. So I told Sydnes, 'Look, we know where the guy is. Let's go sit outside the conference room because, sooner or later, he's got to come out to go to the john.

"So the two of us went and sat outside the conference room and, of course, the guy eventually came out and headed toward the men's room. We grabbed him and dragged him into another office and put this whole business about the ink formula to him. He finally agreed to help us find out what the ingredients were in the formula. Later, IBM's lab found the ingredients were safe."

· 4 ·

Some while later the members of the inner circle would have yet another opportunity to slake their addiction to adrenaline. This time it was the "case of the lacerated power cords." Wilkie and his staff discovered a flaw in the packing boxes used for the PC's power cords, the electrical line used to plug in the unit.

It was reported that by using a knife to open the cartons by cutting around the edges, some people pushed too hard on the knife and nicked a power cord, which could cause a short-circuit. In a box of 2,000 power cords, perhaps a half-dozen cords might get nicked. By this time, IBM had boxes of power cords all over the country, so, again (as in the days of the Power Brigade), Wilkie sent his loyalists into the field to hand sort about 30,000 power cords to replace the few that actually were nicked.

As Wilkie recalled, "Again, when we had to send people around the country to fix problems on short notice, the members of the team would beat the doors down to help. They were all so proud of their product they were willing to do whatever was necessary to ensure that this was the best personal computer in the world."

Although the machine was complete and on the market, it seemed, in some quarters, as if the good old days hadn't passed at all. The wild ducks were still flying.

# 21    Surviving with Success

· 1 ·

The unexpected overnight success of the IBM PC created unforeseen problems. Clearly the wild ducks had flown too far too fast too soon.

To their eventual dismay and the ultimate grief of Estridge, the machine was simply selling much faster than it could be made. By now, Dan Wilkie, as the manager of manufacturing, had only a dim memory of his not-so-long-ago days in the steel mills of western Indiana. "Let's face it," he recalled, "we missed the preliminary sales forecast by almost 500 per cent. But by the same measure, it skewed the bottom line in our favor since, with the volumes way up, the per-unit production costs kept heading down. This meant that from the very beginning we were selling machines at a higher profit than we had ever anticipated."

Since IBM never releases its production figures, the press, Wall Street and all the IBM-watchers could only speculate about how well the PC was doing. At the end of 1981, the experts agreed that some 30,000 to 40,000 IBM PCs had been shipped from Boca Raton. The truth is that exactly 13,533 PCs were in the field when IBM closed its books on the first four months of the PC Era.

Estridge later told *Byte* magazine (November 1983), "We guessed wrong on how many people would order the PC from day one. We thought there would be less demand than there was, so we had to catch up and we passed that point. . . . We didn't think we were introducing standards. We were trying to discover what was there and then build a machine, a marketing strategy and distribution plan that [would] fit what had been pioneered and established by others in machines, software and marketing channels."

117

· 2 ·

During these days, order backlogs increased to intolerable levels. The production line at Boca Raton needed to be modernized immediately.

Also, new workers had to be screened and hired without delay, which is not like conducting a cattle call when IBM is the company. And the personnel staff, while under pressure to hire scores of new workers, was, at the same time, scrambling to add to their own ranks to accommodate the priority hiring.

Meanwhile, real troubles were building in the organization of independent, authorized PC dealers. The original intention was for the dealer to solve all problems with the machine, a responsibility similar to that traditionally assumed by IBM field representatives. But, when customers see the IBM name on a product, calls for help would almost always be made directly to the company, despite the fact that the dealers had been carefully trained to handle their problems.

IBM had built its reputation on unmatched service and support for its customers; the PC team accepted this as a given. As it was, the team now discovered to their chagrin that independence from the organization created a special set of responsibilities. If these were not met, it could be "reliably suspected" that headquarters would quickly step in and seize control of the PC IBU. The International Business Machines Corporation was not about to let its business depend on some wild ducks at the Boca Raton outpost.

There was, for example, the "case of the toll-free telephone lines" feeding into Boca Raton. Hundreds of calls from dealers and customers across the country would come in on the line every week. As Dan Wilkie recalled, "We would personally review every phone call. We wanted to know why people were calling, how we responded, what problem areas were developing."

(As it happened, most of the queries were for operating information and technical support, while only a relatively few calls concerned quality complaints. Eventually, under the direction of a separate group, the call-by-call analyses enabled the PC team to isolate problem areas for special attention.)

· 3 ·

But production problems and customer support were not the only troubles. There was also the vexing matter of the gray market.

All of the major computer manufacturers, including IBM, offer discounts on large purchase orders. Many resourceful retail dealers (and, it is suspected, certain corporate purchasing agents) often buy more products than they need to take advantage of the discounts. Then, when the products are shipped, these customers peddle the excess at a profit to so-called gray market outlets. The outlets, in turn, add a markup according to what they think the customer will pay. The final price, however, will always be less, sometimes substantially less, than what an authorized dealer will have to charge to cover the costs of the service and support that got him the authorized dealership in the first place.

Also, customers sometimes examine a product in the authorized dealers' showrooms but, when it comes time to buy, go to a gray-market outlet. Understandably, this situation upsets the authorized dealers, who have limited power to influence this practice in a free market economy.

From the beginning, the IBM PC marketing staff at Boca Raton was accused of ignoring the gray market. Assured of anonymity, the chief executive officer of a large group of IBM PC authorized dealers explained why he believes the marketing of the machine "ran rampant."

He asserted that retailers of IBM products "operate in a *de facto* regulated industry. We run our businesses under that big umbrella called 'IBM' and we have to react to everything they do. It's definitely in their corporate self-interest to introduce and regulate the industry standards."

The retailing executive stated, "The IBM PC jumped off to an incredible market share because it was allowed to run rampant. There was no discipline at all in the marketplace and so the gray market in the machines just took off and it's still going strong," this retailer said.

"There were several ways IBM could have blocked this, but they chose not to," he asserted. "We complained about it and they gave us a million legal reasons why they couldn't do anything. They'll bring in armies of attorneys who develop any position, any point of view or argument ever known to man to justify what they're doing."

"To shut us up, they said, 'If we find out who's distributing this product to unauthorized outlets, we'll terminate their dealerships.' And, in fact, they did take away the authorizations of a few token dealers, but that hardly made a dent in the flow of products to the gray market."

This executive believes IBM even acted as a co-conspirator in propping up the unauthorized dealers. "They would tell us that we'd get one price for ordering a certain number of PCs and a better price if we ordered more of that number. But the disparity between the two prices wasn't sufficient to accommodate large volume purchasers who would naturally think, 'I'll order a lot of machines to get the best possible price and if I can't move them quickly enough, then I can always off-load them to the guys in the gray market.'

"So what happened is that the dealer ordered so many machines he didn't have any place to keep them if they weren't on back orders, so he'd have to dump them on the gray market so he could show IBM that he was a 'high volume seller' and thus get favorable treatment from the company when, in fact, he was a major conduit for the gray market." (Both Sparky Sparks and officials at IBM vehemently denied these allegations, but many industry analysts agreed with the substance of the retailer's remarks.)

· 4 ·

During the 1981 Christmas holidays, no member of the Estridge family was really relaxed. Instead, there was a feeling that the totally unexpected early acceptance of the new PC had somehow altered their lives.

During the past year, Don had become understandably less involved at home, preoccupied as he was with the progress of Project Chess. Now that the goal of that project had been achieved on schedule and its success was reaching stratospheric levels, there was a new perception of Don by his peers within the corporation and the industry.

Don for years had been this easygoing, free-wheeling, playful guy who liked to kid around on the job and tinker with his little computer at home. He was well thought of at Boca Raton, and even some of the administrators at Armonk knew who he was among IBM's more than 400,000 other employees.

Although recollections blur when particulars are discussed of just who contributed what to the development of the IBM PC, there is no disputing the fact that Don Estridge was the engineer of achievement: He was the man who led the team and made it work. Opel conceived the idea for the PC, Lowe started the project, but it was Estridge who brought everyone and everything together to make the basic machine the most practical innovation of its time, an achievement acknowleged from the day the IBM PC was introduced. It was becoming increasingly difficult for Estridge to follow his own admonition about always staying humble.

The pressure, the problems and even the success—they caused changes in Estridge, and the changes showed.

· 5 ·

In January 1983, Estridge was named a vice president of the IBM Systems Products Division and general manager of entry systems at the Boca Raton site. His hair had been trimmed to a shorter length as his style gradually became tailored to the corporate image.

In the meantime, some members of the early team who hadn't been able to keep up with the pace were also gone and the PC IBU, under Estridge, was being staffed with some of the corporation's more stellar upwardly mobile executives.

In the same month, despite the mounting order backlog, the IBM PC had to be introduced into overseas markets.

Wilkie, devoted as ever to Estridge, was put in charge of the Boca Raton site while his boss traveled to the other side of the world. It was Wilkie's habit to begin his workday shortly after sunrise, so there he was, the designated top gun at IBM's hottest location, settling in to run things on Estridge's first day out of the office when, at half past seven, he got a phone call from one of the Armonk headquarters staff members.

This man, who Wilkie thought was just full of envy of the Boca team, says, "Hey, Dan, I'm sitting here reading my *New York Times* and I'll be damned, but here's a story that says *your* computer can't do divisions by ten. Can that be true, Dan?"

Wilkie closed his eyes, rubbed his forehead and said, "I'll look into it and get back to you." He hung up the phone, muttered a characterization of the caller and decided he'd have to wait for the specialists in such matters to arrive at the office.

He sat there sipping his coffee and planning his day when, five minutes later, the phone rang again. On the other end, also calling from Armonk, was John Fellows Akers, the unchallenged heir apparent to Chief Executive Officer Opel.

"Dan, this is John," he said. "You probably don't know why I'm calling you at this time of day."

Wilkie, canny enough not to groan into the phone, replied, "John, if it is about that article in the *New York Times* . . ."

"Yes, Dan," Akers interjected, "that's just what I'm calling about."

Wilkie continued, "Well, John, I want you to know that I'm already working on this and I'll call you back later today when I figure out what in the hell is going on."

Akers agreed that this would be all right, and he seemed reassured that Wilkie, down in the boondocks of Boca Raton, was already aware of what appeared in the pages of that day's *New York Times*. They wished each other a nice day. When Wilkie hung up, he sat staring at the phone, wondering if this was typical of how Estridge's weeks began. If this is the way it goes, Wilkie thought to himself, then it's a goddam miracle that Estridge doesn't drink, which, as everyone knows, is something else Donnie doesn't do, in addition to not smoking, cursing or driving too fast.

After a few minutes, Wilkie, who has been known to curse a bit and exceed the speed limit, cursed a lot, and ran out of his office and down the hall, where he found a coffee klatch of early risers replaying yesterday's football games. Right there, Wilkie went ahead and "made their day" and set them working on the problem and, before noon, had Akers on the phone with an answer why the IBM PC got bad press this Monday morning in January and what action was being taken to fix the situation.

The story actually began in the Midwest, about a week earlier. A university professor was dabbling with an IBM PC, when he discovered that the machine, upon being pressed to perform a double precision math calculation in an unformulated and unprotected mode, would divide 100 by 10 and give an answer of 9.999999999 instead of 10.

The academic tried for three days to get through to someone at IBM who would be interested in hearing about his discovery. According to Wilkie, "This professor called the company on three different days and he kept getting bumped around by phone operators to people who didn't know what he was talking about. The guy was really persistent, so he kept trying and he got bumped around about 10 times on each of the three days. Finally, he got so mad that he picked up the phone and called the *New York Times*.

"We got right on this and we made a software correction to fix the machine and clear up the defect. Later, on the same day, some other papers picked this up like it was really something, even though it was only a little nit-picking. But after all, this was IBM they were reporting on. If it was one of the imitation PCs from some other manufacturer, the story would never have appeared, but the thing is that people have come to expect perfection from IBM, which, obviously, cannot always be the case."

As far as Wilkie was concerned, the real difficulty had little to do with absolute accuracy in a double precision math problem. "The defect was that the company didn't have a procedure to let this guy communicate his problem. This experience taught us that it is just as important to have the phone answered properly as it is to design the product correct-

t professor had gotten through when he first called the com-
n we could have fixed the defect, communicated the solution
itely to our dealers and the newspaper story would have never
l."

v weeks later, the PC Unit formed an educational system
board and appointed the professor as a charter member. "We
i to Boca Raton on a company plane, wined him, dined him,
le sure he was satisfied. This was only proper because he taught
y important lesson, which was to listen to *all* sources of input in
n to our dealers," Wilkie said. "We also learned that trying to
l inquiries back through the dealers was naive and fundamental-
vrong approach for us to take," he added.

· 6 ·

The experience with the double precision math error and the attendant
publicity caused Estridge and his staff to reconsider their approach to
service and support for the PC.

With their freedom in the balance (and convinced that corporate interference at this time would doom the attraction of their little
machine), Estridge, Wilkie, Sydnes and Sparks took it upon themselves
to establish a service-and-support program for the PC that would be unmatched by any other manufacturer of desk-top computers.

They began by deputizing Wilkie to establish a system to monitor and
report on the quality of every IBM PC throughout the world. The
reports would be gathered throughout the week and summarized at a
meeting scheduled for three o'clock every Friday afternoon.

Years later, these meetings remained clear in Wilkie's memory. "The
meetings were mandatory; nothing else could be on our schedules for
that time.

"Everything that had to do with the product was placed under constant and ongoing review: production schedules, quality control,
delivery, dealer relations, sales promotion, software programs,
customer service, even the way the instruction manuals were
assembled."

Estridge sat in on these meetings when he was in town, but because
he had to spend so much time traveling, Wilkie chaired the meetings on
a permanent basis. The discussion covered all the routine matters and
then such things as customer set-up problems, the choice of wording in

a manual, the way a packing box opened, how the packing material came out of the box and always, always, how the machine itself was performing.

Had it not been for their obsession with details, matched by a compulsion to produce the best machine of its kind to prove that their autonomy was indeed merited, the PC team would have undoubtedly been disbanded before their principal goal was achieved. Now with the goal realized, these same peculiar quirks were focused on achieving perfection even though the PC was in the stores.

With more IBM PCs sold every week, the volume of data for Wilkie's weekly reports began to get out of hand. Although the weekly meetings were still convening at mid-afternoon on Fridays, they were lasting until seven or eight o'clock at night.

Finally, Wilkie went to Estridge and said, "Look, you're getting to be real busy and so is everybody else, so maybe it would be easier for you to just forget about sitting in on the weekly review meetings. Maybe sit in once a month and in the meantime I'll give you regular summaries by memorandum."

Estridge, who had a highly honed ability to sense when he wasn't hearing the whole story, replied, "No way. I learn more about the business in those meetings than from anything else I do all week. Come on, what's the real problem?"

"Well," Wilkie stammered, "the data for my reports has been coming in on Wednesdays and Thursdays and, frankly, I don't have much of a chance to get it together to articulate it well and develop action plans for the Friday meetings."

"That's no problem, Estridge said. "We'll move the meetings to Mondays at three o'clock. That way you can have the whole weekend to get your presentations ready."

· 7 ·

It is now obvious that the instant acceptance of the IBM Personal Computer had everything to do with the way the machine was initially distributed. "We believe the consumer is best served by having the broadest range of distribution options available," Charles E. Pankenier, director of communications for IBM's Entry Systems Division, told a *Fortune* magazine seminar on "The PC Revolution in Business." He said such distribution options allow the consumer to "make the tradeoffs on price, on delivery, on levels of support and on the countless other factors that may be important in an individual purchase decision. . . . It is that emphasis on customer satisfaction across all distribution channels and with every aspect of the transaction that has guided us every step of the way," Pankenier said.

But, as Don Estridge told *Byte*, "Many who wrote about the IBM PC at the beginning said that there was nothing technologically new in this machine. That was the best news we could have had; we actually had done what we had set out to do."

Ever humble, Estridge let it go at that, deftly failing to mention the long-term strategy behind the development of the machine. This strategy, of course, called for IBM's entry in the market to cause a dramatic expansion in the demand for personal computers. As a result, the corporation would be well positioned to take away the major share of the market from weaker and less well capitalized competitors and, in the process, IBM intended that its operating system would be the internationally accepted standard for all desk-top computing.

· 8 ·

Every week the Monday meeting lasted longer because the number of problems kept growing as more PCs were sold. At the same time, under the burden of unfamiliar administrative difficulties, Estridge began to show stress, a circumstance noticed by Wilkie. "Donnie had characteristics—a sort of body language. There was phase one where he would put his head in his hands and get this look on his face like he wanted to say: 'Please tell me what you're saying isn't true.'

"In phase two, he would fold his hands on the conference table or his desk and he would lay his head on top of his hands. That meant the guy giving the report was in very deep trouble.

"Phase three was the absolute end. Donnie would leave his hands on his lap and put his forehead straight down on the table. When he did this, we all knew we were in the deepest possible trouble."

It didn't take long for those he worked with to learn what irritated Estridge. And it became easier and easier, it seemed, to send him to "phase three."

# 22 An Interlude for Intrigue

·  1  ·

Software programmers and manufacturers of accessories for personal computers were wise to suppose that the risk factor was almost nil in designing products for the IBM PC.

While some third-party companies adopted a wait-and-see attitude toward the machine and its possible acceptance in the market, others saw nothing but an IBM nameplate—and that was good enough for them. These companies were the ones that made quick fortunes if they worked hard and fast. These were companies owned by people like Martin Alpert of Tecmar.

As Alpert stated, "If the IBM PC won big, then we would win big. We were protected by their reputation." With his confidence so bolstered, Alpert had his executives waiting outside the main Sears Business Center in Chicago on the morning of Wednesday, August 12, 1981. When the store opened, they rushed in, paid cash for the first two IBM PCs sold anywhere and flew back to Tecmar headquarters in Cleveland.

The machines were immediately disassembled and their workings analyzed in a process known as "reverse engineering." The goal was to find ways to build add-on products for the new PCs and, by eating their meals at the office and working around the clock, this is what the Tecmar staff accomplished in a matter of days.

The next step was to produce add-on products for the IBM PC and to have them ready in six weeks to introduce at Comdex, the largest trade show for microcomputer dealers in the nation.

When the 1981 Comdex opened at Las Vegas in November, Martin

Alpert and his technicians had 26 fully operational products for the new IBM PC, including a high-density storage device, a speech synthesizer for the blind and a unit to control electrical appliances.

The Comdex conventioneers were interested enough in the product line to order them in amounts that, then and later, would make Tecmar, in less than a year, the fastest-growing company in Ohio. What Alpert began in 1974 as a mom-and-pop operation with his wife Carolyn had become the full-scale producer of almost 100 different add-ons for the IBM PC.

Martin Alpert—a 33-year-old doctor with a specialty in biomedical engineering, the son of immigrants who met in a Nazi concentration camp, the designer of a machine to diagnose lung problems instantly—was now the head of a major company with more than 400 employees and anticipated annual sales of $100 million. This was the same Marty Alpert who almost flunked out of college for spending too much time playing pinochle.

The unassuming Midwesterner didn't even realize how much he was fascinating someone else—a man who, until then, had been far more captivated by the affairs of the Orient than he was with the activities of anyone in the state of Ohio.

·  2  ·

While people like Bill Gates of Microsoft and Marty Alpert at Tecmar were becoming independently wealthy and internationally renowned because the IBM PC was a success, the men behind the machine were still toiling away anonymously for six- and seven-day weeks at Boca Raton, dividing their thoughts between dreams of merit bonuses and worries about how to send their kids through college without taking out a second mortgage on their homes.

On the surface, the camaraderie and high spirits of the team—inspired by Estridge's charismatic leadership and the innate sense of security that comes with being an IBM employee—would have seemed sufficient to assure the group's stability.

And, though IBM was hardly ready to let the PC team share directly in the profits from their endeavors, the corporation did give "merit award" cash bonuses to the deserving at Boca Raton.

But these one-shot awards did not upset IBM's graduated pay scales, nor did the payments affect benefit packages, which, at IBM, are calculated on an employee's base salary. Instead, the bonuses were intended to be an incentive for all employees, a prize that can be achieved when someone demonstrates superior performance and gives higher productivity. According to Dan Wilkie, "When we came out with the PC and the company was giving awards all over the place; production and warehouse workers were getting awards, as well as the engineers and managers. It's my understanding that they gave away more awards to people who worked on the PC than IBM ever did with any other product they'd introduced."

· 3 ·

Tecmar's rising star was being tracked with special interest by William Erdman, a Far East marketing director for IBM.

Erdman was planning to leave the company to establish his own consulting firm. Although he had not given formal notice, he did confide his plans to Peter Stearns, a software specialist at IBM. Quietly, and certainly without the corporation's knowledge, Stearns had formed a new company with Lewis Eggebrecht—the same Lew Eggebrecht who was a member of the original "Dirty Dozen," who had joined Bill Sydnes and William Lowe at Armonk to demonstrate the vixen and the rocket display on the prototype in August 1980.

Between themselves, Erdman, Stearns and Eggebrecht colluded to execute a scheme that would be discreetly presented to representatives of Tecmar. Although the three were still employees of IBM, they were acting on their own and for their personal gain when they agreed to make the proposal to Tecmar.

Erdman was the front man. In a conversation with Tecmar's vice president for marketing, Erdman offered Tecmar the design specifications for a device that would expand the PC's ability to communicate with other computers. Erdman's asking price for the specifications was $100,000; he also used the occasion to allude to other IBM products that were still to be announced. He indicated that Stearns and Eggebrecht would be willing to discuss these further breaches of IBM's internal security.

The Tecmar executive immediately reported the conversation to Alpert, and Alpert agreed to meet with Erdman. In the interim, Alpert discussed the proposal with his wife, his attorney and his financial advisor. All three told him the same thing: Report this to IBM.

Alpert took the advice. In doing so, he became deeply involved in IBM's investigation.

Since Erdman was cautious enough not to put anything in writing, it was necessary for IBM to develop evidence by other methods. IBM wanted Alpert to schedule a meeting with the co-conspirators. He would be wired with a concealed tape recorder. There would be another tape recorder in his briefcase. Alpert agreed to cooperate with IBM, explaining later that the Stearns scheme was "grossly unethical" and that, even if he did go along with it, the company Stearns and Eggebrecht wanted to form would compete directly with Tecmar.

Initially, phone calls were recorded. Then, on Saturday, September 4, 1982, Alpert attended a morning meeting with the men in a hotel near the Cleveland Hopkins International Airport. Alpert was "wired" to record the meeting in the hotel's coffee shop. Meanwhile, in an upstairs room, an IBM security agent monitored the meeting and stood ready to intervene if Alpert should be detected. Later, the meeting moved to Tecmar's offices, where Alpert activated the tape recorder in his briefcase.

On Monday, September 13, IBM pulled together its reams of evidence and immediately dismissed Erdman, Stearns and Eggebrecht. On the same day, IBM's attorneys received an injunction that would halt further transmission of confidential information.

In an interview appearing in the May 1983 edition of *Cleveland* magazine, a partner in the New York law firm of Cravath, Swaine & Moore, which handled the case for IBM, said: "In essence an employee leaving a company can use his knowledge and training in a general way, but he cannot use an employer's special skill and confidential information. Often there is a gray area, but this was black and white. Remember, the employees had not even left IBM."

The three men did not go to jail but, as part of a permanent settlement of the case, they agreed, in effect, that they would never again do any work in the computer industry without first receiving IBM's approval. This was a real shame for Eggebrecht, who Bill Sydnes referred to as, "a naive man easily influenced by others, but, the most talented systems architect I ever met."

·  4  ·

Many of those who remained at Boca Raton understood how the discontent of their former comrades had led to the Tecmar episode. They had been allowed to function with extraordinary freedom—like independent businessmen within the corporation—and they had come up with the fastest-selling product of its type in the history of the computer industry. Although revenues from the PC were accounting for less than 10 percent of IBM's total worldwide sales, every one of those little machines was turning a profit.

Thanks solely to the IBM PC, microcomputers and their accessories created the boom business of the 1980s. There were a lot of people—people just like Bill Gates and Marty Alpert—who were building very comfortable futures because Estridge and his teammates had done their jobs so well.

"I remember making a call on the Tandon Corporation," Wilkie said. "They were the people supplying us with disk drives and when I passed the executive parking lot, all I saw were Rolls Royces, Mercedes and Porsches. I did consider that, after all, I was in Southern California, but I also remember thinking, 'I am definitely in the wrong end of this business.'"

· 5 ·

To the astonishment of almost everyone, including IBM's public relations staff, the PC was an instant media darling. Because so many peripheral devices were being made for the machine and so much software written for its operating system, scores of publications were begun to serve the demand to advertise the new lines of merchandise produced by this expanding sub-industry.

Since the products were made especially for the IBM PC, the publications were edited exclusively for users of the machine. Because of second class mailing regulations, the publications had to wrap *some* editorial matter around pages-after-pages of advertising. Hardly wanting to criticize the machine that set them up in business, the publications would rhapsodize on the wonders of the IBM PC. They might pick on a peripheral, or smite some software, but the machine, itself, was not criticized. The editors were keenly aware of how their bread was buttered.

Generally favorable coverage of the PC in the trade publications produced a bandwagon effect among the daily business press and the specialized financial media. These publications also were aware of those new advertising dollars, so they expanded their coverage of the IBM Personal Computer.

But just so much can be written from public relations types, so the trade and consumer media began to focus on the men behind the machine.

Reporters do not decide they are going to do a story on IBM, then simply pick up the phone and talk to the right people at the company if they intend to quote them directly; there is a procedure to follow and it begins with the company's public relations department. When the press began to pester IBM for interviews with the PC team, a curious policy was established.

The unofficial policy stated that Bill Lowe was to give no interviews about the IBM PC, though Lowe was regarded as the single most active force behind the development of the prototype machine. Rather, Lowe was instructed to keep away from the media. It is understood that Lowe accepted this nonrole graciously and, some say, even gratefully.

As one IBM watcher has suggested, "This whole thing may have been Lowe's idea. Maybe he sensed that the PC was an aberration for IBM and an impossible act to follow. Whatever the reasons, it was clear that he didn't want to be a source for interviews on the product. I think he suspected that anyone cleared to be quoted on the PC could easily end up getting his name in print more often than the chairman of the company. Even if that couldn't be helped, it certainly wouldn't look good around headquarters."

With Lowe unavailable to the media, Don Estridge was designated and willingly acted as the official source for press interviews about the IBM PC. This was yet another challenge for Estridge and his communications staff, and they handled it with their typical élan.

· 6 ·

Understandably, Estridge refused all public comment when pressed for his opinions on the Tecmar incident. Privately, he brooded over the affair, saying that the IBM men involved behaved "like a pack of fools."

His psychological barometer, always attuned to the PC team, told him that the incident was a serious blow to morale. Not too many people were acquainted with Erdman, and Stearns had been regarded as something of a nonentity in his contributions to the team. But Eggebrecht! Lew Eggebrecht had been there at the beginning. He was one of those guys who slept on his desk and shaved in the men's room.

It was too hard to believe. But it was a fact, and the memory wouldn't go away. Something had to be done quickly to lift the heavy mood that hung over the staff.

·  7  ·

On one of his Saturday afternoon shopping expeditions with Mary Ann, Don Estridge was idly poking around a novelty shop. On a counter was a display board of small red rosettes reminiscent of the lapel insignia worn by members of the French Legion of Merit, and similar to the red rose that appeared in the "tramp" ads.

Estridge stared at the board for a few moments, then he removed one of the rosettes and fingered it. An inspiration began to take form. Then he broke into that famous grin, reached for his wallet, and bought every rosette.

The following Monday, Estridge showed up at the office with one of the rosettes in his lapel. Intentionally, and quite uncharacteristically, he kept his jacket on. Eventually, Wilkie walked into Estridge's office and, seeing the jacket, asked if Estridge was sick and had a chill, or was he expecting visitors from Armonk?

Estridge just sat there and shook his head. (He did not lay his head down on the desk.) Then Wilkie spied the rosette. "What's that for?" he asked, pointing to Estridge's lapel.

It seemed that Estridge wanted to say, "I thought you'd never ask." Instead, he reached into his briefcase, pulled out a rosette, and said, "Here, take this," dropping the rosette into Wilkie's palm.

"What's this mean?" Wilkie said.

"It means you're a member of the finest, most professional and most loyal team that's ever been assembled in the history of IBM," Estridge replied. "Put the rosette in your lapel and wear it everywhere you go so people will know who you are and what you belong to. Besides," he grinned, "we all need to stop and smell the roses from time to time."

Wilkie, who admits that he was born feeling like an outsider, was overwhelmed. The man he respected more than anyone else in the world was giving him a special insignia to show that he belonged.

Wilkie, the tough-and-gruff big bad bear, felt tears in his eyes. "Now go on. State your business and get out of here," Estridge said, again with that grin. "I've got some more of these things to hand out."


·  8  ·

Every so often, Estridge would call together everyone from every IBM outpost in the company who had had anything to do with the PC. These were typically mass gatherings for production, marketing and administrative people and the sessions—they were really pep rallies—would be held in large auditoriums to allow as many PC people as possible to get together.

The rallies were outstanding examples of the use of mass psychology. To sit in was like being in the front row when George C. Scott strutted on stage at the beginning of *Patton*, or how it was in the locker room at halftime when "The Fighting Irish" were faltering and Knute Rockne was making a speech modeled on a special school of oratory that began with Mark Antony's eulogy for Julius Caesar.

Estridge was straight out of this old school when it came to firing a crowd's adrenaline. He even had a way to get them cheering without opening his mouth.

For example, in January 1983 when his morale meter signaled that the team needed inspiration, he called for a "pep rally" in the main auditorium of Broward Community College, not far from Boca Raton. More than 1,000 PC people were there. Estridge intentionally kept them milling around outside the auditorium until he was ready to begin.

Then, just one door opened. This forced the crowd to enter in single file while loudspeakers played "Hooked on Classics," a record album of 17 familiar classical pieces set to a rock-music rhythm.

Filled with anticipation, the crowd pushed and jostled to squeeze through the door to get inside and down front as the sound system poured out stirring classical music excerpts, including the cannonade from Tchaikovsky's "1812 Overture," "The Hallelujah Chorus" from Handel's *Messiah*, "The March of the Toreadors" from Bizet's *Carmen*, "The Ode to Joy" from Beethoven's Ninth Symphony, Rimsky Korsakov's "Flight of the Bumble Bee," Clark's "Trumpet Voluntary," and Rossini's "William Tell Overture."

All the while, Wilkie and Estridge stood together by the stage, waiting for the crowd to calm down and settle in.

"Just look at the size of this group and the unbelievable excitement," Wilkie said. "Wherever it comes from, I hope we never lose it. It's like magic . . . pure magic."

Estridge looked down at his feet, lifted his head toward the ceiling, then looked back down and surveyed the large room.

"I hope so, too," he said, "I really do hope we never lose it. But from now on, it's going to be tougher and tougher to hold on to this. Let's enjoy it while we can."

# 23　Validating the Acclaim

· 1 ·

During 1982, the Soviet Union named a new chief of state, Israel invaded Lebanon and Britain repatriated the Falkland Islands. But to the editors of *Time* magazine, nothing matched the significance of the personal computer. For the first time in 55 years, the editors eschewed a human being for the cover of their first issue of 1983 to name the personal computer as its "Machine of the Year."

*Time* announced: "The 'information revolution' that futurists have long predicted has arrived, bringing with it the promise of dramatic changes in the way people live and work, perhaps even in the way they think. Americans will never be the same. In a larger perspective, the entire world will never be the same."

Explaining their decision, *Time*'s editors said, "There are some occasions when the most significant force in a year's news is not a single individual but a process, and a widespread recognition by a whole society that this process is changing the course of all other processes. . . . *Time*'s Man of the Year for 1982, the greatest influence for good or evil, is not a man at all. It is a machine: the computer."

As if to assure readers that the editors were in solid company, *Time* quoted Austrian Chancellor Bruno Kreisky, "What networks of railroads, highways and canals were in another age, networks of telecommunications, information and computerization are today." Further, they quoted French Editor Jean-Jacques Servan-Schreiber, who sees the computer as ". . . the source of new life that has been delivered to us."

Although "The Machine of the Year" cover story did not necessarily dwell on IBM, it did note that the corporation "has launched itself in a new direction by marketing a small, low-cost personal computer. The creamy white PC (for personal computer), introduced in August 1981, has set a standard of excellence for the industry. . . . With PCs now selling at a brisker rate than ever, the marketplace apparently agreed that IBM had built the Cadillac of the 1982 class."

· 2 ·

Aside from correctly crediting John Opel with the original decision to build the machine, the *Time* cover story did not mention any other personalities at IBM by name. It did note that the machine was designed by "an engineering team, cloistered at a plant in Boca Raton, Fla." and as far as Estridge was concerned, this attribution was adequate.

Estridge was grateful that *Time* had overlooked the very real possibility that IBM would already be working on the design of a hot new addition to its PC product line.

As intended, the basic IBM PC was embraced by businessmen; only relatively few of the machines were being used as "home computers." Even this limited acceptance apparently gratified Opel, who told the *Time* "Machine of the Year" cover story writers, "Who would have believed ten years ago that we'd have computers in the home?"

While Opel was dropping such "gee whiz" remarks, Estridge and a sworn-to-secrecy group of supervisors drawn mainly from the original PC team were already designing new machines intended to be used at home as its predecessor PC was at the office.

This way, IBM could be present at every level of the industry. Besides, if the boys at Boca could turn out a winner like the IBM PC within a year, how much of a challenge could it be to build a junior version of the same machine adequate for the applications in a typical American home?

But the truth was that the original IBM PC proved to be an act that was all but impossible to follow.

· 3 ·

In February 1982, with the PC on its way to becoming the industry standard, IBM moved to expand upward and downward from it.

Three product charters were established, with each charter headed by its own manager, in much the same way that Estridge managed the PC's development. This time, though, the standard was in place, and Estridge, in Wilkie's words, "Knighted the product managers to give them power across the board, but without the overall authority Estridge held. The concept was modeled after the corporation's approach; that is, the managers had a certain autonomy, but there were a series of built-in checkpoints along the line. The concept looked good, it was simple enough, but the problem was that there weren't three identical clones of Don Estridge to manage the products which ultimately became the PC/XT, the PC Junior and the PC AT."

Of course, before any work began, funding had to be approved. The PC team drew up three presentations reviewed during many grueling sessions at IBM's Armonk, New York facility. Wilkie was present, and he recalls sitting with the other key members of the team in a hotel at White Plains in the early morning, concerned about the impact of all three approvals coming simultaneously. "We put in a lot of work to position the XT and the Junior in their markets," he recalled, "but the AT was covered with little more than a few days of discussions. The AT would depend on an advanced microprocessor, the Intel 80286, which, at that time, was an iffy proposition at best. The only reason we even brought the AT into the discussion was to plant the seed for *future* funding; the XT and the Junior were what we wanted money for on the spot.

"I said to no one in particular, 'My God, what happens if the CMC [Corporate Management Committee] approves all three programs now? Do you realize what that means in work and how thin we'll be spread?' There was a long pause and we all looked at each other. Finally, Estridge said, 'That's something we'll worry about if and when we get the order.' Well, we got the order, all right. All three programs were simultaneously funded. When we returned to Boca, Don called the product managers together and gave each of them stars to put on their badges and he told them to 'Go and do good work.' But not all of those stars were to shine brightly and life around Boca was never the same after that."

· 4 ·

As applications software for the PC continued to be written, a new demand was created for effective ways to promote these packages. In large measure, this demand was met by the burgeoning subindustry of PC-oriented newspapers and magazines.

Dan Wilkie recalled, "By 1983, there were at least a dozen monthly or bi-monthly magazines and maybe as many as 20 weekly publications, all devoted exclusively to the IBM Personal Computer. After a while, these people ran out of things to write about, so they sent investigative-type reporters to Boca Raton with the sole purpose of finding out what we were up to.

"By then, the XT was announced and word got out that we were designing a new version of the PC, so all these editorial snoops were running around Boca Raton trying to scoop one another. When they weren't dodging in and out behind palm trees, they'd hang out in bars trying to stay sober long enough to pick up on any conversations they might find interesting. They had inside sources, outside sources and sources that were somewhere in between. It was like a little version of Watergate. It got so every time we turned around, there was a reporter lurking in the shadows. After a while, they started to annoy the hell out of us, especially the guys from *Fortune* and the *New York Times* who were never strong advocates of IBM. *Electronic News*, the major weekly newspaper in the industry, wasn't really kind to us either, but they seemed to be generally unkind to everybody else in the business at the time, so it didn't bother us so much when they got on our case."

As has been noted, IBM believes in selective application of the First Amendment when revealing the extent of the corporation's activities. Ever aware of this fact, Estridge had a way of manipulating IBM's policy of secrecy to achieve extraordinary results with the press.

With few exceptions, the editors and reporters covering the operation at Boca Raton had an unusual, if sometimes grudging, affection for Estridge. It was as if the media knew they were being used—but they would just lay back in the Florida sunshine and let it happen.

There is reason to believe that a lot of the press's attitude was influenced by the image Estridge presented. He had long since changed to a more tailored appearance and he had a mystical ability to distance himself from the inbred bureaucracy and policies of the very organization to which he swore unwavering allegiance. Most people attempting such a maneuver would be scorned for hypocrisy and duplicity. But not Don Estridge—to interview him was to love him.

And so he used the press to promote the PC, to extol entrepreneurship at IBM and—perhaps, most important—to help him maintain a high level of morale at every layer of the rapidly expanding organization under his command.

Those who look back on these days as the zenith of their careers never fail to mention how the effect of so much attention inspired their work and their lives. Dan Wilkie, for one, would later say, "The magnitude of the promotions and the advertising and all the publicity combined to galvanize the lowest level people all the way to the top of the group.

Publications like *Time, Fortune, Business Week*, the *Wall Street Journal*, the *New York Times*, the various PC magazines—they were all coming into the factory, taking pictures of people at their work stations, including people loading at the back docks and working in the warehouse. It was like the press was all over the place. It was just incredible hype. Everybody was fired up. We were all celebrities."

This, of course, had its own effect. Suffused with their new-found recognition and never knowing when a photographer would pop up, dock workers and warehousemen took to having their hair styled. Meanwhile, the secretaries at the site were every bit as stylishly turned out (by Boca Raton standards) as their counterparts at corporate headquarters. This was doubtlessly the premier showplace of the IBM organization, for a while.

The publicity fed on itself. The press would analyze the new products and marketing strategies. This alerted independent organizations which, in turn, conducted their own critiques of the products and strategies, and these critiques would garner their own round of publicity.

But at Armonk it was making some very influential people unhappy. Blue Magic was heading toward a conflict with the Green-Eyed Monster. After all, it was one thing to break nearly all the rules to build the PC and get it to market, but then to boast about this to the world and make it seem that all IBM had to do was build little desk-top computers—now that was going too far!

For example, when the corporation announced a major improvement to its line of highly promoted Sierra mainframe computers, the *Wall Street Journal* tucked the announcement in the back pages of the same issue that prominently featured an up-front roundup story on *rumors* about the new home computer Estridge and his staff were *supposedly* developing.

This particular issue of the *Journal* caused quite some consternation at Armonk. The topic of that day was what to do about Estridge and his band of publicity hounds. The solution, if it can be called that, was to give them enough rope until they hanged themselves.

· 5 ·

From the beginning, the IBM PC was never meant to be a one-shot proposition. If the machine was successful, then it would naturally lead to new products in the PC line and improvements on the basic model.

Since Project Chess and its purpose, the Acorn, might have been abandoned at any time during development, the specifics of follow-up products were academic. The point was to get the PC built the right way the first time and to see how it was received by the market.

When the machine succeeded beyond the most optimistic of expectations, then it was time to consider new and advanced models of the product.

Although certain fundamental improvements would be made to the basic PC (such as boosting its random access memory capacity and making the machine easier for the dealer network to service), advanced models would have to offer striking improvements over the PC. The advanced machines then would be clearly differentiated in the market. This strategy of technological enhancement has enabled IBM to take a few fundamentally distinctive machines and mature them simultaneously into full product lines. This had been proven to be a brilliant strategy, and was one Estridge was not about to alter.

Joe Sarubbi, the veteran engineer who used his long-established contacts in the company to bring out the original machine on time, was put in charge of a team to develop a PC that would use hard disk data-storage technology. Sarubbi and his team had a year, and they stayed on schedule, the only one of the products chartered in February 1982 to do so.

In New York in March of 1983, IBM announced the PC/XT. Later, in a related story in *PCjr.* magazine (February 1984), Contributing Editor Lindsy Van Gelder recalled the circumstances surrounding the machine's introduction:

> IBM summoned us all by Mailgram, rented a hotel conference room and hired a pair of linebackeresque security guards to stand outside the doors, arms folded, until the press conference began. No one was allowed past the sacred portals, even reporters who promised to go in and stay in, and who didn't appear to be sporting Dick Tracy wristwatches.

It was explained at the press conference that XT stood for Extended Technology, which was an apt description of the machine since it had nine times the memory capacity of the original PC, with room to expand that capacity to nearly 22 million characters of information because of its hard disk. The PC/XT had a color display and an integrated communications adapter that enabled it to communicate with other IBM computers, or to tap into the growing number of outside data banks that were proliferating.

While the PC/XT quickly found a niche, it did so without having a serious impact on the sales of the earlier, less high-tech models. The PC/XT became a successful addition to the PC's product line because it answered the professional computer user's need for a quality machine with the advantages of high-capacity data storage.

But the PC/XT was most definitely not a home computer. There was still another gap for IBM to fill, this time in what was basically the very low end of the market.

How and when would Estridge and his team come up with a suitable product to fulfill Opel's pledge to make IBM a factor of consequence at every level of the computer market?

It was certainly no secret that such a product—the ultimate home computer—was being designed by the very same capable mavericks who built the machine that became synonymous with personal computing and established the IBM system as the only standard to follow in the hottest industry of the early 1980s.

Meanwhile, the hotels and motels on Florida's Gold Coast were filled with reporters and photographers, each one eager to get "the real story" about this wondrous home computer.

But the media couldn't even learn the name of the product. If the "Acorn" had fallen from the "Oak" of IBM, then what would be the logical declension of an acorn? Would it be a nut? Not even IBM would call one of its products "The Nut." So what was next? If not a nut, then maybe a peanut. The new home computer from IBM would be called "The Peanut."

And so they took this and ran with it, and wrote stories about "The Peanut," and they called it a "home computer" and predicted all sorts of successes for the machine.

# 24    Discontent and Defection

Bill Sydnes, brilliant engineer, dedicated workaholic and core member of the original PC development team, was given charge of developing IBM's home computer.

Significantly, Sydnes was not a charter member of the Don Estridge Fan Club. Some observers speculate that Sydnes was miffed because Estridge was brought in from "outside" to head Project Chess after Sydnes had been the first one invited to join the original "Dirty Dozen" when it was formed to design the prototype PC. There was also the matter of rewards received for a job more than well done. As Sydnes later confided, "When I worked in the Datamaster group, the IBM salary plan would allow me to get up to a 16 percent raise in seven months; instead, I would get a seven percent raise in 16 months." Of course, it didn't help when Sydnes saw those *real outsiders*, like Bill Gates and Marty Alpert, becoming rich by selling operating systems and add-on peripherals for the machine that he had devoted so much of himself to.

While Sydnes was filling up with resentment, opportunities were again opening, and when one came along to be the man behind the development of what would be the most-awaited computer in the history of IBM—well, what kind of hard-driving engineer could say no?

So Sydnes took over the home computer project in early 1982. Certain nonengineering aspects of the original PC project had slipped past him, but now he wanted control of both design and development and a say in how "his" machine would be distributed and marketed.

Sydnes had to get Estridge to agree, and when they sat down to talk out the details, the boss's head bobbed up and down at almost every suggestion from Sydnes.

"Sure." "Okay." "You've got it." Estridge had never been so agreeable. Still, not too much of that grin, but after all, wasn't Sydnes getting his way? Did Estridge have to smile every time he made a concession?

But Sydnes was smiling when he left the office as Estridge asked him to "Please close the door"—which gave Estridge an opportunity to place his hands on the desk and lay his head face down on his hands.

·  2  ·

It wasn't long before the rug was pulled from Sydnes. He'd wrongly assumed that he'd have relative carte blanche when it came to staffing his new project, but this was not to be. As he later recalled:

"I did the original staffing for the PC project, but when I did the Junior [as the machine came to be known] I wasn't allowed to take anyone with me from the PC group. That was frustrating because there I was with a ton of responsibility and a very aggressive schedule to meet on the project and I wasn't given any resources to do the job. This meant I had to start from scratch and assemble every resource myself." In fact, there it was, spring 1982, and he was to complete the machine for a July 1983 announcement.

As far as Sydnes was concerned, the Junior was going to be "a magnificent machine" that would mark IBM's entry into what he envisioned as "the consumer markets served by mass merchandisers." It would be a low-end machine that competed head-on with the Apple II Plus and the Apple II E, but which would be priced significantly below the II E. Sydnes said,

> Our machine would have a fairly limited capacity, but it would still be compatible with the original IBM PC. This would be made up for by a significant upward expansion capability defined in its architecture. With add-on capabilities, the machine could be totally compatible with the PC. It was designed to permit addition of a second disk drive, plenty of add-on memory modules, and even a controller for a Winchester (hard disk) drive. These things, at least, were in the original plan.

Bill Sydnes had some very firm beliefs on how this low-end computer should reach its brand-new markets—markets that computer maker IBM had never before attempted to reach.

Estridge himself described the markets they were going after during an interview with *Personal Computing* magazine (September 1984). Referring specifically to home computers, he said:

There will be more and more people who use the machine to process their own personal information, but [they will do so] by using the same applications as businesses use today to process work. . . . When you say doing work in the home, people sometimes think taking work home is what you mean. That is not what we mean at all. It means using the application tools to apply them to the information at home. And the people I know who are doing that are getting leverage on their situations. They are either more careful with their money or getting more out of their money.

Just like the people who shop at K Mart and J.C. Penney, Sydnes reasoned. And so, because he was so deeply involved with every aspect of this project—design, engineering and marketing—Sydnes developed thoughts of his own on how and where the final machine should be sold. "We had numerous discussions with mass merchandisers," he would recall. "The sales channels were all pretty much lined up and recruited, but when it came right down to it, Estridge wouldn't allow me to go forward because he felt it wasn't proper for IBM to be in those channels."

Sydnes believed he was designing the absolutely right home computer for markets alien to IBM but, when problems arose, Estridge backed down. The IBM PC Junior, according to Sydnes, was originally designed as a home computer to be sold at a competitive price at the thousands of mass-merchandising outlets throughout North America. It would be the first time a product with the high-class name of IBM would be promoted and sold to the masses. But after six months into the development of the concept, Estridge decided he did not like it at all.

Although the project was assigned to engineer Sydnes, Estridge, as a corporate vice president and head of the IBM PC operation, remained in control. When he impressed this fact upon Sydnes and vetoed the merchandising plans, Sydnes, who was not without ambitions within the corporation, pursued a promotion by requesting a transfer to New York, where a new job had opened up.

According to Sydnes, "Don let me interview for the job in New York. I interviewed for the job, I was offered the job, then Don told me I couldn't take the job after all. Meanwhile, I was under the impression that Don had moved me to a higher level when I took over the home computer project. Later, I found out that I was at a much lower level than I thought, which meant I couldn't get the kind of raise I wanted to go with the transfer. And all this was happening at the same time he was telling me I couldn't market the machine the way I wanted to."

Although he was never told as much, Sydnes still believes, "IBM was afraid that the Junior was going to grow up to kill the low end of demand for the PC, which was now being sold in 47 countries around the world.

"The difference in marketing overhead through the proposed new channels of distribution caused certain well-placed people in the company to insist that there was no way the price of the machine could be brought down to the promotional entry level figure I had in mind."

Until then, Sydnes had been in confident control of his project—just as Estridge was when he shepherded the PC to market on time. But there were essential differences between the two projects: Estridge was a pioneer, and the people he reported to were in Armonk, away from the day-to-day action when the PC was being built. On the other hand, Sydnes was more or less following in Estridge's footsteps with Estridge, himself, very much on the scene. It is reliably understood that this situation strained a relationship that had never been that warm to begin with. There is no question that Sydnes was chosen on the basis of his competence. And it is to Estridge's credit that he made this recommendation with concern for Sydnes's professional abilities and not on the basis of Sydnes's skills in traversing the byzantine pathways of IBM. Sydnes, as they say, "was set in his ways"—but so was Estridge, and he held the authority.

Sydnes was neither cowed nor obsequious when confronted by authority. Looking back to these tense times in early 1983, Sydnes recalls, "Did Estridge and I argue? I'd say there were some fairly heated discussions.

"When you find out that you have been essentially misled after everything you worked for, when your reputation and your career is on the line with the Junior and you know there is no way the machine is going to succeed if it doesn't go through the right marketing channels—well, you'd have to be pretty weird not to get mad," Sydnes said.

The Junior Sydnes conceived "was a dynamite product that could have blown the Apple II series off the map." He wasn't at all worried about Apple's Lisa computer, which had been introduced at the beginning of the year and had received a lukewarm reception because it was considered overpriced and undercapable. Nor did Sydnes lose sleep over Coleco's Adam, an enthusiastically anticipated home computer which, for one reason or another, kept missing its intended introduction dates.

But the highly regarded Apple IIs were worth IBM's competition. These machines were sold through conventional computer outlets, which, to Sydnes, was a strategy that automatically restricted their markets. He wanted the Junior to capitalize on the market's embrace of the IBM PC's operating standard, but to be completely compatible with the PC only through the addition of add-on accessories. By the time these peripherals were added on, the Junior would end up costing about as much as the basic PC. While the machine's architecture would be "opened" for the benefit of third party suppliers of peripherals (as was done with the PC), this time the essential add-ons would be in-house products. In fact, by the spring of 1983, about 20 peripherals were already defined and developed by IBM staff engineers under the direction of Sydnes and his top aides.

Estridge had been aware of this design strategy all the time. Initially, he did not interfere. But then, for precise reasons that have not been made clear, Estridge became convinced that Sydnes's overall strategy for the Junior was unacceptable.

A consensus claims that Estridge had already made the decision not to use cost-cutting outlets to sell the machine and that Sydnes simply did not want to accept this decision. It is not likely that Estridge would want to go to Armonk with the radical notion that IBM should start selling its products through mass-merchandising outlets that would show little or no enthusiasm for going through the rigamorole of qualifying as "Authorized IBM Dealers." It had been battle enough to convince the corporate staff that respected outlets like Computerland and the Sears Business Centers could be trusted with official authorization—but to bring in retailers like K Mart and J.C. Penny would inevitably lead to IBM products being legitimately sold by people like Crazy Eddie, The Wiz and such aggressive merchandisers as New York's 47 St. Photo, the king of the gray market.

Estridge was also at the center of the debate over the compatibility issue. Battle lines developed between two highly vocal camps. One group argued that if the Junior was completely compatible with the IBM PC, the lower end of the market for the senior and more profitable machine would be lost forever. In effect, they insisted, IBM would be competing with itself, a strong argument against compatibility.

In the other group, defenders of compatibility (like Bill Sydnes), declared without equivocation that the Junior would have to be compatible to attract businessmen with a PC at the office who would now be able to take projects home to complete on their Juniors.

Although Estridge was right in the middle on this debate for a while, there were strong positions within the PC inner circle holding that anything short of compatibility would be unacceptable. In his interview with *Personal Computing* (September 1984), he stated that spreadsheet work and word processing are "the easiest two examples" of personal computing applications that transfer readily between the office and the home. "And," he told the magazine, "using those tools in the home for your own personal information will become more and more popular as more and more people become uninhibited about doing that. . . . I [also] think using personal computing in the home will be a means of collecting and analyzing [the output of] data base services and information delivery services."

· 3 ·

Sydnes was furious.

To begin with, he was still angry because Estridge let him apply for the job in New York and then refused to let him take the job when it was offered. At the same time, Estridge vetoed Sydnes's carefully conceived retail marketing strategy for the PC Junior. Finally, it seemed that every time Sydnes came to work he saw new faces in the plant and more cars in the company parking lot. By this time, he later said, "Estridge was allowing the organization to grow far past the point of profitability. In my professional judgment at the time, there was no earthly reason to have thousands of people working on the IBM Personal Computer. That much overhead has to be supported by an enormous revenue base and profit stream. I mean, My God! look at Apple; they had more than half our revenues with about a third of the people we were carrying on our payroll."

Despite what Sydnes at the time called Estridge's "delusions of grandeur," he continually stressed the need to cut the payroll and increase efficiency. "I was very opinionated about this," he recalls. "I told Estridge he was crazy to let the organization grow well past the point where it could continue to be profitable. But his attitude was like, 'Go away, little boy.'"

By now Sydnes saw no hope. Estridge was becoming more remote, inserting sublayers of managers between himself and those who, at one time, had direct access to his office, where the door was now usually kept closed. "When he started cutting off the guys that had made major contributions to the PC that, in my opinion," Sydnes said, "was the start of the fall of the PC group. A lot of people were getting very uptight and angry."

To this day, Sydnes blames pressure from above for the transformation of Estridge from Mr. Good Guy to Just Another Management Clone in a Blue Suit. "He very obviously was saying what the people above him wanted to hear," Sydnes said. "What Don did in the initial phases of the PC program was absolutely magnificent. What he did after the group became much larger was, in my opinion, unforgivable to the people and the product."

Ironically, according to Sydnes, the very success of the PC attracted attention from corporate management, which now wanted Estridge to find positions at Boca Raton for tried-and-true-blue upward strivers from the middle ranks of management. Estridge did as he was told, and the result, Sydnes says, "Caused the structure to collapse, or—worse yet—the structure got built up the way IBM wanted it to be."

The operating euphemism at IBM for Sydnes's actions at this point was to "escalate his concern." This he did to no result, so he escalated his concern even more by offering his resignation, which Estridge accepted without chagrin.

By this time, the factory was coming on line to build the first preproduction models of the IBM PC Junior—the machine that would have made or broken Bill Sydnes's career at IBM.

# 25    Into
Bureaucracy

All this while,  the IBM PC was delivering data-processing power that was adequate for the majority of applications in thousands of business offices across the country. A lot of work that would have gone to mainframes held under the tight control of "office information systems (OIS) specialists" was work that could now remain within its own little universe. Here it was controlled at the source, finally freed from the in-house tyranny of the OIS Merlins who collaborated with their Blue-Suited Allies at IBM to throw a cloak of mystery over computers in general and information access in particular.

But the PC wasn't just one more project. It was delivering data-processing power that was adequate for the majority of applications in thousands of business offices across the country. A lot of work that would have gone to mainframes held under the tight control of "office information systems (OIS) specialists" was work that could now remain within its own little universe. Here it was controlled at the source, finally freed from the in-house tyranny of the OIS Merlins who collaborated with their Blue-Suited Allies at IBM to throw a cloak of mystery over computers in general and information access in particular.

When office workers sat down at the keyboard of an IBM PC they were more often than not astonished at how adept they could be with these wonderful machines. The PCs themselves were hardly more challenging than operating an electric typewriter, and the applications programs—the software itself that made the machines make magic—transformed workers into wizards when it came to enhancing efficiency and boosting productivity.

In some large corporations, departmental budgets were sufficient to allow managers to buy their own PCs without "justifying" the purchase or clearing it through the OIS. In time, across the United States and throughout much of the Western world, the personal computing revolution, made possible with and advanced by the IBM PC, was threatening the empires so carefully constructed by the self-appointed custodians of information within the corporations. These, of course, were the very same people who form the power base of allegiance to and admiration for the IBM Way of business conduct.

By 1983, it was apparent to the Armonk IBMers that Don Estridge and the boys at Boca had indeed planted a Trojan horse with a microprocessor heart within the walls of IBM.

· 2 ·

The strategists at corporate headquarters wisely reckoned that it would be a public relations disaster to follow traditional ways and disband the PC operation. Their reasoning was influenced by the unrelenting media attention focused on Boca Raton, especially at this time, when curiosity about the new home computer was at its peak. There was also the morale factor—and employee morale is a factor IBM never lightly disregards. It would be one thing to merge the PC with a me-too product, but here was the most successful project ever formed in the history of the corporation—a unit, acting independently, that had come up with a product which, for once, really did exceed the most optimistic expectations of nearly everyone. But, even then, the PC was never believed to have the potential to become the basic workstation of the entire IBM line of computers.

Proving that there is more than one way to solve a problem at IBM, the decision was made not to disband the team at all. Instead, it would be upgraded. The PC unit would become a *division* of the corporation. This way, it would be too big and too important to be the sole responsibility of Don Estridge and those other freewheelers in Florida.

Besides, there is no such thing as an "independent" division within IBM.

· 3 ·

On August 1, 1983, the new Entry Systems Division (ESD) was created. Don Estridge was named its president.

The corporation's official announcement said the division would have "U.S. product management and manufacturing responsibility for general-purpose, low-cost, personal-use computer systems."

The new division was given responsibility for the 6,000 employees at the IBM plant at Austin, Texas, which had opened in 1967. As the company later explained, "In essence, the idea was to pull together two major sites, Austin and Boca Raton, which had similar missions—to make computers that would end up on top of a desk—but which had been in slightly different orbits in IBM. Austin came at micro-computing from the traditional data processing point of view—heavily office oriented. Boca Raton came at it from a wide open, do-what-you-will-with-the-product orientation."

The division's responsibilities also included operations at an IBM plant in Greenock, Scotland, and one in Wangaratta, an Australian city north of Melbourne. The division became fully integrated into the corporation, and had responsibilities for forecasting, pricing, terms and conditions and the management of supply and demand. In this sense, IBM commented, "ESD is unique in the general computer business in IBM."

Additionally, the company explained, when the ESD was established, production rates on PCs had already increased several times "with more systems shipped in the first five months of 1983 than in all of 1982. Daily manufacturing volumes have increased 600 percent with high quality. Retail outlets have doubled. Sales have risen to the point that would rank ESD [as] eligible for the Fortune 500 index."

In just one day, the number of employees under Estridge increased from 4,000 to 10,000. Some 6,000 applications programs for the IBM PC were being written by more than 2,000 software houses. The new division's Dealer Support Center was ready to handle as many as 700 phone calls a day, and a computerized support system would soon generate 20,000 inquiries a month from more than 70 percent of the network of IBM PC retail outlets. Meanwhile, plans were being completed to sell the division's products in 74 countries.

Joe Bauman returned from Rochester to become vice president in charge of manufacturing for the division. Dan Wilkie became the division director of quality assurance and technology. Joe Sarubbi was appointed director of technologies, reporting to Wilkie. Other IBM heavyweights came in from throughout the organization to take over operations, product management, plans and controls and legal matters.

Now things were starting to hum the IBM Way. Estridge, mollified by his promotion, had accepted the inevitable, but apparently not without some misgivings, as is evident in his message in *Currents*, an IBM in-house publication:

"The business we are generating is large enough to warrant more central management in terms of planning and measurement, but we will still be walking a line between being an Independent Business Unit and a more conventional IBM division.

"Personal computing and workstations are very dynamic areas of our industry. Advances, enhancements and new products are introduced in rapid fire succession. To compete in that marketplace, we have to be able to act and respond quickly. Our management style is geared to eliminating overhead, unnecessary meetings and discussion; to operating with lower costs, fewer people and shorter development cycles.

"What we accomplish is based on trust, not inspection. Individuals have to feel they can do the job and then be given the latitude to do it. This places a heavy burden on employees and managers because they have the responsibility for getting something done—and done right. . . . Maintaining an environment in which we trust and respect each other becomes more challenging as our numbers grow and as our business increases."

Clearly, he was using a company publication to challenge the company's management. Then, as if to remind any detractors of what had been accomplished *before* the division was formed, Estridge coyly observed:

"I believe we have the leadership position. If you assess leadership as the variety of programs a customer may buy for a specific brand of personal computer, we are already the leader with more programs available for the IBM Personal Computer than for any other PC. If you assess it [leadership] from a customer satisfaction point of view, our products have been rated as high as or even higher than other IBM products."

Estridge knew his promotion and expanded authority was not necessarily an indication of his team's total acceptance by the men at Armonk.

# 26    Hubris and
# Humility

· 1 ·

As Dan Wilkie was fond of saying, "There sure as hell were no virgins on the Junior project."

Translation: Anyone who had anything to do with that project carries a share of the blame for what became of IBM's first failed attempt to build a home computer.

Intoxicated by the can-do spirit that brought the original PC to market on time, Estridge and the team behind the home computer reasoned that they should be able to match the same timetable for the little machine that finally was known as the IBM PC Junior. After all, the original PC group had performed its mission with the same resources, and Sarubbi and his product charter group had completed the XT in a reasonable time.

The engineers, instead of creating a product, set about achieving an assumed triumph, which was, of course, to perfect the machine that would introduce practical computing to the American consumer. They were wrong from the beginning.

· 2 ·

With the benefit of hindsight, Dan Wilkie now says, "The Junior development group simply had too much freedom for a team that wasn't nearly as capable as the people behind the original PC. For one thing, the timing for announcement of the product was too ambitious. The plan was to have the machine ready for unveiling in late spring, or by mid-summer at the latest. This was about the time Sydnes left and that

152

created confusion about the status of the program, such as the final resolution of the compatibility issue and who would be responsible for Sydnes' former responsibilities. Much later, it became evident that Sydnes was way behind schedule and he was making significant unilateral changes in the machine's design without informing Don Estridge, or the other people in the group."

Apparently the investigative reporters sent to Boca Raton missed the real inside story—the story of frustration and confusion surrounding the home computer's development. The machine's design was far behind schedule and there were serious problems with vendors. But even as late as August 1983, IBM's deceptive ploys were working, because the press hadn't even discovered what the machine was named.

A story in the August 1 edition of the *Boston Globe* carried the headline, "Peanut' Expected to Make Big Splash." Eighteen days later, the *Wall Street Journal* declared with some equivocation: "IBM's 'Peanut,' a.k.a. 'Hercules,' 'Sprite,' 'Pigeon' and 'Pancake,' Nears Market Bow." And on August 29, a reporter on assignment in Boca Raton filed a story in the *Miami Herald* under the headline: "Aroma of 'Peanut' Escaping Though It Remains in Shell."

The media speculated that the new home computer from Big Blue was delayed because, this time, IBM was having trouble with its outside suppliers. Of course, nobody at IBM would confirm this. Besides, the suggestion was ridiculous, considering the original PC team's outstanding success in contracting for parts outside the company. IBM always knows what it's doing.

· 3 ·

The original PC team's successful relationships with outside suppliers did not hold for the developers of the Junior.

Although he was not directly involved with the early development of the machine, Dan Wilkie still vividly remembers what happened when he volunteered to help solve a manufacturing problem with the Junior.

"A corporate vice president from Armonk had come down to Florida in September after stopping off at the Teledyne plant in Tennessee where the Juniors were being built. The meetings in Tennessee turned into an absolute disaster when our people found serious design problems with the machine's engineering and the vendors' capabilities, which meant there was no way it would be ready to announce before late fall or even by the end of the year.

"We were all to get together for dinner one night at the Brooks Restaurant in Deerfield Beach and the problems with Teledyne were certain to be the main topic of discussion. I arrived a few minutes early," Wilkie said, "and Tom O'Donnell, IBM's vice president for development, came in soon after. He looked like he had been just dragged behind a truck. I asked him what the trouble was and he replied that the review in Tennessee had gone very badly and that matters were far worse than he had been led to believe. I offered to go to Tennessee the following week to spend a few days to see what I could do to work things out. O'Donnell's eyes lit up and he accepted my offer on the spot."

Within two days, Wilkie had assembled a team of loyalists to go with him to Teledyne to do a "quick fix." The quick fix took three months and required direct assistance from almost 50 members of the IBM engineering and manufacturing staffs.

As Wilkie recalls, "Joe Sarubbi set up a war room in his office at Boca and he coordinated the work with me at Tennessee. We held daily meetings by phone for three months. Many of the systems had to be re-worked and re-boxed in new packages two or three times. The press was speculating that the vendors were causing the delays, but not all of the blame fell on them because we had to make hundreds of engineering changes to meet the FCC [Federal Communications Commission] Class B emissions requirements. Circuit designs and board layouts had to be redone to dampen electrical noises. This took weeks to accomplish. Meanwhile, the inside covers of the machines had to be coated with a special formula we call 'silver paint' that sells for $700 a gallon. The first few hundred units were painted by hand in a makeshift area and the coverage was so poor we were finishing only eight to twelve sets of covers per gallon of paint. Eventually, the painting was handled by robotizing the operations and that led to affordable yields."

The Junior clearly had many design flaws that had not been corrected. And, quite simply, IBM mistook the capabilities of Teledyne. Wilkie explained, "It was another example of the old syndrome that says we should stay at arm's length because, if we're paying a vendor to deliver something and if they have difficulties, then that's their problem. Obviously, in this case, we were completely naive because the vendor didn't have the skills to do the job and we should have been helping out right along. So we got in there and slowly straightened things out, but it took a lot longer than we expected and there were some very painful sessions in the process."

Wilkie managed to delay IBM's top management from intruding despite the threat of a visit from John F. Akers himself, the new president of IBM, the man whom *Fortune* magazine described as "handsome, charming, articulate, supremely self-confident and relentlessly self-disciplined, a chief executive from central casting, direct, decisive . . . [with] sharp instincts, sure grasp of the big picture, and undoubted ability to lead."

Gone were the relaxed invitations to Boca Raton. Instead, prospective visitors got responses like, "Stay home. Everything is under control. Thanks for thinking of us. We'll call if we need you. Goodbye. (Click.) Whew!"

Besides, there wouldn't have been time even for wanted visitors. The workday was typically 14 to 16 hours, six or seven days a week. Ask Wilkie how it was with Teledyne, and what the mood was around Boca Raton, as the Junior sputtered and wheezed its way to market in 1983, and the big bad bear's scowl warns, "Don't ask."

After a chance to reflect, Wilkie will go into a Monday-morning quarterback routine and wistfully admit, "We poured a lot of money into the Junior trying to get it to work—more money than any other company could afford under similar circumstances and certainly more money than the product ever deserved. We ended up putting more money into advertising the Junior than it would have taken to develop another product. This, combined with the unbelievable hype in the press and sales forecasts predicting that we'd sell over a million units in the first year meant that the pressure to build the product at any cost was intense. We should have just taken our lumps, admitted our mistakes, and gone on to develop a replacement product. But our real error was in letting the development team run unchecked until we were past the point of no return and found ourselves stuck with a single, less than competent vendor."

· 4 ·

Even now, Wilkie is indignant when he recalls that painful time. "Early on, Sydnes was determined to be as close to Estridge as he could get," Wilkie said. "However, the reality was that Sydnes wasn't even in the same league. There was, for instance, far more to developing a product and making it successful beyond designing a few circuits.

"Bill [Sydnes] wanted this to be a Commodore or Atari type of product with no focus at all on service or quality. By contrast, the original PC was a model of quality and performance. For example—and not many people know this—the original IBM PC was completely redesigned in the late fall of 1981 to correct some circuitry problems to be in compliance with FCC Class B emission requirements. At that time, Joe Sarubbi and his product engineering team made more than 100 engineering changes in the machine to enable components to be used from multiple sources and to resolve a number of marginal ground loop errors in the original design.

"But Bill Sydnes' concept of design was to find the cheapest component from a single source and if the vendor can't deliver to specifications, then send the shipment back. In theory, this may sound great, but in practice, it's a total disaster waiting to happen. "Unfortunately," Wilkie continued, "too many of Sydnes' concepts went into the Junior, despite the fact that early charter requirements were very specific regarding the Junior's compatibility.

"Eventually, several factors led to design and delivery delays with the machine. For instance, we were all hot about doing our work and growing the business. But over a six month period, about 95 percent of all the key people in the group had been in their assignments for less than three months and we were still bringing on new people.

"At the same time, Estridge was preoccupied with issues relating to product positioning, marketing and sales. Sarubbi was working full-time on the XT and I was deeply involved with my responsibilities in manufacturing and quality control. Meanwhile, Sydnes was separating himself and the Junior team from the rest of the group."

In the spring of 1983, the Junior's design problems became shockingly apparent when a succession of engineering release dates were missed. Clearly, the compromises that were made on the machine until then had coalesced to all but destroy the project. At the same time, Sydnes was frustrated by his inability to earn higher pay for systems design work. Finally, according to Wilkie, "Sydnes came in my office one morning at 7:00 and told me he was going to meet with Estridge at 8:00 and resign. I believe the thing that bothered him most was that no one tried to talk him out of it.

"With Sydnes out of there and with Sarubbi buried on issues with the XT, a guy named Dave O'Connor was assigned to head up the Junior program. Only then did the real magnitude of the Junior's program delays come to the surface and any hope for a summer or early fall delivery date was doomed."

· 5 ·

IBM knows it's not perfect. After all, the company probably spends more money in a year on false starts, aborted projects and dead-end ideas than a lot of companies within its industry make in annual sales.

IBM, of course, does not discuss funded projects that have not succeeded and (as has been noted) it is prudently nonresponsive even when it seems that one of these projects may be surviving all the way to introduction on the market.

The cometlike history of the PC Junior is precisely the sort of embarrassment IBM seeks to avoid. If, in the most ideal of IBM worlds, no one knew that there was going to be a Junior, then, when the trouble began, the company could have quietly ended the project and, as Wilkie later suggested, the company's time, brains and money could have been poured into a new home computer project, staffed with innovators and a slogan urging, "Let's get it right the second time around."

Perhaps some other corporation that does not so manipulatively keep itself out of the spotlight might have frozen the project, reviewed the situation and cut its losses without the world being the wiser. But the Junior backed IBM into a corner. IBM had almost *invited* speculation about the machine. Ever since the *Wall Street Journal* became the first publication to report rumors of a new IBM machine in early 1983, the market anticipated a wunderkind, a miraculous machine which, even in the best of circumstances, could not possibly have lived up to its advance reputation.

· 6 ·

Because of the overwhelming success of the original IBM PC, Estridge continued to believe that his prime source of knowledge came from the lips of others, even if they weren't so-called computer experts.

Accordingly, in September 1982 he had Sparky Sparks enlist a cross section of top-notch PC retailers and organize them into a Dealer Advisory Council (DAC). When the Council spoke, Estridge listened. The problem is that he heard too much and trusted what he heard. When members of the DAC signed their nondisclosure agreements, they were shown working prototypes of the PC Junior. Aside from some suggestions here and there, the dealers were remarkably enthusiastic over the machine and its prospects.

The Junior's keyboard—which became infamous for its spongy-to-the-touch keys that resembled pieces of Chiclets chewing gum—drew a few negative comments from the dealers, but not enough to send the board back to its developers. But then, who was to know that *this* keyboard would become an object of embarrassment?

Dan Wilkie recalled, "We had input from software houses, dealer advisory groups and consultants and, of these, no one said outright that they didn't like the Junior's keyboard. Before we introduced the original PC, we showed that keyboard to certain people and some of them had negative things to say about it. People still went out and bought the PC faster than we could make it, then they'd complain that the keyboard didn't match the Selectric standard, but the thing is, they kept on buying the PC and its keyboard eventually became the industry standard.

"So what are we supposed to think when a handful of dealers tells us the Junior's keyboard stinks? Did we tell them they were full of it, because some other guys had said the same things and worse about the original PC's keyboard and look at how that turned out? I mean, it's like what are you going to do? The first time the dealers were wrong; the next time they were right. Our error was in not fixing it quickly. A new keyboard could have been out in 60 days if we hadn't taken so long to decide what to do."

Since dealer relations for a new product introduction are taken very seriously, the priority was to get 1,700 models of the Junior ready for the dealers, most of whom, by the late fall of 1983, still had no idea what the machine was called, what it looked like, or even what it was supposed to do.

· 7 ·

Three weeks before IBM finally admitted that such a product as the PC Junior even existed, the Ziff-Davis Publishing Company in New York City had ready a promotional issue of its *PCjr* magazine. As its editor explained at the time, "We can brag just a little. Our inside sources are very, very good."

Along with scores of other computer trade publications and members of the general business press, the editors of *PCjr* received an invitation from IBM on the day before Halloween 1983. With IBM's customary restraint, it was worded simply as "a demonstration of a new product." The event was held on Tuesday, November 1, 1983, in a wing of the

Gallery of Science, a special exhibition area at the corporation's new office building in midtown Manhattan.

Lindsy Van Gelder, contributing editor for *PCjr*, attended the product demonstration and reported:

"There were no barred doors on November 1, although there was a lady at the entrance who asked to see your credentials (and let you in, even if you didn't have any). Next stop was down a flight of stairs, and a right turn into a reception room. Beyond this area was a hall, discreetly closed off by a velvet rope of the sort used in movie theaters. At the end of the hall, we could see another room, where presumably, IT was. Every step along the route made us flutter a little harder in giddy anticipation of IT. In fact, except for the absence of a big sign on the wall warning pregnant women and people with heart conditions to turn back, it felt exactly like snaking along the lines waiting to ride Space Mountain in Disneyland."

Van Gelder recalls helping herself to "pastries, juice and coffee . . . served on tables graced with the by-now-de-rigueur-bud-vases-containing-single-roses. . . . At 10 a.m. on the nose, the velvet rope swung open, and we did another locust imitation, zeroing in on IT. . . . The initial five minutes of our very random access to the PCjr was bedlam, with flashbulbs popping like grenades, oohs and ahs of the sort usually heard at fireworks displays, dailies' journalists sprinting back down the hall to the telephones, and the TV and radio news crews (who'd been asked to wait until the print press was finished, but thought better of it) charging in like killer bees."

After the first rush of enthusiasm, Van Gelder wrote, "True to its word, IBM proceeded not to give us the standard Q-and-A-type press conference. What followed was more of a cross between a computer show and a college mixer. While we wandered around looking at the merchandise, we got chatted up by dozens of unfailingly polite, well-dressed IBM employees, each wearing a single rose in his or her lapel." Reporter Van Gelder also points out that "Each booth area . . . was staffed by at least one member of the rose brigade."

Van Gelder also told of visiting a "Technical Information" booth at the unveiling ceremonies where, "The knowledgeable fellow with the flower in his lapel patiently answered all questions . . . Finally, someone asked him what seemed to be the inevitable question: 'From what you're saying, would it be possible to upgrade [the PCjr.] to the functional capability of a PC or an XT?' We waited for Mr. Petal-Pectorals to toss off an IBMism: 'I wouldn't care to speculate on that.' Actually what the fellow said was: 'Yes.' Amazing!"

· 8 ·

It was IBM's fault that the PC Junior was not built to be more compatible with its predecessors, which, many observers now say, was the principal reason why the machine was not a success. But it was certainly *not* IBM's fault that the press and the microcomputer industry "made" the machine much more than it was.

In announcing the PC Junior, the company issued a straightforward press release that stated (in part):

"The IBM PCjr features a 16-bit 8088 microprocessor, 64KB of permanent Read Only Memory (ROM), 64KB of user memory, a cordless 62-key keyboard, a desktop transformer, two slots for ROM cartridges, an audio tone generator and a 12-month warranty.

"The enhanced model includes an additional 64KB of user memory for a total of 128KB, as well as a 360KB, dual-sided, slim-line diskette drive. It also has the capacity to display up to 80 columns of information."

What the press didn't know—and really couldn't have known—was that many members of the so-called rose brigade at the Junior's debut weren't convinced themselves that the machine had a remarkable future. Beyond the carefully orchestrated style and dignity that is a hallmark of every IBM product introduction, the men and women with the roses in their lapels were polite, informative, but not carried away by the magnitude of what they were doing on that first day of November 1983.

On the other hand, the press was determined to find more in the product than was there—even if truth was a casualty in the process. There was, for instance, an analysis of the Junior in an early issue of *PCjr* magazine that declared, ". . . the design of PCjr reveals it to be a capable machine. . . . Junior is something much more than a scaled-down business computer. The hardware itself points in the direction that IBM believes personal computers are going (and have so far gone) and it shows what IBM expects Junior to do and where it expects it will do it." The magazine further predicted that "PCjr is designed to be a part of a home entertainment system, not just a glorified typewriter or adding machine."

Meanwhile, the legions of outside entrepreneurs that had been getting rich by building add-ons for the original IBM PC had great plans for the PC Junior. According to *PCjr.* magazine, "The consensus on the PCjr in the aftermarket industry is unanimously positive—they believe Junior will be a runaway success and that backing it will help support their firms. As a group, the aftermarketeers see the PCjr as being more successful than most other computer introductions. They believe it's in the same league as Junior's million-selling forebear, the IBM Personal Computer."

Indeed, one of the "aftermarketeers" told the magazine, "We are committing our resources to the PCjr." Another sagely noted, "The more limited the features of the computer, the greater the opportunity for us." And yet another of these optimists enthused, "Just as the PC legitimatized computers for medium and small businesses, Junior will show the world that everybody is going to have a computer. The first month, people will buy them and stare at them. After that, the PCjr will invade the PC market. . . . The PCjr is wonderful because everybody in the world is going to make things that go on it. Eventually, it will be able to do everything. That's what happens when you're IBM."

It is also an example of what happens when almost-pathetic, un-questioning faith in IBM blocks good sense of many of the would-be suppliers of peripherals for the Junior. For them, every Junior sold represented an opportunity for an add-on. They were on IBM's coattails and IBM was never wrong. As far as these suppliers were concerned, they were on their way to becoming millionaires.

As it turned out, more than a few of them are no longer in business.

· 9 ·

Dan Wilkie recalled the flurry at Boca Raton to get the 1,700 demonstration models of the Junior out to the dealers in late fall of 1983. Some members of the team questioned this decision, including Wilkie, who said, "Because of our problems with the design and the vendors we had low levels of finished products on hand, so some of us wanted to hold the volume shipments until January—after the holiday season—to let the news coverage die down and to see how the product was being positioned in the market."

"We announced the Junior about two months before it would be shipped. In the meantime, the dealer advisory councils said their people needed demo models so they could start placing orders for the machines. So we busted our chops getting the demos out by early December. It wasn't until later that we found out that 80 percent of the demos just sat in the back rooms at the stores because the dealers were not about to have their salesmen pushing a machine during the Christmas season that they couldn't possibly deliver until after the first of the year."

Not experienced at the time with the vagaries of low-end computer retailing, the IBM ESD simply followed orders and got the machines to the dealers in early December 1983. Meanwhile, according to Wilkie, the influential Dealers Advisory Council for the Junior and the IBM marketing group were both insisting that at least 1.2 million Juniors could be sold during 1984. "I can remember Paul Rizzo, a corporate vice president who had been around for a long time, saying to me, 'Why don't we gear up to just build maybe 200,000 or 300,000 of the machines, wait and see what happens and, if it takes off, we'll let the supply chase the demand?' Rizzo was a very, very smart and perceptive individual. If the ESD had taken his advice, we would have been much better off.

"What we did was kind of meet the dealers and Rizzo halfway. We kept modifying the production plans until we ended up with a plan to build about 600,000 Juniors. By June of '84, we stopped making the machines and with about 350,000 units in inventory, we still had enough machines to handle the demand for another year and a half. That just goes to show how little the dealer channels and the ESD knew about the market for home computers.

"Don Estridge was always reminding us to be humble, but this was our first visible experience outside of IBM at learning to be humble. It's tough to be humble when you think you're good."

# 27 Where All Roads Lead

· 1 ·

Don Estridge had two favorite aphorisms; one was about staying humble, and the other was a flat statement that, as far as upward strivers at IBM were concerned, "All roads must eventually lead to Armonk."

Translation: Personal ambition was not necessarily served by using IBM as a stepping-stone to better-paying but less secure jobs elsewhere in the computer industry.

He practiced what he preached. With the success of the PC, Estridge became the target of corporate recruiters for the management-starved microcomputer industry. For any of them to lure Estridge—the biggest name in the industry—away from IBM would have been the coup of their careers.

Estridge himself was tempted by an apple—that is, Apple Computer, Inc. In late 1985 when Steve Jobs, Apple's chairman and principal stockholder, was looking for a new chief executive, and according to sources close to Estridge, Jobs offered him the job, with a starting annual salary and benefits package that topped $1 million. (The Apple job eventually went to John Sculley.)

At the time, Estridge was believed to be earning somewhat more than $175,000 a year, though with IBM's generous bonus arrangements, his total compensation package for 1983 probably came close to $250,000. Nevertheless, this was much less than chief executives were earning at many companies put in business by the IBM PC. Estridge was also offered the presidency of SUN Microcomputers, a fast-growing workstation company, which is now partially owned by AT&T.

To accept the Apple offer would have meant a move to the company's headquarters at Cupertino in the heart of California's Silicon Valley, far away from Don and Mary Ann's family, friends and roots in Florida. So he told Steve Jobs "Thanks, but no thanks." Besides, Estridge was still getting a kick out of telling strangers he worked for IBM, just so he could see the look of respect and admiration on their faces. And, simply, he had an unquestionable loyalty and devotion to IBM.

His attitude affected his close associate, Dan Wilkie, who rolled his eyes heavenward when Estridge would return to the office with little anecdotes of how he impressed some nice old couple he met in an airport when he told them, "I'm with IBM!" Wilkie, the streetwise scruffy kid from the steel mill cities of western Indiana, used to say he was also proud to be with IBM, but he felt he could easily adjust to a truly fat paycheck and that Estridge's super "Gee Whiz" enthusiasm for good old Big Blue was based on his personal success and rewards at the company.

Anyway, that's what he used to say but, in his own tough-and-gruff way, Wilkie too was totally loyal to IBM. There was a time, though, in early 1983, when he was tempted to jump ("What the hell, what did I have to lose? I could always say, 'no'"). So Wilkie talked to the Compaq Computer Corporation about the possibility of new employment for the sort of money and stock options he'd probably have to hang around IBM for another 10 years to make.

He didn't say yes or no right away, but went home and discussed the prospect with his wife, who asked him if the pressure at work had caused him to lose his senses. He mentioned it to his kids, and their eyes started to water and their lips quivered. When he told his mother that he was thinking about—just "thinking about"—leaving IBM, Wilkie swears that she would have reacted more calmly if he had said he was divorcing his wife. So Wilkie told those other people "thanks, but no thanks." Explaining afterwards, Wilkie said, "Don Estridge was the real factor in my decision to stay. I'd never be able to tell him I was leaving and, besides, I was learning more with him than at any other time in my career. I never worked harder and I never had more fun. There was no good reason to leave at that time and so I didn't because I couldn't."

· 2 ·

In January 1984, Don Estridge was named a vice president of IBM. It's not that Estridge didn't deserve the promotion, but it's amazing that it came so quickly and without the promotion makers at IBM waiting to see how the Entry Systems Division (ESD)'s latest venture, the PC Junior, was going to fare in the marketplace.

As it turned out, the machine wasn't doing so well at all. The wag who said its keyboard was full of Chiclets gave an appraisal that stuck. There were also the legions of disappointed customers led by the media to expect the Junior to handle all of the major software they were using on their office PCs. But, instead of seeing that they had been the dupes of overeager journalists, this significant, potential market for the PC Junior inspected the machine, shook their heads and walked away by the thousands.

Meanwhile, the ESD had been impressed by the response to some of the portable computers that had cloned the PC's operating system. In what came across as a halfhearted attempt to grab a share of this unanticipated market, IBM introduced its own version of a portable PC on February 16, 1984.

This machine received a lukewarm reception that led to sluggish sales. This time the division's market research could be blamed for concluding that a strong demand existed for PC portability. The fact is that the competitive portables sold well not because they were transportable, but because they were available when the supply of IBM PCs was lagging behind demand.

Again, as with the Junior, IBM was so anxious about the Portable affecting sales of the original PC and the hard disk XT that they made the machine less competent than the PC and XT. Meanwhile, the best of the competitive portables was almost every bit as capable as the original PC. Since the market was far more concerned with capability than portability, the IBM Portable PC became a classic case of too little too late. Sixteen months after its introduction, the machine was quietly phased out of the IBM product line.

·  3  ·

As spring 1984 approached, Estridge would say in private conversations that the ESD had been going its own way for too long, and intervention by the corporation was inevitable.

It was like déjà vu for Wilkie, who remembered the pep rally at Broward Community College in what seemed to be the distant past but was actually not quite two years ago. There he was, once again pacing the stage with Estridge, both of them waiting for the fired-up members of the old IBU to file in and settle down while the rock-music version of *Carmen* or "Flight of the Bumble Bee" was playing and excitement was filling the hall and he turned to Estridge and said he wished this could last forever, and Estridge said that could never be so.

They were sitting around again on a Saturday morning at the office when Estridge leaned back in his chair and put his feet on the conference table. "You know, there will never again be anything like the PC group in IBM."

Wilkie asked, "Why not? We're growing a $4 billion a year business."

Estridge said, "I'll tell you why not. It's because another group like that might be another success and the company is not about to let something like this get out of hand again. They don't want to lose the control. It's a shame. It really is. But that's the way it is as I see it."

"I can't believe we would be the last of it," Wilkie said. "I think the reverse should happen—IBM should try ten more of these groups and if three of them hit, then the company still comes out a big winner."

"Nope. You're lookin' at it," Estridge said, breaking into the grin that hadn't been seen around the ESD headquarters for quite some time.

"So where does that leave people like you and me?" Wilkie asked.

"Well, don't forget," Estridge advised, "all roads still lead to Armonk. I have a feeling I'll be heading there before long and maybe you'd better think about getting your bags packed, too."

· 4 ·

In early 1984, John Akers, president of IBM, appeared at Boca Raton to address a meeting of the influential New York Society of Security Analysts, whose members had been flown to Florida as guests of the corporation.

After a few perfunctory remarks about the corporation's ambitions, Akers warned the analysts against engaging in what he called "PC myopia." Referring directly to the principal product of the Entry Systems Division, he said, "We must keep an eye on planning its integration into the full IBM product line and carefully manage its role in our total business."

If anything, the formal remarks of John Akers are never to be taken lightly. As a 12-year veteran of the company and a close IBM observer later commented, "Anybody familiar with how IBM works knew that the company wasn't going to leave the PC project alone forever.

"It was one thing when the guys forming the original PC group could pick people like themselves to work with, but when the PC took off like a rocket, more executives had to be brought in from throughout the corporation and, in most cases, these were people well grounded in the IBM traditions."

Continuing, the observer said, "When it became obvious that the PC group had struck gold, the rest of the company sat up fast and took notice. Some of them must have said things like, 'Hey, wait a minute. There's that hard core of people down in Florida who created the PC and now they want to set themselves apart from the rest of us. We can't allow that. It's disruptive to the company.

"I can look at this from the outside," he said, "and I can almost see the Old Guard resisting the success of the upstarts, while all the time they were singing out of the same hymnal about how wonderful it was that the PC was such a success and only IBM could do something like that and ain't IBM grand?

"After all, it's one thing to change something if the mold isn't working. It's another thing to take something that's very successful and mold it into a bureaucratic nightmare that's not so successful. It's amazing what IBM can do to bring individuals and groups of independent thinkers into line. What I mean is, well, it's kind of like sour grapes."

Another ex-IBMer and former member of the PC team recalled, "Most of the turmoil we started to encounter in late 1983 and into the next year was a direct result of the company eroding the team's autonomy. The type of thinking that went into developing the original PC now had to bend to the authority of the corporation. Obviously, at least in my opinion, this had a negative impact on the ESD's ability to develop the right products for the marketplace. The failures of the Junior and the Portable PC are good examples of what caused the corporation to start making its influence felt. Then Estridge got spread too thin when he was saddled with taking over an entire division, including declining products like 'The Displaywriter' (a stand-alone word processing system that became an anachronism with the advent of practical PC technology). There was no way Estridge could afford the same focus as he had when he directed development of the PC and the XT. The guy was a brilliant programmer and engineer, but he started to do some strange things when he was required to handle more complex business issues."

As Dan Wilkie recalled, "One of Don's faults was that he was naive as hell about how far he could go in breaking IBM's traditions as far as rewarding individuals. He'd tell us that he was going to get the company to make special considerations beyond merit pay for certain people.

He'd talk about getting us special cash and stock incentive bonuses. I knew what he was doing; he was trying to keep our morale up during the time when the company was starting to move in on our division and he also truly believed some of us deserved special recognition.

"But at the end, Don couldn't deliver because there was no way the company was going to make special concessions that would get its compensation and bonus programs out of whack. So when his promises didn't happen, Don would backtrack. After a while, when he kept having these delusions about getting us bonuses and the like, we'd say, 'Yeah. Right.' Then we'd go and forget about it because we knew he couldn't do it, even though, in his heart, we knew he wanted to do it, so that was okay, but it still wasn't putting any money in our pockets."

By early 1984, money was filling the pockets of independent software developers and builders of the so-called PC clones that were capitalizing on the open architecture and nonproprietary operating system of the PC and the XT. When the stock market began its recovery in August 1982, the first of the microcomputer entrepreneurs were well on their way to becoming millionaires many times over. And they had no qualms about flaunting their wealth. Nearly all of them were under 30 years old.

The disparity of how money was distributed in the computer industry created deep dissatisfaction among the "old timers" at the ESD. Nor were matters helped by the corporation's intrusions and the fact that most of the key director and vice president positions in the PC group were now being held by executives recently brought in from elsewhere in the corporation.

Several core members of the PC group felt betrayed. They had been let alone to do their job, and they did it so well that they not only met their deadline but they created a machine that revolutionized the computer industry and changed for all time the way business is conducted throughout the world. For this, after working 70-hour weeks, they received one or two merit increases and a bonus or two in three years. Otherwise, all they had was the satisfaction of a job well done. For most of them, oddly enough, this might have been enough if only they had been allowed to continue to be "the wild ducks at Boca Raton."

But to have the corporation come in and make changes as if the PC team had fouled up instead of succeeded—that was the final insult. No real money, no more autonomy, keep smiling and mark the days till retirement. If this was the IBM Way, they wanted no more of it after experiencing what Wilkie called "the excitement and freedom of the early PC environment."

So they left. Sparky Sparks left in February 1983 and, also in 1983, Jim D'Arezzo departed for Compaq Computer Corporation. Both said it was a lot easier to leave the company than to give notice to Don Estridge. Others soon followed Sparks and D'Arezzo.

Sparks later explained, "I left because I had earned and deserved a bigger and better opportunity than IBM was able to give me considering that I had proved my ability to deliver. The fact is that most of those on the PC project weren't sharing in the rewards to the extent that they deserved to. This didn't include Don Estridge, who deserved everything he got out of the project."

· 5 ·

Whenever someone of consequence was ready to leave the PC team, the ESD and IBM, their first stop, as a matter of courtesy and protocol, was at Estridge's office. They would suck in their breath, go in, sit down, and tell Don Estridge how sorry they were to leave (and they meant it). They mentioned their families and how college educations would have to be paid for and mumbled about not being able to "pass up this opportunity." What they didn't want to hear from Estridge and what he would never be so mean to say was that "this opportunity" would not have been theirs if he hadn't picked them for the PC team in the first place.

# 28    Dealing with Disaster

· 1 ·

When 1984 arrived the IBM PC Junior was having very serious difficulty in the stores.

The basic machine sold for $699, a price that the media said was too high for a home computer. The advanced model sold for $1,269—a figure bordering on the outrageous for a home computer, but it was a price that paradoxically promised commissions too low to excite salespeople in IBM's vast network of computer retail outlets.

Another problem at the consumer level was that the major PC retailers, such as Computerland and the Sears Business Centers, soon learned that their true market was the small businessperson who could be counted on to buy multiple PCs once he understood the advantages of personal computing. Very often, it took no more time to sell as many as half a dozen IBM PCs to a small businessperson than it did to convince an amateur that the PC Junior might make a good "starter" machine.

For reasons that are still unclear, IBM, with all of its vast marketing expertise, failed to grasp the fundamental fact that its major retail outlets had quickly and smoothly developed into sophisticated, full-service operations with outside sales staffs well-tuned to the needs of their commercial customers. Only as an incidental did the stores pay much attention in 1984 to off-the-street, walk-in business.

IBM's marketing and product development specialists at corporate headquarters also failed to grasp the obvious fact that the market for the basic 8088 and 8086 microprocessor chips was far from exhausted. Instead, they became infatuated with the Intel 80286 chip—a powerful microprocessor that was unquestionably on the leading edge of pc technology.

The problem was that this chip, though "discovered," was still being perfected, which meant it was inevitable, but not yet practical. Estridge understood this, so in early 1984, he comissioned Dan Wilke and two other men on the pc team to develop three advanced products that would still be based on the accepted 8086 technology. The development would take place within the framework of the Entry Systems Division at Boca Raton and would, for the time being, be insulated from the corporate bureaucracy—similar to the way the original pc project was organized.

The three new projects were aimed at developing microcomputers that could take advantage of IBM's high-flying leadership in the field. The eventual products were intended to be "clone killers" in the XT marketplace, that is, original IBM PCs that would come head on against the machines that were copying Big Blue's technology to make machines that sold for less than the bellwether IBM products. One supposition pointed to the remarkably extended life of the Apple II and IIe microcomputers which, after some five years, were still selling well; the other supposition was based on the perception that the advanced 8086 technology was, itself, still very viable.

The three projects proceeded apace until Monday, July 2, 1984, when Estridge called the project directors together for a special meeting at the Sheraton Hotel in Boca Raton. The highlight of the meeting was a presentation straight out of Armonk abetted by management "moles" within the ESD. These factors indicated that the market was exhausted for 8086-based products and that now was the time to switch to development of machines that would be based on the high-performance 80286 technology.

Estridge heard this argument, then he turned to Wilkie and his peers. They lobbied vigorously and vociferously for their projects, insisting that the market proved there was still plenty of life in the "old" technology and that applications programs based on the 80286 chip were still far from ready for introduction.

"We have to go on. We've got to finish what we're doing. Product lives don't just stop like that," Wilkie persisted. Estridge sat quietly. listening to one side and then the other. When the cases were finally closed Estridge tucked his fingers beneath his glasses and rubbed his eyes. Then he looked down, looked up, sighed and said, "The 8086 projects are finished. We're moving toward the 286 now. That's it."

Wilkie and his peers were flabbergasted. Quickly they collected themselves and started shouting in unison. Wilkie—the big, bad, tough bear—was not about to give up without a fight and his eyes blazing, his body shaking, his voice rising, he shouted, "Now, Goddamit, Don, wait a minute!"

"No!" Estridge shouted back—even more loudly and firmly than Wilkie.

But Wilkie, the riled bear, persisted, "Don, you're wrong. You're absolutely dead wrong."

Estridge replied, "Well, that's your opinion."

"I guess you're not always right, but you're always the boss. Right?" Wilkie countered.

"That's right," Estridge snapped. "I am the boss. I respect your opinion, but I've made my decision and that's it. The case is closed. Do you understand? Closed!" Then he stuffed his papers into his briefcase and walked out of the room.

With that decision IBM walked away from a market it created—a market which would, in time, create hundreds of millions of dollars in revenues for the skilled imitators of a technology that might have belonged almost exclusively to the largest computer corporation in the world.

· 2 ·

The press had been remarkably fickle in its treatment of the PC Junior. After predicting the wonders of the machine before its introduction, the general circulation business press now felt obliged to report every detail of the Junior's downfall.

The *Wall Street Journal* was the first publication to break the story that the machine was in the works; now it became among the first to chronicle its troubles. In late February 1984, the *Journal* ran a story under the headline, "IBM's Hotly Touted PCjr Receives Cooler Than Expected Reception." In May, the newspaper followed this up with another story headlined, "IBM Says Sales of Its PCjr Model Below Expectations."

In April, 1984, *Business Week* ran a story on "How Apple is Bullying IBM's PCjr." The following month, a story syndicated through the Knight-Ridder Newspapers said, "Market is Unforgiving for 'Junior' Computer." The same month, May 1984, *USA Today* noted, "PCjr Problems Force Cracks in IBM's Wall of Corporate Silence" and the *New York Times* ran an inventory of what it called "IBM's Problems With Junior."

Looking back to those days when the ESD and the Junior were being inundated by harsh press coverage, a professional IBM-watcher remarked, "It really makes no sense to blame the press for the Junior's problems, but, nevertheless, we have to recognize that the media had a hand in this. First, they made the machine out to be more than it could ever live up to; then, when the machine failed to take off and soar into the stratosphere like the IBM PC did, the media couldn't wait to start dancing on the Junior's grave. It's really hard to feel sorry for IBM, but, still, there was something unfair and even kind of vindictive about this, especially since Estridge had always bent over backward to be cooperative with the press. But then nothing sells newspapers like bad news—especially when it has to do with a company like IBM that's not used to dealing with failure."

· 3 ·

IBM held a special reception at the Plaza Hotel in New York City on the last day of July 1984 to introduce an advanced version of the PC Junior.

The advancements included a new typewriter-style keyboard with a harder touch, expanded memory capabilities for more than 500K of storage, an emulated disk drive and a speech synthesizer with a vocabulary of 196 words. The company even agreed to give the new keyboards without charge to owners of the spongy Chiclets models. In all, this was clearly an aggressive effort by IBM to salvage at least a share of the educational and home office markets for the Junior.

Improving the Junior was unquestionably a sincere move to penetrate what the company still stubbornly perceived as an actual market. But a major retailer of IBM PC products saw matters otherwise:

"IBM misread the direction and maturity of the market, but then, so did everybody else. The Junior was overpriced for the home market," he explained, "and when the whole market collapsed, it did so for very good reasons because no one has yet been able to penetrate the market with practical uses for a computer.

"I'm not talking about people who use a computer as an adjunct to their professional lives, or to run a business—those are not 'home' uses at all. What I'm talking about are the machines like the Commodores and Ataris. A lot of these machines were sold, but there was no depth of continuing use to that market. Parents would buy these little machines because they thought their kids had to become 'computer literate' to get good grades and move on to high class academies and Ivy League colleges. But the kids looked at the home machines as glorified toys because, at school, they had access to more capable computers. So the so-called 'home computer' market is just kind of hanging there—the machines are still around and they are being used for some quasi-business applications and there's no doubt that they have educational value for the kids. But that's about it for home computers in the 1980s."

Any other computer manufacturer might have made quiet apologies and withdrawn from the market for home computers. This was not an easy thing for Big Blue to do.

· 4 ·

Since the press was on a roll pointing out IBM's mishaps with the hapless Junior during the spring and summer of 1984, there was hardly any space left to speculate on rumors that the company was readying an advanced desk-top computer with a high-powered microprocessor and twice the storage and data manipulation capacity of any other personal computer.

Eventually (and nearly 18 months behind its original schedule), the ESD introduced the PC/AT on Tuesday, August 14, 1984, at a Texas-sized party in Dallas—just three years and two days after the unveiling of the original IBM Personal Computer.

Phillipe Kahn, president of Borland International, a leading software developer, recalls being invited to dinner at Dallas by several IBM executives during the AT introduction festivities. Kahn said they showed interest in Borland's "Turbo Pascal" programming language and also used the occasion to pick his brain on other companies that would be suitable third-party software developers for the AT. According to Kahn, the dinner broke up with lots of enthusiasm, good fellowship and promises by IBM to stay in touch. That was the first and last time Kahn heard from IBM on the AT matter.

The AT stood for "Advanced Technology" and not for "Attractive Tag," since the machine carried a price just shy of $4,000. The company said the AT was designed to be a multitask, multiuser computer. To meet this description, the machine had up to 3 million bytes of main storage and more than 40 million bytes of on-line storage. Its Intel 80286 microprocessor enabled the AT to process information (such as spreadsheet calculations and data-base retrievals) up to three times faster than the PC/XT or its antecedent, the "old" bare bones PC.

There were eight slots in the machine's chassis to handle the type of add-ons that had significantly enhanced the capabilities of its predecessors. As many as three megabytes (three million bytes) of RAM could run on boosted-up versions of the machine, and it could also handle up to three disk drives.

Since the keyboard on the original IBM PC created so much criticism and because the Chiclets keyboard on the first models of the PC Junior was the cause of so much mockery, IBM finally took the hint and introduced the AT with a streamlined, sensible keyboard based on the widely accepted Selectric standard the company had established years before for its line of typewriting machines.

The AT was a good, sturdy and powerful machine. It deserved the enthusiastic reception it received from the IBM dealers. The trouble was that the company had once again and quite inexplicably botched its forecasting, and demand for the machine was underestimated. Some observers believe that IBM, embarrassed by the surfeit of PC Juniors clogging its inventories, opted for the formula Paul Rizzo had sagely suggested for the Junior—that is, let the supply chase the demand. As it was, the demand built, but there was almost no supply at all to chase it.

It seems that the earliest models of the AT had 20 megabyte hard disk drives that would suddenly and unpredictably grab stored data and destroy it. This, of course, was an absolute disaster. Weeks of work were lost by users, and they complained mightily. Yet, despite the evidence, IBM insisted that no such problem existed. And yet, with no satisfactory explanation, the company stopped shipping the AT and announced that further deliveries of the machine would be delayed indefinitely.

According to *PC World* magazine (August 1987),

> Fingers were pointed at CMI, manufacturer of the drive, then (Microsoft) DOS 3.00, and finally Western Digital, maker of the drive's controller board. As reputations left and right were being bashed (especially CMI's), IBM denied that any problem existed—but recalled the disk controllers anyway. By the time Western Digital confessed that a faulty Texas Instruments chip on the board was to blame, the public was losing faith in the AT.

After the exasperating experience with Teledyne and the PC Junior, it would seem that the ESD would have learned not to place too much reliance on just one outside supplier; indeed, it is something of a policy at IBM always to have at least one backup supplier waiting in the wings. But the decision makers at the ESD were singularly distracted by how the AT would be priced and marketed ("Our biggest mistake with the AT was to underprice it," Wilkie commented some time later). Apparently they were blinded by the disk drive supplier's guarantees of competence. When serious problems with the drives arose, they caused the initial deliveries of the AT to be stretched out for an unacceptable nine months after the August 14 introduction.

"It was crazy not to have a second source for such a critical part," IBM watcher Robert T. Fertig, president of Enterprise Information Systems, later told *Business Week* magazine (February 11, 1985). "It is definitely not like IBM, and it's an example of ad hoc management." But he does not fault management itself: Division President Philip D. Estridge "simply had too much responsibility," Fertig said.

# 29   IBM Moves In

· 1 ·

Ever since the PC group lost its independence and became the Entry Systems Division (ESD) of IBM in August 1983, the Boca Raton facility became a different place to work. During the new division's first year there had been the Junior disaster, the IBM Portable embarrassment, and the AT fiasco. Nevertheless, with its insistence on cloaking reality as far as its resources allowed, the company proclaimed on the occasion of the division's first anniversary, "ESD has proven it is organized for fast track performance. The organizational accomplishments of ESD's first year are remarkable. . . [it has] a cross-pollination of original thinking from people throughout the division and an impressive record of innovation, quality and cost-control achievements."

In the same announcement intended for circulation only within the company, Dr. Robert L. Carberry, the no-nonsense executive hand-picked by Armonk to take over the ESD's Systems Architecture and Technology, clearly scolded the team of disgruntled upstarts from the old PC group: "Development in ESD is like a series of entrepreneurs running for the door to get their products out," Carberry said. Further, "Our role is to put an environment around product managers that says, 'Let's preserve their ability to run to completion as quickly as possible. But let's coordinate for compatibility among products. . . and make certain our timing is correct.' In short, we want to keep a balance that allows our entrepreneurial operations to be contained in the larger structure needed to manage the business."

At the same time, Robert K. Moesser, the newly appointed division director for quality, remarked that the ESD must maintain its momentum "by focusing on a new attitude toward control systems and processes."

177

But "control systems and processes" contradicted the spirit of the PC operation. According to Wilkie, "The guys on the PC team who had been around for a while were getting the impression that bigness was settling in and many of us didn't like it. We were spending too much time communicating instead of producing. The company came in and set up multiple levels of managers, multiple disciplines, new policies and procedures, and reviews upon reviews.

"By now, of course, Estridge was a division president and a corporate vice president and when these guys from up north began to come on board, the next thing we knew is that Don had reporting layers between himself and some of the people down the ladder who used to get much of their motivation by working closely with Don.

"After a while," Wilkie continued, "it was like a big cloud gradually engulfing us one day at a time. It used to be when you had something to show Don, you could take it right to him; now, there were three or four other guys that had to review it first.

"This protocol and discipline started to cause problems because Don was spending almost 80 percent of his time in Armonk, with just unbelievable traveling back and forth to report to all the people he now had to deal with in IBM."

The sign of the corporation is the presence of controls. And now, there were controls covering operations, manufacturing, marketing, logistics, inventories and anything that could be subjected to controls. Then the controls themselves were audited, that is, *reviewed for control*.

It's not that the veterans of the PC IBU were unfamiliar with IBM's desire for controls, but, as Wilkie explained, "We were running so fast for so long that we didn't have time to put controls in place. Shortly after I was promoted from being plant manager for the PC group, the corporation came in and found all sorts of controls that were inadequate by their standards. These were controls that were influenced less by cost than by the need for a quick response and speed of tasks. I went to Estridge and apologized for the trouble this was causing and he told me, 'You've got absolutely nothing to be sorry about. I knew the risks, you knew the risks, we took these as calculated risks and the result was that we grew an incredible business at the fastest rate in the company's history. So go and help them fix things. We have to do it their way because we're a big business now.'

"This all came about when we were starting to take off as a business," Wilkie recalled. "We were talking to the other divisions about software and technology and we were starting to come together with the rest of the company, so, of course we had to run into checks and balances and the bureaucracy, all of which was very aggravating and time consuming for the people who were used to taking risks and running fast.

"But with the PC, whether we intended to or not, we had come up with the workstation of the IBM universe. Our success made the corporation sit up and take notice of what we were doing. We had become essential to the company, so the company found itself forced to pay attention to us."

· 2 ·

By the fall of 1984, the company had stuck with the Junior until it found itself stuck with the Junior.

The improved version of the machine with its new keyboard and enhanced memory evoked a ho-hum response from consumers. Some sources say that the beefed-up model had no effect at all on the Junior's anemic sales.

The challenge to find a solution to the Junior was given to Estridge. There is reason to believe he sensed the machine would never make it, but he also had to maintain his reputation and defend his position from the criticism now known to be coming from IBM's Communications Products Division (CPD).

The CPD resented Estridge and the Entry Systems Division (ESD) because he held on stubbornly to his division's independence and refused to cooperate with other divisions, such as the CPD, which had been struggling to develop an office automation strategy for the corporation, with the PC as its workstation. Estridge did not want the PC to become subservient and be used only as a workstation; he wanted it to be the centerpiece of a complete line of self-contained computer products.

The people at the CPD had another opinion—an opinion that was more acceptable to the corporation and would reflect more favorably on their role. They complained about Estridge's attitude to top management, but by now Estridge was well known and well connected among the people of consequence at corporate headquarters. As a result, when they came up against this man, whom they thought was an easy-to-push-around engineer from the Florida boondocks, they learned that Estridge was as tough as any of them—though no match for their collective power—when it came to playing the game of corporate Darwinism.

Now he was being severely tested. The naysayers and policy-compulsives adopted a fresh refrain: "Scrap the Junior. Kill the machine. Be contrite. Cooperate. Conform."

### · 3 ·

The test was finding a way to sell the Junior while saving face for IBM and the ESD.

A series of meetings held at the ESD during late autumn of 1984 concluded with the decision that it was too early to abandon the Junior because contracts with the principal supplier for the machine ran through the following spring. This situation gave the ESD breathing room to make one last big push, and the Christmas season was starting.

To create enthusiasm for the machine in fall of 1984, IBM began a direct mail campaign that offered PC Junior and software incentives to nearly two million households known to have college-bound children.

Next, a second PC Junior mailing went to eight million professional and business prospects many of whom, IBM assumed, would go to a store to look at the Junior before upgrading to the IBM PC or XT.

Then, for Christmas 1984, IBM launched a PC Junior special promotion aimed at 10 million of the nation's most affluent households—a market that could afford to spend a few hundred dollars more to buy a "real" personal computer.

Finally, in order to do *something, anything* to sell the Junior, IBM simultaneously mounted the most intense television advertising campaign in the corporation's history and followed up with ads in 80 magazines and 160 daily newspapers. The strategy behind this effort was to reach 98 percent of the potential buyers for the Junior at least 30 times by the end of the year.

"You just can't succeed in this business without a substantial and continuing investment in advertising," said David McGovern, the ESD's advertising manager. Of course, having the right product at the right price doesn't hurt either.

In the meantime, authorized IBM dealers were allowed to sell the Junior with a color monitor for $799. At this price the dealers were soon begging IBM for more Juniors. Sales soared. Finally, it looked like the Junior was on its way into the American homes it was designed for.

### · 4 ·

In 1981, the year the PC was introduced, the machine accounted for not quite $43 million in revenues. By the end of 1984, the PC and the division's allied products were responsible for more than $4 billion in sales—a figure that almost matched the corporation's *entire* revenues in

1966. If the Entry Systems Division's sales had not been combined with IBM's revenues, the ESD would have ranked as the 74th largest industrial company in the nation during 1984, according to the Fortune 500 index, and the third largest computer company behind IBM itself and Digital Equipment Corporation.

No other company in the history of the Fortune 500 had ever risen so far and so fast as the division that created and marketed the IBM Personal Computer.

The division was a success. The PC Junior, the source of negative publicity and embarassment, was finally performing the IBM way.

As happy IBMers from the ESD gathered to celebrate the New Year, few tears were shed when "Auld Lang Syne" was played. They were all looking forward to 1985.

# 30 An Erosion of Autonomy

· 1 ·

In January 1985, reports all but confirmed that IBM President John F. Akers would soon assume the title of chief executive officer of the corporation.

It was also the month that IBM's National Distribution Division (NDD) succeeded in wresting retail dealer sales of all PC products from the ESD. This significant erosion of Estridge's empire came about when the dealers' outside salespeople clashed too directly and for too long with the efforts of IBM's National Accounts Division (NAD) and the National Marketing Division (NMD). Essentially, one division of IBM, the ESD, was selling products to organizations that resold the products to customers, who were being solicited by two other IBM divisions to buy the same products. The circumstances leading to this overlap came about early on in the history of the PC when the big-ticket sales reps in the Information Systems Group (ISG) (which encompassed the NAD and the NMD) turned their backs on the "toy" of a personal computer. By the time it became evident that the PC wasn't a plaything, the ESD had a sales strategy independent of the ISG.

By taking over the dealer sales, service and support, the NAD sought to protect IBM's marketing force and, ostensibly, be able to dismantle the network supplying PC products to the gray market. As a concession to Estridge, the ESD was allowed to keep its control of pricing and sales promotion, including advertising.

In making the announcement, IBM corporate headquarters never really said which division—the NAD or the ESD—would have ultimate responsibility for the profitability of PC products. Instead, the corporation insisted that the only motivation behind the transfer of authority was to sharpen the focus on new products while enhancing customer support and opportunities for all divisions of IBM. But what also wasn't made clear in the announcement was that this action was a return to the corporation's traditional way of operating, that is, with product development and manufacturing clearly separated from the marketing and sales functions. Until now, the ESD had been an exception.

Edward M. Esber, Jr., now chairman and chief executive officer of Ashton-Tate, a large software company, welcomed the changes at IBM. "I, for one, was glad to see the pc operations folded into IBM's corporate computing operations," he said. "As a result, the pc became the integrated work station for a variety of sophisticated business networking applications, which was a direct benefit to IBM's national account customers. This would probably not have happened if the pc had remained as an independent entity within the corporation."

In a letter of explanation to the more than 2,000 authorized retailers of IBM products, the corporation reasserted its commitment "to the reseller channel as an integral part of IBM's product and marketing strategy. Day-to-day business relations with your dealer account manager and other IBMers will remain the same."

What didn't remain the same was the reception for the PC Junior. When the special holiday promotion ended, sales of the machine simply collapsed. Estridge and the ESD had failed to pass the test. The Junior was a failure.

· 2 ·

On February 1, 1985, John Akers was named chief executive officer of IBM. The title was passed from John Opel who continued as chairman of the corporation.

A former aircraft-carrier fighter pilot in the navy, the 50-year-old Akers was known for his dedication to paramilitary organization and discipline. Sometimes accused (behind his back) of harboring a cold and arrogant attitude, Akers has skillfully hidden this part of his character.

According to *Business Week* magazine (February 18, 1985): "It is easy to see Akers's appeal. He is confident, quick-witted, and extroverted—a ruddy faced salesman's salesman with a firm handshake, a robust laugh, and an intrinsic grasp of his company's $46 billion business. . . . (He) seems to have the right blend of charm and aggressivess to succeed."

The report also quoted a colleague who called Akers, "a steel hand in a velvet glove."

· 3 ·

"Because we are big and successful, we'll always have dissatisfied individuals. But the problems are usually ones of (their own) execution, as opposed to someone goring their ox," Akers told *Business Week*.

Perhaps an ox was not being gored, but during these days in the spring of 1985, a bear was certainly being provoked.

Dan Wilkie, the big bad bear, knew Big Blue had definitely taken over. The bureaucracy was in place, along with all those new faces and calls for reviews and controls. "Many members of the early pc teams were saying, 'That's it. There's no way we're going to move back to the old mode when Estridge was running things.'

"There were a lot of people at the ESD who really resented the changes," Wilkie said. "But the fact was, it probably would have been stupid for us to run the division in 1985 the same way it ran during '81 to '83. I don't know if it would have worked; after all, these were different times and different situations. But the ESD was not a traditional division and trying to run it according to traditional IBM ways was just wrong. For the people who were used to going after something and getting a quick response—well, this new order just drove them up the trees."

For almost four years, for the ESD, a-crisis-a-minute had been their way of life. Now IBM had taken over with what Wilkie called "its gray cloud" of policies, procedures and controls, the same that he had adapted to for 14 years until the ESD showed him what he saw as a better way of working.

And so, with the onset of order and organization, came a slowing of the pace. Gradually, the ESD was being transformed into a model of propriety, a cog in the wheel, a quiet contributor to the corporation's bottom line.

It was like hell on earth for the old guard with the lapel rosettes at Boca Raton. They'd mutter against the new order and long for the old days and say they weren't going to work 70 hours a week anymore because they couldn't see the results.

They had been superb at what they did best, and now they had to ask to be able to do it. Instead, they were told to work on presentations, or status reports, or presentations that were like reports, or reports on how presentations can be more like reports. So they rebelled. "Hey," they'd say. "We're just going to sit back for a while and watch things go along." They came to work on time at eight o'clock and actually took lunch breaks and headed home at five o'clock and now they always took their weekends off. They marked the days till they could again find something exciting to work on. Meanwhile, more than a few started to look outside IBM for employment for the first time in their careers.

Of course, since most were young with a big slice of their careers yet ahead and families still to feed, they kept this discontent to themselves.

· **4** ·

Don and Mary Ann Estridge built a new house in Boca Raton to be both showplace and a center for their family, where Don could sit back one day in his rocking chair and play the role of paterfamilias. With his own hands, he was building a playhouse for his grandchildren behind the main house when, one late winter day in early 1985 and quite without warning, the men with the real power at Armonk released a new announcement.

Don Estridge would become vice president in charge of worldwide manufacturing for IBM, with headquarters at Armonk. Bill Lowe would leave Armonk, where he had been serving as an executive in the group that directed the activities of the Entry Systems Division (ESD). Lowe was to go to Boca Raton, where he would succeed Estridge as president of the ESD. The changes would be effective immediately.

Some observers speculated that Lowe was still in awe of the early accomplishments of the PC team and would be more of an administrative than an operational influence on the daily activities at Boca Raton. But others more correctly reasoned that the Junior's problems, coupled with the AT's ongoing difficulties, meant that Lowe had no other choice than to revert without delay to the corporation's traditional methods of management, marketing and organization. This, of course, was not made entirely clear when the top-rung changes at the ESD were announced in March 1985.

IBM timed the announcement to coincide with a meeting of the ESD staff at Boca Raton. Estridge and Lowe appeared together at the meeting to announce the shifts in management. Estridge's people rose twice to give their old boss standing ovations. There were tears in

Estridge's eyes as he hung his head and took off his glasses and wiped his eyes with the tips of his left thumb and index finger. Then he replaced the glasses, blinked a few times, tugged at the rosette in his lapel, looked up and there it was—the wide grin, ear-to-ear—just like it was that day, more than a thousand days ago, when the same Bill Lowe who was here at his side now (and looking uncomfortable) had asked, "Don, do you think you'd be interested in taking over the PC Project?"

· 5 ·

Less than 600 days after its entrance, IBM shut its door on the PC Junior on Tuesday, March 19, 1985—just moments after the closing bell rang the end of the trading day at the New York Stock Exchange.

Sales had fallen off by as much as 20 percent after the holiday promotion ended on January 31. If nothing else, the PC Junior had shown that an enthusiastic market existed for a quality computer system with a list price under $1,000. The problem, though, was that the Junior couldn't be sold for less than four figures and still return the profit margins IBM demanded.

Industry sources estimated that the two-month promotion accounted for sales of 80 percent of the quarter of a million PC Juniors sold in 1984. In all, IBM sold slightly more than half a million of the machines during the Junior's brief existence.

Later some industry insiders speculated that the costs of the components in the Junior, added to the massive advertising expenditures (divided by the number of machines sold), indicated that IBM was taking a loss on each machine just to move it out of inventory. Essentially, the company was "dumping" its goods.

In an interview with the *New York Times* (April 2, 1985), C. Michael Armstrong, a senior vice president of IBM responsible for the company's small-computer and workstation operations, said IBM's decision to stop production of the Junior had been misinterpreted. "They all use the same words: the PC Junior has been killed, orphaned, abandoned. We did nothing of the kind."

In a rambling, convoluted style, the mastery of which seems to be a requirement for high office at IBM, Armstrong explained that the corporation had merely stopped making the Junior, though marketing, service and software development for the machine would continue.

He said that when IBM introduced the machine, "We thought that the applications appealing in the home would be checkbook managers and programs that keep track of recipes and menus." But what most potential buyers were looking for was an inexpensive way to handle word-processing and spreadsheet work.

Armstrong admitted that IBM had misjudged its market. "Maybe we didn't understand the data we were seeing," he told the *Times*. "That can happen when you are new to a business."

When the newspaper's reporter pressed Armstrong to comment on rumors that the collapse of the Junior led to Estridge's transfer, the IBM executive bristled and snapped that the reports were "gossip" and "rubbish." He called Estridge "a hero in the IBM company" and added that he was being "broadened" in a staff job "in recognition of the success he achieved."

Other sources saw it otherwise. Their collective comments indicate that Estridge had drifted into a "them-against-us" posture, that is, Armonk-against-ESD. By nature, Estridge was fiercely loyal to his team, and he had a very special and warm regard for those who returned his loyalty.

"But he never let fame get to his head," *InfoWorld*, a weekly publication for microcomputer users reported in its August 19, 1985 issue. "Following a speech he gave in San Francisco, Estridge was surrounded by industry executives clamoring for his attention. A 14-year-old boy broke through the crowd and asked if he could talk to Estridge about developing a program for the PC. The executives had to wait," according to *InfoWorld*.

With as high a profile as Estridge had, he was bound to have detractors—but, apparently, he had no outright enemies. The detractors accused Estridge of being "arrogant," "aloof," and "remote." Actually, the most frequent personal defect ascribed to him was that he did not bother to return all of his phone calls.

Estridge was competent at politics, though, perhaps, his greatest political oversight was the failure to cultivate a mentor, or "sponsor" of established senior rank within the corporation. Estridge apparently had a friendly relationship with Bill Lowe, who was always a step ahead on the promotion ladder. But Lowe could not really qualify as a mentor to Estridge because Lowe himself was still very much upwardly mobile within IBM; as a result, their relationship was based more on near-equality, rather than on seniority.

Estridge learned from Lowe the value of exposure at Armonk. For example, during the year before his transfer, his associates estimated that Estridge spent no less than 80 percent of his away-from-the-office time at corporate headquarters.

Whether it was his fault or not, the division he headed brought highly publicized embarrassment on the corporation with the failure of the Junior, the foolish judgment behind introduction of the PC Portable and the policy-defying oversight of not having a back-up drive manufacturer for the long-delayed AT.

That was three strikes, and in any league that means you're out. The truth is that his transfer to Armonk was not in any sense a "demotion." The timing was for him, most certainly, a disappointment and cause for anger because the transfer was announced within days of when the corporation knew it was going to shut down the PC Junior.

John F. Akers, many years later, said that he believed Don Estridge had the potential to head up all of IBM or certainly to be one of the top six executives within the company.

Estridge, of course, had been saying for years that "all roads lead to Armonk" for the ambitious at IBM. And it was to Armonk that his road led him.

# 31    Estridge
Moves On

## 1

Don and Mary Ann Estridge set aside their plans for spending their retirement years in the Sunshine State. Instead, they once again resigned themselves to the maxim that says the corporation's initials really mean: "I've Been Moved."

They traveled north to look for a house near Don's new offices at corporate headquarters, and eventually found one at New Canaan, Connecticut, less than an hour by road to Armonk.

Meanwhile, at Boca Raton, Bill Lowe was going through a charade of house hunting. By now, in the spring of 1985, he was already in command at the ESD and, from time to time, he'd make a half hearted survey of the local housing market before lapsing into a state of indecision that was not at all typical of the resolute Lowe.

The people at the ESD began to wonder about his behavior. How could it be, they'd whisper, that Estridge could so quickly find a decent home in one of the country's toughest housing markets, while Bill Lowe couldn't seem to find anything to suit his tastes in or around beautiful Boca Raton?

## 2

In April, during his first appearance before an IBM annual meeting as CEO of the corporation, John Akers told the stockholders that the company was being challenged to integrate "a constantly changing product line that runs the gamut from typewriters and supplies to the most complex worldwide systems." Observers of the company took this as a sign

189

that IBM was going to begin to bring its array of incompatible computers under the control of a central authority. This interpretation was in keeping with Akers's known preference for centralization, as opposed to his predecessor John Opel, who welcomed experiments with decentralization and decision-making autonomy on a divisional level. But Akers was in charge, and he had begun a series of moves that would eventually disorganize the old-timers at the ESD.

Less than two months after the annual meeting, IBM revealed its intention to transfer Bill Lowe and 200 key members of the ESD staff to an IBM satellite facility at Montvale, New Jersey. This move would take all of the division's administrative activities and principal decision making out of Florida and bring it to within a few miles of Armonk. Not affected by the announcement was the development of the automated PC assembly facility at Boca Raton, which would remain in place.

By bringing the the once-maverick ESD within beckoning range of headquarters, IBM was revoking any commitment to localized, hands-on authority. There would be no more of the "them-against-us" attitude that had inspired the spirit of defiance in the old days at Boca Raton. The "them" in the equation had put up with enough of the sullen insolence and muttered innuendos of the "us" ever since the PC group became IBM's Entry Systems Division.

The ESD was simply absorbed.

Now it was apparent why Bill Lowe had so much "trouble" finding a house in Boca Raton. He wasn't looking. He was waiting until the move to New Jersey was officially announced by the corporation.

· 3 ·

Estridge had been on the firing line for nearly five years—first as the major motivator behind the original PC, second as the high-profile head of IBM's most publicized operation.

As his responsibilities increased, so did his time spent away from home. Often he'd leave on Sunday afternoon, return late on Friday, then repeat the process less than two days later.

His assignment as director of worldwide manufacturing for the corporation in its bid to retain a majority share of the $28 billion office equipment market was a major step forward in his career. He would oversee the work of 116,000 people at 41 IBM plants in 15 countries. (At the ESD, Estridge had been responsible for about 10,000 IBM employees at four plants in three countries.)

But by July 1985, Estridge was exhausted and on the way to burnout. The years of unremitting activity and anxiety from coping simultaneously with the crises at Boca Raton and the peculiar politics at Armonk had affected his nerves, turned his hair gray and put lines on his face, though he was still two years from reaching his 50th birthday.

After 26 hectic years with IBM, he was ready to step above the conflict. The new job at Armonk would be less demanding, a relief from being pushed to make promises he could not fulfill and from expectations to achieve impossible goals. He had accepted the promotion with mixed feelings, aware that he would be less visible as a leader, but soothed by the certainty that he would now be functioning within the safety of the corporate structure and the predictability of its traditions.

But in the meantime, the move from Boca Raton to Armonk brought the pressure of quickly finding a new home, preparing for unfamiliar career challenges and bidding farewell to old friends in Florida.

Parties with family and friends were held for the Estridges throughout July at Boca Raton. At the ESD offices, small, informal meetings were held so Don would have many chances to say, "Well, goodbye for now. Good luck. Stay in touch."

Then it would be off to to New Canaan with Mary Ann to get the new house in order. And back to Florida to close down the old house, which was, of course, their "real" house. In between, he attended to the preliminary business of his new post at Armonk.

Finally, Don and Mary Ann found a way to take a real vacation. They would spend a few days at Sanibel Island, on the Gulf of Mexico off the southwest coast of Florida. Then they would return to Boca Raton for one more farewell party before heading off with some close friends for Jackson Hole, Wyoming, where Don could play the dude in his fancy cowboy boots and Mary Ann could strum her guitar around campfires under the Big Sky.

After the vacation, it would be on to Armonk. That was the plan. Until then, it was difficult to pin down the Estridges.

# 32   The Dark Day at Dallas

· 1 ·

On Friday, August 2, while cool, arctic air was drifting from Canada to whistle among the canyons of the Teton Range near Jackson Hole, heat—shimmering heat resembling ripples of rising moisture—was baking the runways at Dallas-Fort Worth Airport, 800 miles from the southernmost border of Wyoming.

"This particular afternoon, from the patchwork of farmland and parking lot that is northwest Dallas County, a hot spot was spawned," writes author Jerome Greer Chandler in his book *Fire & Rain* (Austin, Texas: Texas Monthly Press, 1986).

Chandler's book describes a bizarre series of circumstances which, before the day ended, would cause a catastrophe that would affect the lives of the executives of one of the most influential corporations on earth.

Referring to that hot spot, Chandler wrote:

> Surrounded by a relatively cooler circle, the pocket of warmer air rose. As it did, atmospheric pressure lessened and the pocket began to expand. At the same time, it cooled, although more slowly than the air around it. The higher the pocket ascended, the cooler it became. And simultaneously, its ability to hold water vapor lessened. Eventually, it reached a point called the *convective condensation level*, where the relative humidity is 100 percent. The product was a cloud.
>
> . . . Seen from a distance, it resembled the mushroom cloud of a thermonuclear explosion. The mimicry was apt, for hidden within the gangrenous giant was a heat engine, a furnace of enormous power. The hotter the day grew, the more malignant the monster became. On August 2, the thermometer registered above 100 degrees.

192

· 2 ·

Shortly before 4:00 PM, Eastern Daylight Saving Time (EDST), Delta
Airlines Flight 191, a Lockheed L-1011 TriStar jumbo jet, began to
board passengers at Fort Lauderdale, Florida. Among the 152 were
eight IBM employees, seven members of IBM families and two college
students who had worked as temporary employees of IBM during the
summer.

Weather at the Dallas-Fort Worth Airport was reported to be "good,"
with only the possibility of widely scattered thundershowers around
8:00 PM—a full two hours after Flight 191 was scheduled to be safely on
the ground in Texas.

The flight departed on time at 4:10 PM and flew westward, while the
cloud forming at Dallas was, according to author Chandler, " . . . No
longer a puffy white pocket, it [had] turned cumulonimbus. Condensa-
tion was by now a runaway nuclear reaction, as water droplets grew and
collided with one another. The higher the process propelled itself, the
cooler the droplets became. Some became crystals of ice. Some of the
remaining moisture adhered to them. The result was hail that danced
about in the mounting maelstrom until it was heavy enough to
overcome the dervish updrafts and fall to earth. And so it was that
accumulated moisture—frozen and liquid—overloaded the capacity of
the creature to carry it."

This was the birth of a thunderstorm. As Greer explains: "Every
thunderstorm produces a downdraft, a rush of air preceding and con-
comitant with rain and hail. In perhaps one in a hundred cases, the
downdraft itself mutates. . . . When conditions are right, [the
downdraft] can assume the velocity of a freight train."

Flight 191 ran head-on into this freight train. As it descended to the
approach runway, the copilot, who was flying the plane, brought the
craft directly into the path of the downdraft. At this point, he lost control of the plane. It crashed to earth, split in two, and the forward portion of the fuselage burst into flames, killing 137 passengers.

· 3 ·

Dan Wilkie, who was then the site general manager at Boca Raton,
came home on Friday night, August 2, kicked off his shoes, and picked

up the evening newspaper. He did not turn on the radio or the television set.

At 7:30, the phone rang. The first news came through that IBM employees from the Boca Raton site were believed to be on Delta Flight 191, which had just crashed at Dallas. The call came to Wilkie because he was the site general manager at Boca Raton at the time.

He called the site general manager of the ESD facility at Austin. More often than not on Friday nights, the division had people returning to Austin after spending a few days at Boca Raton. They usually took the same Delta flight that left Fort Lauderdale in the late afternoon bound for Austin via Dallas. But that was not the case this Friday. The Austin-based executives had stayed in Texas because the top managers from Boca Raton were in New York.

Wilkie and his counterpart at Austin compared notes. Apparently, there were some IBM sales reps on the plane returning to Los Angeles through Dallas. They also learned that an IBM employee was traveling on the flight with his wife and daughter. Two college students who had worked during the summer at IBM in Boca Raton were returning to their homes on Flight 191, though one of the students planned to stop off at Dallas for a sorority meeting.

Wilkie spent the next four hours staying in touch by phone with Delta Airlines and the IBM facilities at Austin and Armonk to organize a task force that would verify identification of the bodies and notify the families.

At 11:30 PM, a call came through to Wilkie from the manager of the IBM sales office at Fort Lauderdale.

"Dan," he said, "do you know about the plane, the Dallas flight?"

Wilkie said he was aware of the flight and had been working to get positive identification of those on board. Then he asked, "Did you have anybody on the flight?"

There was a long pause, then the manager at Fort Lauderdale said, "No, we didn't have anyone on the plane, but Patty Estridge, Don's daughter, just called me and said her folks were on the plane."

Wilkie was speechless. He recoiled as if he had received a punch in the stomach. The manager at Fort Lauderdale said he understood that one of the Estridge's daughters was at the Dallas airport planning to meet with her parents when they changed planes. "I don't know what to do," the manager said. "I'll take care of it and keep you posted," Wilkie replied. Then he sat alone, his head in his hands, stunned by the horror of the crash—already aware that Estridge was dead.

## · 4 ·

When Wilkie regained his composure, he consulted his confidential corporate phone directory and phoned John Akers at his home, shortly before midnight. He told Akers that Don and Mary Ann Estridge were probably on the plane, and they were not identified among the survivors. After a long pause Akers asked, "Have you talked to any of the key people involved? Do you know this for sure?"

Wilkie replied, "Well, I can't confirm that they're dead, but they're supposedly not among the survivors. That's all I know now. I'll stay on this and keep you posted."

Finally, the phone calls slowed down, and Wilkie slumped in his chair. It was now 3:00 AM, Saturday, August 3. As Wilkie later recalled, "I knew in my heart that Don and Mary Ann had to be dead, but there was still some doubt. So we kept it really quiet, everybody at Delta did too, until we could get solid confirmation."

Understandably, Wilkie could not sleep that night. He had to stay busy. He had to do something, so, through the night, he made phone calls.

On Saturday morning, the reports of the Estridges's deaths were confirmed. They had been on the way to Jackson Hole, via Dallas, on the last leg of their long-anticipated vacation before settling down near Armonk.

Wilkie was among the first to know that the report of the deaths was now a fact. Rather than have those who were in the pc group and close to the Estridges hear about this tragedy on a newscast, Wilkie took it upon himself to phone them.

He called Jeanette Maher, the public relations director for the ESD who had been with Estridge since the early days of the original PC group. She broke into tears. He contacted others, including Joe Sarubbi, one of the original inner circle from the Saturday morning sessions of a time that seemed so long ago. Sarubbi, rough and tough, himself, was overwhelmed with grief.

Wilkie tried unsuccessfully to reach Joe Bauman, one of the first recruits on the original PC development team. He shared the news of Estridge's death with Mrs. Bauman and asked that her husband phone when he arrived at home.

Joe Bauman had been traveling by automobile to Rochester, Minnesota. It wasn't until early Saturday afternoon that he would reach his wife. He had stopped at a roadside inn to phone her. Bauman told her that he heard about the plane crash on his car radio. Mrs. Bauman, assuming that the radio report had given names, said to her husband, "Isn't it tragic about Don?" This was the first Bauman had heard of Estridge being on the plane. Bauman broke down.

Mrs. Bauman then phoned Wilkie's wife who, in turn, phoned her husband in his office at the ESD. When she told Wilkie that Joe Bauman had finally been reached and how he had reacted, Wilkie was stunned.

All this time—it had been nearly 36 hours—Wilkie had gone without sleep, making phone calls, breaking the news, keeping busy, running on adrenaline and resistance to shock. Now, weakened by the accumulation of his experiences, his resistance to grief gave way. He left his office and went to the men's room and cried for a quarter of an hour. Then he washed his face and returned to the office to coordinate more arrangements for family members to claim the bodies of their loved ones.

· 5 ·

IBM is second only to the Roman Catholic Church when it comes to ceremoniously burying its dead.

Akers gave Wilkie and others full authority to do whatever was necessary to ease the grief of the IBM families who had lost loved ones on Flight 191.

Looking back to that awful time, Wilkie recalled:

"The roommate of one of the college girls killed on the flight was so upset that she was sleeping in the hallway outside the room they once shared on campus. The girl had no affiliation with IBM, but we saw to it that she was flown home to her family.

"We paid for the funeral of one of the other students who had been with us that summer because her parents were separated and her mother didn't have enough money to pay the expenses herself.

"I had everything and everybody in the company at my disposal. I had permission to use the company planes to fly anybody anywhere. We were flying people and families into Dallas from all over the country. Meanwhile, John Akers and the other top corporate officers were calling me every couple of hours to see how the arrangements were going.

"Don's death, of course, wasn't the only one getting headlines around the world, but it is to IBM's eternal credit that the company went out of its way to take the focus off Don. This was because the company did not want to in any way demean or belittle the loss of anyone else on that plane. The other losses were just as tragic and those families were hurt just as much as the Estridges's survivors.

. "Hundreds and hundreds of people came to Boca Raton to pay their respects. It was a great loss, not only from the company's standpoint, but for the community as well."

· 6 ·

The funerals began on Monday, August 5, and did not end until the following Friday. Wilkie and his task force worked 18-hour days to complete the arrangements.

The funeral for Don and Mary Ann Estridge was held on Wednesday, August 7, at the Ascension Roman Catholic Church in Boca Raton. More than 1,000 people attended the Mass, including John Akers and other senior officers of the IBM corporation.

Don Estridge's casket had a wreath of red roses on top. Mary Ann's casket was topped with white orchids. Each of the pallbearers wore a red rosette in his lapel.

The choir sang Mary Ann's favorite hymn, "The Church in the Wildwood." This was followed by Don's favorite, "Swing Low, Sweet Chariot."

Jim Strothman, editor of *MIS Week*, an information management trade publication, attended the funeral and later reported in the publication (August 14, 1985):

"Bob McMullin, a manager of strategy for IBM at Boca Raton and one of two people to give eulogies at the funeral service said, 'When I think of Don and Mary Ann, I think of four priorities which guided their lives—family, friends, tradition and success. Don and Mary Ann placed family first. Their love formed the basis of one of the most solid families I have ever had the privilege to know.

'They were always there when any friend needed them and there were many annual holidays to which they gave meaning, from the black-eyed peas and pork dinners they served on New Year's to the Fourth of July barbecues. They had a tradition of good humor,' McMullin said at the funeral service, as family members and friends wiped tears from their eyes."

·  7  ·

The funeral cortege stretched for over a mile to the Boca Raton Cemetery. Dan Wilkie was a pallbearer and, when the graveside services were being conducted, he kept his gaze on the roses lying atop the casket of Don Estridge.

When the services ended, no one moved to leave. Hundreds of people stood still, waiting for someone else to make the first move. To say something. To do something.

Wilkie had helped to make the arrangements for the funeral, and he was a pallbearer and also the site general manager at Boca Raton, which meant many heads were turned toward him. They waited and watched for him to make the first move. But Wilkie continued to stare at the roses on the casket.

Finally he stepped forward and removed the red rosette from his lapel—the very rosette Estridge had given him years ago—and he placed it on top of Don Estridge's casket.

As if on cue, another pallbearer stepped forward, removed his rosette and gently laid it on the casket. Then another did the same thing, and another came forward through the crowd and another, until the red roses—the symbol of the PC team—were surrounded by a cluster of eight tiny red rosettes.

When the last rosette was placed, Wilkie slowly turned and moved away from the gravesites. As he walked from the cemetery in the warm noonday sun, inhaling the soft Florida air, Wilkie felt compelled to look back one final time toward the rosette on the casket, the symbol of his finest days. Instead, he set his chin and kept his gaze forward.

There was work to be done and the day was still young.

# 33 The Last
# Man Out

· 1 ·

Activity as therapy for grief performed its healing for Wilkie and his PC
teammates at the ESD. "The best thing we could do was stay busy and
that's exactly what we did," Wilkie said.

The temporary attitude about an eight-to-five day with an hour for
lunch and weekends off was a worthless one for people who had to keep
their minds busy to avoid what had been happening in their lives.

Wilkie was one of those who used work as more than a way to support
his family. He dove in, stayed busy and, when thoughts of the days with
Estridge at IBM interfered, he would tell himself, "Well, this, too, shall
pass." He waited for nature to take its course and, of course, that is what
it did.

· 2 ·

About two weeks after Don and Mary Ann Estridge were buried,
Wilkie's dreams began.

"For months, I dreamed every night about Don, or Don and Mary
Ann," Wilkie said. "These were 'third party' dreams; I'd be standing
outside of what was going on, like being at a play, but there I was—in
the play!

"My wife and I had spent some time with Don and Mary Ann in San
Francisco. Now, I would have those dreams and I would see the
Estridges and my wife and myself shopping in San Francisco, or going
to a tennis tournament, or standing on a street corner looking for
directions.

"Then there would be other dreams with just Don and I and we'd be at business meetings, or we'd be in a hotel room somewhere, or sitting together talking to each other on an airplane.

"It was the weirdest thing," he says. "I would always be looking on and seeing us. It was like I was outside of my body physically, as if I was someone else. I can't explain it."

In every instance, Wilkie recalled, the dreams were remarkably vivid. To this day, he can still remember details of those dreams that occurred without fail nearly every night during the early fall of 1985.

· 3 ·

During the workdays, Wilkie grew steadily more discontent. The rules and regulations, audits and procedures, had robbed him of his independence and stifled his spirit.

The dream that he would someday work again with Estridge on another new and exciting business venture was shattered. It would have been like old times all over again. But that dream died with Estridge—while the dreams about Estridge continued every almost night.

So when Wilkie was approached this time by another company with an offer to come in, take control, and start a new computer systems business—well, this time, he listened carefully. They offered him the presidency of the company, stock options, the freedom to run his own show, unlimited international travel and the sort of salary he would probably never achieve if he stayed at IBM until he was too old to get out of bed in the morning. But, of course, it meant he might have to do some explaining when people asked him what the new company did, and he would also have to move his family from Florida to California.

Wilkie accepted the offer. On Thanksgiving Eve, 1985, he resigned from IBM. That night, the dreams about Estridge stopped.

· 4 ·

From time to time, Wilkie still meets young engineers who fall all over themselves when they learn he was a member of the team that developed and built more than three million of the original IBM PCs.

"They look at it as the round table of IBM, with Don Estridge as King Arthur and the rest of us as knights in the days of Camelot," he said. "I get the idea that they want to say, 'God, it's just incredible to be talking to one of the key guys who was in the PC group!'"

When they ask him how it was and what it was like, Wilkie smiles, swells with pride and usually goes to his bobsled analogy:

"It was like being on top of a long hill riding a bobsled. You take off and you gain speed and gain speed and about three-quarters of the way down the hill, you're just holding on, because that bobsled is going at Mach 2 and bouncing all over.

"And there you are, holding on for dear life, and you see woods coming up. So now you have to stop just holding on, you have to steer because the woods are full of product strategies, life transitions, rules to follow . . . and you're on a vehicle that isn't geared to get through these woods.

"This is what happened to us. We were going very, very fast. We were gaining a tremendous amount of speed and there was a momentum we couldn't control until we ran into the woods and hit a few trees. The trees were the checks and balances and the audits, and, yes, our own mistakes.

"There were no trees in the way when we started. There were no standards to follow, no end-of-product-life strategies, or product transitions, or systems architectures, or interfacing problems with other machines. When we began, we didn't even think about world trade in dozens of languages and we sure didn't worry about replacement products, because we were working on a brand new machine.

"So, okay . . . we were racing down an open hill and we hit some trees. But none of us wanted to go down that hill in a wheelbarrow."

The young engineers shyly laugh and shuffle their feet nervously as Wilkie always adds:

"The most important thing has nothing to do with the fact that the PC group doesn't exist anymore. What's important to remember is what the group stood for and what it accomplished. By God, we were a team that created an industry for IBM and put the company's name on more products in more places than it had ever been before.

"No one can ever take that away from me and the other people who built the first IBM PC."

Then, ever so absentmindedly (because it has become a habit), Dan Wilkie gently strokes the lapel where he once wore the proud symbol of his allegiance—the rumpled rosette now lying buried with his beloved leader and the lost dreams of Camelot.

# Epilogue

By the time of Don Estridge's death, many key people on the PC team were gone except for Dan Wilkie and Joe Sarubbi. They all knew that they wouldn't have been as marketable outside IBM if Estridge hadn't picked them for the project. But most didn't feel that they had been rewarded for their success at IBM. Others left because their jobs were finished and they knew they could never duplicate their success and stay with the company.

· 1 ·

Jim D'Arezzo left IBM in late 1983 to join Compaq Computer Corporation as vice president of corporate communications. He has since been promoted to vice president of corporate marketing.

Just as at IBM, D'Arezzo is responsible for product introductions at Compaq. He has overseen the introductions of all of Compaq's computer lines, with the exception of the original Compaq Portable.

D'Arezzo supervises Compaq advertising, marketing and sales support programs, product documentation and packaging, including company and product positioning.

Compaq has a reputation for superiority among the IBM PC-compatibles and has achieved outstanding success in the computer industry.

There is no question that IBM lost a great deal when D'Arezzo left. Most of Compaq's success has been at the expense of IBM. And most of Compaq's marketing has been orchestrated against IBM.

· 2 ·

Joe Sarubbi was among the last to go, retiring after 33 years with IBM. In February 1986, he joined the Tandon Corporation as senior vice president of manufacturing operations, reporting to his friend Dan Wilkie. With Wilkie and other ex-IBMers Bill Sydnes and Sparky Sparks, Sarubbi helped launch Tandon's line of PC-compatible computers.

It was very important for Tandon to hire Sarubbi, since manufacturing is key in keeping the price of Tandon computers as low as possible. And since Tandon computers are a late-comer on the PC scene, the major way the company has differentiated its products has been through a lower price.

To keep manufacturing costs down, Tandon has tried to incorporate as many functions as possible into a few main components. To its further advantage, Tandon makes its own power supplies and disk drives. The more efficiently the company makes these components, the more margin they and their dealers can realize on computers.

Sarubbi took charge of manufacturing at Tandon and helped the company get through a shaky start in the PC business. He has since left Tandon and now lives in Florida, where he does consulting for his friend Dan Wilkie at Dynabrook Technologies.

· 3 ·

Sparky Sparks brought his marketing genius to Compaq Computer Corporation in Houston as vice president of sales and service. He helped to make Compaq one of the most successful start-up operations in the history of American business. It was Sparks who masterminded Compaq's sales philosophy of selling strictly through dealers. He used his contacts to get the Compaq Portable Computer into nearly every dealership that sold IBM PCs.

Compaq and Sparks helped build dealer loyalty by not using a direct sales force to compete with dealers. The fact that Compaq was the first company with an IBM clone didn't hurt either. Due in large part to Sparks's marketing genius, Compaq achieved sales of $110 million in its first year of business (1983), and $289 million in its second year and posted $1 billion in sales for 1987.

Sparks then helped to start up a new Compaq division, Compaq Telecommunications in Dallas. While there, he launched the Telecompaq, a combination telephone and computer system that was generally conceded to be ahead of its time. Compaq sported a dubious marketing strategy for the Telecompaq, selling it through telephone companies such as Pacific Bell. No one understood the computer, not the people who were selling it nor the potential customers. Add to this the fact that two different departments generally make buying decisions for telephones and computers in corporations, and it was clear the Telecompaq was doomed. It is Compaq's only "mistake" to date. In late 1985, Sparks left Compaq to join Tandon Corporation as senior vice president of sales and marketing.

Sparks quickly lined up dealers like Entre Computer Centers, Sears Business Systems Centers, a number of Computerland franchises and several smaller chains. The main selling points Tandon offered dealers were 42 to 47 percent margins (five to 10 points higher than most other vendors) and lower retail prices.

But Tandon got off to a less-than-auspicious start as a name-brand vendor, and Sparks resigned "for personal reasons" just 11 months after joining Tandon.

His sabbatical didn't last for long. In March 1987 Sparks was named president of Amdek Corporation, a Northern California company most noted for producing computer monitors. Sparks was also named vice president of Amdek's parent company, Wyse Technology, a corporation that manufactures microcomputers and terminals. His charter at Amdek was to help broaden the company's product line into system products and to establish its line in worldwide markets. He eventually left Amdek to become vice president for sales and marketing of Next Gen, a new company.

IBM's marketing staff has gotten along fine without Sparks, but there is little question that IBM was hurt by his departure. Compaq never would have achieved the success it has without Sparks's marketing genius.

· 4 ·

During the middle of the PCjr debacle, Bill Sydnes left IBM to join Franklin Computer Corporation as vice president for product development. After Franklin declared Chapter 11, he became an independent consultant. Sydnes was later recruited to join Wilkie and Sparks at the Tandon Corporation. He left almost a year later, however, to return to consulting and freelance product development.

· 5 ·

Dan Wilkie, one of the most important members in the Tandon-IBM connection, joined Tandon in late 1985 as president and chief operating officer. Sirjang Tandon, founder of the company, was impressed by Wilkie's manufacturing experience and hired him to direct the effort to capture a significant share of the personal computer market in the United States.

Before joining Tandon, Wilkie was general manager of the IBM Boca Raton site. Tandon specialized in producing private-label (OEM) systems, and Tandon-brand systems. Despite the expertise it accumulated from IBM, the company, burdened by insufficient cash, was slow to gain a foothold in the United States market, and had limited success.

Ex-IBMers Sparky Sparks and Bill Sydnes left Tandon within a year after joining the company. But Dan Wilkie persisted and was instrumental in launching Tandon's line of low-cost PC clones in the United States, though the company's highest-volume products are sold in Europe.

In August 1987, Wilkie resigned as president of Tandon despite a four-year contract worth more than $1.2 million. Industry speculation blamed the Wilkie resignation on Mr. Tandon, an entrepreneur who found it difficult to relinquish day-to-day control of his company, and on disagreements over the company's expenses and the direction of its marketing and sales.

In November 1987, Wilkie became one of the founders of Dynabook Technologies, a maker of high-performance MS-DOS-based lap-top computers funded by Silicon Valley's leading venture capital firms. As the company's founder, president, chief executive officer, Wilkie said, "This is another opportunity for me to create a new set of products and standards in our industry. I believe Don Estridge would be proud of me."

· 6 ·

The computer industry has changed markedly since November 1985.

Most personal computers until then were based on the same 8088 microprocessor that was at the heart of the then-four-year-old IBM PC. However, the faster and more powerful 80286, introduced by IBM in 1984 for the PC AT, was quickly becoming popular with corporations.

The staggering 50 and 60 percent growth rates the microcomputer industry considered "typical" during the early 1980s came to an abrupt halt in 1985. Growth leveled out to an annualized rate of approximately 15 percent, causing a massive rise in inventories for the companies that had expected growth to continue. Among those disappointed optimists was IBM. The market wasn't experiencing phenomenal growth rates anymore, and smaller companies found themselves competing vigorously for the few dollars still around that hadn't been earmarked for companies such as IBM, Compaq and Apple. As a result, a shakeout occurred, and many companies either went out of business or were absorbed by large, well-capitalized corporations.

Curiously, many new, small, garage-based companies also came on the scene in 1985. These vendors generally promoted generic Asian-manufactured "clones" of IBM computers, which sold for a fraction of the price of IBM's computers and put a big dent in Big Blue's market share.

These small vendors, plus larger companies like Compaq Computer Corporation, Houston, Texas; Tandy Corporation, Fort Worth, Texas; Apple Computer Inc., Cupertino, California; and others were determined to take market share away from IBM. And take it they did, slicing IBM's share of the personal computer market from 63 percent in 1984 to 38 percent by 1987, according to Infocorp, a market research firm.

Many factors were responsible for IBM's loss. Four of the most important were Apple, Compaq, the proliferation of low-cost clones, and IBM itself.

· 7 ·

One of the companies most affected by economic change in 1985 was Apple Computer. Apple was a company without a focus. Its Macintosh line of computers was unwanted by both consumers and business users. Its aging Apple II line was aimed at a home market that had shrunk dramatically. Apple suffered the first quarterly loss in its history during the third quarter of 1985, and the company's stock dropped to $14 per share. Many analysts wondered if Apple would survive. Others speculated that a larger company like AT&T would move in and take it over.

Some of Apple's problems had to do with organization. There were too many redundant tasks at the company. Support departments, like management information services, marketing, finance, manufacturing and personnel, were essentially triplicated for the Apple II Division, the Macintosh Division and the Accessory Products Group. By eliminating redundant tasks, Apple reduced the number of employees in the company by 21 percent, or more than 1,200 people, with 700 of these in manufacturing alone. Apple thus was able to close three of its six factories. While this was painful, it made Apple leaner and more efficient.

Apple also restructured the approach to its markets—corporate, education and in-home personal computing. Rather than organizing sales and marketing around products, Apple President John Sculley wanted product development to be more market driven.

The most prominent casualty of the reorganization was Apple's founder and chairman, Steve Jobs. After Don Estridge chose not to accept the offer to become president of Apple, Jobs hired Sculley away from Pepsico in 1983 to guide Apple through its transition from an entrepreneurial start-up to a mature company. Ironically, Sculley and his management team quickly realized that Jobs was one of the main obstacles toward achieving that goal.

Jobs had been head of the Macintosh Division before the reorganization. His more favorable treatment of the Macintosh employees, compared to the Apple II employees, was hurting morale. At the company's annual meeting in January 1985, Macintosh employees got front-row seats to hear Jobs speak about Apple and its future. Apple II personnel watched the event on closed circuit television.

Disagreements over the direction of the company and disputes over product strategies caused a bitter feud between Sculley and Jobs. Obviously, Sculley won. With little support among top executives, Jobs resigned as chairman of the board and left the company.

He started a new venture, called Next, and took several Apple employees with him. Apple sued Jobs to prevent him from using Apple technology, but the matter eventually was settled out of court.

With reorganization achieved and Jobs gone, Sculley set out to rebuild Apple and establish its Macintosh line of computers in corporations.

· 8 ·

Apple's biggest problems were IBM and the scores of IBM-compatible computers. The overwhelming percentage of personal computers in corporations were based on the IBM standard, with Intel 8088 or 80286 microprocessors and Microsoft's MS-DOS operating system. Apple Macintosh computers used the Motorola 68000 microprocessor and a proprietary operating system. As a result, they didn't work with the same software as IBM-compatible computers.

So Apple promoted the advantages that the Macintosh enjoyed over IBM and the compatible PCs. Apple called the Macintosh "the computer for the rest of us" because it featured an easy-to-use graphic interface that bypassed most of the difficulties inherent until then in learning to operate a personal computer. It duplicated the concept of a desk-top on the computer screen. Pictures, or icons, were used to represent programs, data and operations. A mouse, or pointing device, could be used to tell the computer what to do.

File handling was elegant and consistent: files were put in folders, and data that wasn't needed anymore was put in a trash can on the screen. Plus, the interface was consistent, so every software program from every vendor featured similar commands. Once a user learned one program, he or she was well on the way to learning another. This was not so in the IBM world, where each program was different, and a new learning experience in itself. Apple pointed to the Macintosh's ease of operation and claimed that corporations could save a lot of time and money by choosing this practical and well-thought-out machine.

In 1985, few companies were intrigued by Apple computers. The MIS managers were put off by Jobs's arrogance in selling the computers as technological wonders. Corporate executives retorted that the Macintosh was a toy and that Apple didn't understand their needs.

There was a general sigh of relief when Jobs left the company. But more importantly, the deficiencies in the Macintosh computer itself had to be resolved. The 1985 version of the Macintosh was slow, didn't have very good business software, didn't connect well to other computers in an organization, and it wasn't expandable. Users couldn't easily add more functions to the computer by opening the box and putting in an expansion board. While the IBM PC featured multiple expansion slots for this purpose, the Macintosh had none. Jobs, in his arrogance, had proclaimed the Macintosh a perfect computer that didn't need to be expanded.

In January 1986, however, Apple introduced a faster, more powerful computer, the Macintosh Plus, which had 1 million bytes of random access memory. This was more than was usually available in the IBM-compatibles, which typically had 640,000 bytes. The Macintosh Plus could also be connected more easily to other computers than its predecessors. Apple also introduced a new term to the computer industry—desk-top publishing: the ability to produce a newsletter, newspaper, technical manual, or even a magazine with a personal computer. Apple's Macintosh was considered to be more efficient at desk-top publishing than any Personal Computer produced by IBM.

The Macintosh also allowed users to display text and pictures on the screen exactly as they were to appear on paper, by using a concept called WYSIWYG (what you see is what you get). Software like Pagemaker from Aldus Corporation, Seattle, let users combine text and graphics into one document and display it in newspaper format. Meanwhile, the Apple LaserWriter printer allowed users to print their documents in any format and with any fonts they chose. The letter quality was much better than printers for the IBM computers.

Desk-top publishing represented Apple's first clear advantage over IBM. And Apple exploited it to the fullest, employing a Trojan horse-type of marketing to reach large corporations. Corporations started to buy the Macintosh for special applications like desk-top publishing. Others in the company would see what the Macintosh could do and how its printout looked, and they'd want to buy one.

This strategy worked, partly because users became exposed to the Macintosh and what it could do and partly because Apple and third-party vendors continued to increase the versatility and applicability of the machine.

Apple, employing a strategy called desk-top communications, worked on making it easier to connect the Macintosh to other computers. Users of a Macintosh, for example, could access information from an IBM PC, an IBM mainframe, a Digital Equipment Corporation minicomputer, or any other device. In 1985, the Macintosh did not share data very well with other machines. But by late 1987, the Macintosh was equal to IBM's personal computers in connectivity, or data sharing.

IBM enjoyed a good reputation with third-party vendors and thousands of software programs were available for its machines. Apple lacked these advantages. But Apple started to foster relationships with IBM software vendors like Microsoft and Lotus Development Corporation to create more and better software programs for the Macintosh. By 1988, a wide variety of powerful Macintosh software was available.

For example, Microsoft Excel is a spreadsheet program judged more powerful than the venerable Lotus 1-2-3 on the IBM side. Microsoft Word, a versatile word-processing program, has been favorably compared with such powerful word-processing programs as WordPerfect and MultiMate, designed for IBM. And database management software like

Helix from Odesta Corporation, and Fourth Dimension, from Acius, in Cupertino, California, made the Macintosh equal to or better than the PC in that application as well. While Macintosh software was once a joke compared to offerings in the MS-DOS world, in many instances it was now surpassing IBM.

A leaner, meaner Apple also became much more efficient in 1986. While Macintosh sales soared, Apple II sales dropped. The company as a whole had nearly identical sales in 1985 and 1986 ($1.9 billion). But profits were almost three times higher ($300,000 versus $120,000).

In March 1985, Sculley was quoted in the *Wall Street Journal* as estimating that Apple had two years to prove that the Macintosh is a serious alternative to IBM. In March 1987, Apple introduced two very serious alternatives, the Macintosh SE and Macintosh II. Both computers featured expansion slots and were capable of working with IBM software. The Macintosh II in particular was extremely powerful and versatile. Apple wasn't replacing the IBM standard in corporations, but the company did present a serious alternative.

· 9 ·

Compaq Computer Corporation came a long way fast from its beginnings in a Houston pie shop in 1982. By 1985, some observers were saying that the company even made better products than IBM. Unlike its competitors, Compaq didn't just clone an IBM product, it worked to improve it while remaining 100 percent compatible with IBM, or, as the company president, Rod Canion, liked to say, the "industry standard."

Compaq was the first vendor to clone an IBM PC. But even its first product offered certain advantages over IBM's PC. The Compaq Portable could be carried around, it boasted a more versatile display, it was less expensive and it was IBM compatible.

Compaq was also first to clone an IBM PC AT. Its Compaq Deskpro 286 was 25 percent faster and 10 percent less expensive than the PC AT. For good measure, Compaq introduced the Compaq Portable 286 at the same time. These computers, too, were IBM compatible.

Unlike other clone vendors, Compaq wasn't afraid to sell its products at or near the hallowed IBM price point. Compaq stuck to its competitive Texas roots by always trying to be in the same dealerships as IBM. Compaq wanted to "shoot it out" with IBM and let prospective buyers compare its products with IBM's, confident that customers would choose Compaq.

In late 1986, Compaq took its biggest gamble. IBM had postponed introducing a computer based on the powerful Intel 80386 microprocessor. And since IBM hadn't released a computer, the rest of the industry also waited. After all, the world waited for IBM, didn't it? This time, Compaq didn't.

Compaq introduced its Deskpro 386, the first computer from a major vendor based on the Intel 80386 microprocessor. Compaq's Deskpro 386 maintained the industry standard because it ran all the software written for other IBM-compatible computers. It made Compaq a market leader, and gave it the reputation of a company that was not afraid to introduce a product before IBM.

A flurry of vendors introduced 80386 machines at Comdex in Las Vegas in November 1986. That is, instead of introducing computers compatible with *IBM* machines, vendors were offering computers compatible with *Compaq*'s. IBM was still the leader, but "David" had hurt "Goliath."

According to Phillipe Kahn of Borland International, IBM's stubbornness in staying with 80286 technology long past its point of usefulness is retarding the overall growth of the microcomputer industry. "There is unquestionably more power and functionality in the 80386 technology," Kahn insists. He adds, "It's ironic that IBM's success with the '286' chip is acting to hold back the whole industry."

On the inside, Compaq is a button-downed clone of IBM. Its corporate culture is more reminiscent of the blue suit atmosphere of IBM than the blue jean environment at Apple. This is understandable, since many of its executives come from traditional corporations like IBM and Texas Instruments.

But on the outside, the company can be downright glitzy. Compaq product introductions are often multimedia events. In 1985, the company hired the Pointer Sisters to help debut the Compaq Deskpro 286 and Compaq Portable 286. In 1986, the company "settled" for popular singer Irene Cara, Houston Mayor Kathy Whitmire, and the Houston Symphony Orchestra to help inaugurate the Compaq Portable II. The company also used the event to celebrate making the Fortune 500 in its fourth year in business, after qualifying for 461st place out of 500 with $505 million in sales for 1985. No other publicly held company in the history of the Fortune 500 had made its way onto the list so quickly.

Due in part to its 80386 product, Compaq sales continued to soar in 1986, rising above $600 million and to more than $1 billion for 1987. Unfortunately for IBM, it looked like David was becoming a Goliath.

· 10 ·

When IBM used third-party parts and hardware in building the IBM PC, it knew that other companies might eventually copy its technology and build competitive machines. However, it's doubtful IBM anticipated that a flurry of "generic" computers from around the world would be introduced, as they were in 1985.

These PCs were often built by moonlighters in their basements. The names of the computers didn't matter, they were simply "PCs." They may or may not have been 100 percent compatible with the IBM PC, and they might not have worked as well. But they were cheap, often selling for less than $1,000 for a complete system, a fraction of the cost of similar IBM offerings. Thus, the concept of a disposable machine was introduced.

At first, the clones were so cheap and poorly built that few prospective buyers took them seriously. But these computers, generally built with parts brought in from the Far East and assembled in the United States, quickly improved in quality. As a result, computers from companies like Leading Edge, PC's Limited, and PC Designs got the attention of IBM's favorite customers—the directors of management information systems (MIS) in large corporations.

Why, an MIS executive wondered, was his or her company spending $3,500 for an IBM computer when it could purchase a clone with similar capabilities for $1,000 or $1,500? Often, the company would have their own in-house maintenance and repair facilities, which meant that if the computers broke down, the company could fix them.

PC's Limited of Austin, Texas, thrived under this arrangement. The company was started with $1,000 by 19-year-old Michael Dell in his college dorm room. It grew to a $70 million company in 1986, and the following year, it sold more than $150 million worth of products, almost exclusively through mail-order sales. The company marketed a variety of IBM-compatible personal computers at a fraction of the price of a comparable IBM machine. Dell, a computer genius, generally designed most of the computer himself.

Most of the prosperity of PC clones has been at the expense of IBM.

While Compaq, Apple and generic clone makers increased market share between 1984 and 1986, IBM's dropped. Part of this was due to increased price competition, but much of it was due to IBM itself.

·  11  ·

If any other company than IBM had released the products it did in 1986, it would have gone out of business. That year, IBM released no fewer than three lines of disastrous personal and business computers. Each machine was poorly conceived for the marketplace, fraught with manufacturing defects, poorly positioned and ridiculously priced. If nothing else, 1986 proved that IBM had indeed been hurt by the defections of early members of the PC team.

Released in January 1986, the IBM RT PC was intended for the engineering workstation market. This market has been growing by leaps and bounds in the last few years and is dominated by Apollo Computer, Chelmsford, Massachusetts and Sun Microsystems, Mountain View, California. Engineering workstations are used by technical professionals—engineers, scientists, mathematicians, geologists and others who use complex calculations or complex graphic images in their jobs. The machines are also intended for computer-aided design and manufacturing applications (CAD/CAM).

The RT PC employed reduced instruction set computer (RISC) technology, an approach developed by IBM in the 1970s to reduce the complexity of computer operations and improve performance.

At a starting price of $11,700, the RT PC was not cheap. In fact, it was approximately twice the price of a PC/AT, which represented the top of IBM's personal computer line at the time. Not only was it expensive, but the RT PC was limited in both graphics and networking, two of the most important factors in the engineering workstation market.

The development of the RT PC line paralleled that of the PC in that a relatively small group of engineers—in this case IBM's Milford, Connecticut-based Engineering Systems Products Independent Business Unit—developed the computer. IBM used an open architecture in the computer so that other companies could develop software and hardware for the machine.

But IBM also included much proprietary hardware and software for the machine. The microprocessor was IBM's. Most of the parts were

IBM's. Even the operating system was IBM's, albeit a redesigned version of the UNIX operating system that was popular among technical professionals.

IBM allowed the RT PC to emulate a PC AT through a co-processor board. But the co-processor board didn't work as fast as a PC AT, so MS-DOS software ran slower on the more expensive RT than it did on a PC AT.

The RT PC was less of an engineering mistake than a marketing failure. IBM tried to create a second standard with the RT PC. But the engineering workstation market didn't need another standard. Apollo, Sun, and even Digital Equipment Corporation, were doing just fine without IBM's help.

And the PC marketplace didn't need another standard either. IBM's own standard was performing excellently there as well.

The RT PC was a computer without a home. Few software or hardware developers bothered to offer products for it, and the computer continues to flounder toward oblivion.

After months of industry hoopla, the PC Convertible (code-named "Clamshell") was introduced in April of 1986. The PC Convertible was a lap-top computer: it weighed 12 pounds, was very portable and took up little desk space.

Priced at $1,995, the PC Convertible included 256K of RAM memory and two 3.5-inch disk drives. It was called a "convertible" because it could work as either a lap-top (as is), or a desk-top computer with the addition of a larger monitor and an expansion box.

As a lap-top computer, the PC Convertible was a failure. It was too slow and its liquid crystal display (LCD) monitor did not show text clearly. The modem for the computer, which let users send and retrieve information over phone lines, was not ready for months. A modem is critical for lap-top computers because users generally take them on business trips and often need access to office computers or information services while on the road. Another problem was that the machine's 3.5-inch drives were not compatible with industry-standard 5.25-inch drives, making it difficult, if not impossible, to use data and application software generated on, or intended for, larger drives.

As a desk-top computer, the PC Convertible was also a failure. To outfit it as a desk-top model cost more than $4,000, or twice the price of comparable desk-top models.

Worse, less than one month after IBM announced the PC Convertible, Toshiba America introduced the T3100, a laptop with a better monitor, faster processor and more storage space in the form of a hard disk drive. While it cost $4,500, the T3100 truly answered business needs and hence sold well.

In September 1987, Compaq introduced the sixth portable computer in its history, the Compaq Portable 386 (the first three computers—the Compaq Portable, Compaq Plus and Compaq Portable 286—were the same size and a similar weight; the Portable II and Portable III represented size and weight reductions; and the Portable 386 was the same size and weight as the Portable III). This was Compaq's lightest, most powerful portable yet, but it still wasn't a lap-top computer. Although Compaq has been very cautious in entering this market, it dominates the market for portable computers.

IBM released the XT-286 in August 1986. It reportedly was the PC2 that was rumored to be readied in April of 1985. If it had been released 16 months earlier, the XT-286 might have been a successful product. But 16 months is a long time in the computer industry, and the XT-286 was a disaster.

Selling for $3,995, the XT-286 combined the technology of the PC XT and the microprocessor of the PC AT in a lower-cost package: It sold for approximately $1,500 less than a similarly equipped PC AT. But it had exceedingly slow disk drives, it was relatively high priced compared to the AT clones then available and it was poorly designed. Embarrassingly for IBM, the circuit cards designed for the bigger PC AT were too tall to fit in the XT-286 and couldn't be used unless the lid to the new product's casing was permanently removed.

In all, this humiliating trio were in great measure responsible for IBM's dramatic loss of market share in 1986. But were these entirely product faults?

Part of IBM's problems have to do with its marketing communications strategies. The company is notorious for poor press relations and uses a strategy of disinformation that keeps the public guessing until the product announcements are made. Meanwhile, press and industry speculation only creates rumors, usually about products that will be so revolutionary that they will destroy the competition. What company could consistently live up to this reputation?

· 12 ·

IBM announced its PS/2 computer series in April 1987. After months of industry speculation, four new machines were unveiled by IBM. For a change, the products were truly impressive.

They were smaller, faster and more powerful than their predecessors. They featured a new operating system (Microsoft OS/2), a graphics-oriented display like the Macintosh, a proprietary bus structure called Micro Channel and a completely redesigned motherboard that included serial and parallel connections for use with modems and printers. (Many other computers require serial and parallel connections to be placed on expansion circuit cards.)

The PS/2 can use most software available for IBM-compatible machines, but it is not an industry-standard computer. Its use of 3.5-inch floppy disk drives, like the PC Convertible, meant that its software would have to be repackaged by vendors. Its Micro Channel bus was not compatible with add-in devices like the circuit cards available for IBM-standard computers.

IBM acknowledged these incompatibilities, but claimed the series' superior features more than made up for the loss of compatibility: better graphics, more efficient data processing, faster processors, competitive pricing and smaller computers.

IBM was right—to a degree. The Model 30, for example, is 25 percent smaller than the IBM PC-XT and 2.5 times faster for a price that is 25 percent lower.

The Model 50 is considered to be the best value in the new line. At $3,595, it includes a powerful Intel 80286 microprocessor, 1 megabyte of RAM, a 1.44 megabyte floppy disk drive, and a 20 megabyte hard disk. It is extremely competitive with similar computers now available.

The Model 60 is a floor-standing version of the Model 50. It offers much more storage capacity than the Model 50, which has limits of 7 megabytes of RAM and 20 megabytes of hard disk space. The Model 60 can handle 15 megabytes of RAM and 185 megabytes of hard disk space.

The Model 80 was IBM's first computer based on the Intel 80386 microprocessor. Even though it was announced seven months after Compaq unveiled its Deskpro 386, the Model 80 impressed potential buyers. This top-of-the-line model arguably is faster and more powerful than any other microcomputer.

Probably the most important feature was a new operating system for the computers, called OS/2, from Microsoft. OS/2 is compatible with other computers in the IBM line and with industry-standard computers. The only requirement is that those computers have to include an Intel 80286 or 80386 microprocessor.

The industry had been waiting for a new operating system ever since the day IBM announced the PC AT in 1984. MS-DOS was limited by the 8088 microprocessor for which it was written. Users wanted a system that took advantage of the capabilities of the PC AT, or even more powerful microcomputers. MS-DOS couldn't do this. Essentially, it limits users to 640K of RAM and 32 megabytes of hard disk storage and forces users to run only one application at a time.

Writing an operating system is a difficult undertaking. It took Microsoft nearly three years to write OS/2. Unfortunately, while OS/2 was announced in April of 1987, it wasn't available until late 1987.

The OS/2 appears to be an operating system that is worth the wait. It lets users and software developers exploit up to 16 megabytes of RAM and much more hard disk space, and it is capable of multitasking, so users can run more than one software program at a time. It also includes a "friendly" interface that makes the IBM PC and its software behave more like a Macintosh and its software.

OS/2 in a standard configuration is available to the entire industry, though OS/2 Extended Edition is proprietary to IBM. Extended Edition includes "hooks" that make access to IBM minicomputers and mainframes very easy.

The PS/2 family has achieved success with more than 1 million units sold. But most corporate users are still waiting for the OS/2 and Extended Edition before buying. In any case, the PS/2 represents a completely different product family for IBM and a new chapter in the history of personal computing. It also closes the book on the IBM PC and its product family.

## ·  13  ·

The success of the IBM PC was somewhat of a fluke. IBM didn't expect it to have the impact on corporations that it did. The company created the computer merely to remain competitive in the growing low end of the market. Little did IBM know in 1980 that within seven years it would release a personal computer (the PS/2 Model 80) with more power than its minicomputers.

Personal computers are much more powerful than anyone expected they'd be. Bill Gates of Microsoft, the principal architect of MS-DOS, never believed the 640K RAM barrier that has caused so much trouble for computer users and developers would ever be a problem. Yet it became an obstacle within three years of the release of MS-DOS.

The incredible success of the IBM PC and other MS-DOS computers made nearly every professional get a personal computer for his or her workspace, hence the 50 percent and 60 percent growth rates for personal computers. In those days, there was an anti-MIS feeling in many corporations, where users felt they could do more with their personal computer than they could with the corporate mainframe that the MIS owned, operated and maintained. It soon became apparent, however, that they were wrong.

Corporate managers using Lotus 1-2-3 spreadsheets for financial analyses found that they couldn't keep all the information they needed on their personal computer. Personal computers weren't (and still aren't) powerful and storage intensive enough to do this. Besides, large databases of financial and other information are best kept on the corporate mainframe, where everyone in the corporation can gain access to it then.

Mainframes have always been more powerful than PCs and have always been able to sort large amounts of data faster and more efficiently. So the professional was forced to make up with the MIS director, and ask him or her how to get information from the corporate mainframe for use on the IBM PC.

Users also soon wanted to share data with other personal computer users. Copying the information onto a diskette and bringing it to a colleague's office got old in a hurry. Again, MIS came to the rescue, hooking up the computers on local area networks.

Connecting to the corporate mainframe and to other personal computers, then, became almost as important as having the power of a personal computer on one's desk. That's why IBM created the PS/2 line and the OS/2 Extended Edition, computers with built-in connectivity for corporate America's needs.

Mainframes have become devices that store and manage large amounts of data quickly and efficiently, while personal computers have become the tool of the corporate manager. Managers get the information they need from the corporate mainframe and use it on their PC. They then share the results of their analyses with other managers in the corporation via local area networks.

Despite its initial disdain, the personal computer's importance to IBM is now accepted as a painfully proven fact. IBM's loss of market share in the personal computer segment of its business led to less profit for Big Blue in both 1985 and 1986, the first back-to-back slump for the company since the Great Depression.

IBM is still mainframe oriented. It lives or dies by the success of its mainframe computers. But its minicomputers are less important than they used to be. The personal computer line, however, is more important than ever before, both in profit and reputation.

The IBM PC revolutionized the electronic processing of words and data. A multibillion dollar industry grew up around it. IBM established the standard, then challenged others to improve on it. The company made people think differently about all kinds of computers—micros, minis and mainframes. Personal computers have become an important factor in IBM's future, and the only one in companies such as Compaq and Apple. The days of the PC as the "renegade" of the computer world were over a long time ago.

# Appendix

## Timeline of IBM PC-Related Product Introductions

**IBM Personal Computer**
Introduced: August 1981
Price: $2,880
Features: Intel 8088 microprocessor, 64K memory, one 160K floppy disk drive

**IBM Personal Computer XT**
Introduced: March 1983
Price: $4,995
Features: Intel 8088 microprocessor, 128K memory, 360K floppy disk drive, 10 megabyte hard disk

**IBM PCjr**
Introduced: October 1983
Price: $1,269
Features: Intel 8088 microprocessor, 128K memory, 360K floppy disk drive

**IBM 3270 PC**
Introduced: October 1983
Price: $4,290
Features: Intel 8088 microprocessor, 256K memory, one 360K floppy disk drive, built-in 3270 terminal emulation facilities

**IBM PC XT Model 3270**
Introduced: October 1983
Price: $8,995
Features: Intel 8088 microprocessor, 768K memory, one 360K floppy disk drive, 1 10 megabyte hard disk, built-in 3270 terminal emulation facilities

**IBM Portable Computer**
Introduced: February 1984
Price: $2,795
Features: Portable computer with Intel 8088 microprocessor, 256K memory, one 360K floppy disk drive

**IBM Personal Computer AT**
Introduced: August 1984
Price: $5,795
Features: Intel 80286 microprocessor, 512K memory, 1.2 megabyte floppy disk drive, 20 megabyte hard disk

**IBM RT PC**
Introduced: January 1986
Price: $11,700
Features: IBM 32-bit RISC processor, 1 megabyte memory, 1.2 megabyte floppy disk drive, 40 megabyte hard disk

**IBM PC Convertible**
Introduced: April 1986
Price: $2,995
Features: Lap-top computer with Intel 80088 microprocessor, 256K memory, two 720K floppy disk drives

**IBM PC-XT Model 286**
Introduced: August 1986
Price: $3,995
Features: Intel 80286 microprocessor, 640K memory, 20 megabyte hard disk

**IBM Personal System/2**
*Model 30*
Introduced: April 1987
Price: $1,695
Features: Intel 8086 microprocessor, 640K memory, two 720K floppy disk drives

**IBM Personal System/2**
*Model 50*
Introduced: April 1987
Price: $3,595
Features: Intel 80286 microprocessor, 1 megabyte memory, 1.44 megabyte floppy disk drive, 20 megabyte hard disk

**IBM Personal System/2**
*Model 60*
Introduced: April 1987
Price: $5,295
Features: Intel 80286 microprocessor, 1 megabyte memory, 1.44 megabyte floppy disk drive, 44 megabyte hard disk

**IBM Personal System/2**
*Model 80*
Introduced: April 1987
Price: $6,995
Features: Intel 80386 microprocessor, 1 megabyte memory, 1.44 megabyte floppy disk drive, 44 megabyte hard disk

**IBM Personal System/2**
*Model 25*
Introduced: August 1987
Price: $1,395
Features: Intel 8086 microprocessor, 640K memory, 720K floppy disk drive, monochrome monitor

# Index